345.73 Silverman, Milton
SIL   J.

Cop.1   Open and shut

DATE			

Also by Ron Winslow

HARD AGROUND

OPEN
AND
SHUT

OPEN
AND
SHUT

Milton J. Silverman

with RON WINSLOW

W · W · NORTON & COMPANY · NEW YORK · LONDON

Library of Congress Cataloging in Publication Data
Silverman, Milton J
Open and Shut.
1. Winters, Norma. 2. Trials (Murder)—California.
I. Winslow, Ron, joint author. II. Title.
KF224.W56S54   345.73′02523   80–28908
ISBN 0–393–01442–8

W. W. Norton & Company, Inc. 500 Fifth Avenue, New York, N.Y. 10110
W. W. Norton & Company Ltd. 25 New Street Square, London EC4A 3NT
1 2 3 4 5 6 7 8 9 0

To my wife, Maria, who believes in miracles, and to my
children, Richard and Rose Ann.

M.J.S.

Shortly after the jury returned with a verdict in her case, Norma Winters suggested that I write the story of her trial. She believed, and I did too, that her case was unique, that it said something important about the American system of justice.

Whether justice was served in the case of the *People of the State of California* v. *Norma Winters* is a question that the reader must decide. Yet, the trial itself was only part of the story. *Open and Shut* is also a mystery and a tale of human tragedy. It could not have been told in full without the willing cooperation of Norma and her family, particularly Beth. They wanted to tell the whole story. Indeed, that is the only way it could have been told.

Milton J. Silverman
San Diego, California

"The story has, I believe, been told more than once in the newspapers, but, like all such narratives, its effect is much less striking when set forth *en bloc* in a single half-column of print than when the facts slowly evolve before your own eyes, and the mystery clears gradually away as each new discovery furnishes a step which leads on to the complete truth."

The Adventure of the Engineer's Thumb

PART I

The Crime

"The most commonplace crime is often the most mysterious."

A Study in Scarlet

CHAPTER 1

Beth Winters lay still beneath a blanket on her bed, holding a pillow tightly to her ear. It was nearly midnight, but she couldn't sleep. She had tried to lock the door, but he had jimmied it so that the inside knob couldn't be turned. All she could do was wait and listen, and pray—pray that the stillness would not be broken by any sound.

It had started nearly six years ago, when she was twelve. He had asked her to lie down next to him on the bed. Suddenly he was breathing hard and holding her tightly. And he was moving his hands around on her, rubbing and feeling her. She didn't know exactly what he was doing, but she knew it was wrong. When he stopped, she got up quickly and ran out of the room. She told no one what had happened.

It continued infrequently over the next two years, but by the time she was fourteen and developing sexually, he would come after her nearly every day for weeks at a time.

Now she heard his quiet footsteps on the carpet and a slight twist of the knob on the door.

Her pulse raced. She felt nauseated. "Please God, make him leave. Make him disappear, evaporate, die."

She huddled, knees to her chest, at the far corner of the bed, her back to the door. A sliver of light traced the wall and then retreated as the door clicked shut. His footsteps were almost silent on the *carpet, but she could feel him moving toward her in the darkness. She gripped the headboard with her fingers and choked back the urge to scream, to cry. When the bed sagged under his weight and he reached across to pull back the blanket, she lay still, pretending to sleep, hoping that somehow he would go away.*

She felt his hand on her back just below her right shoulder and twitched to avoid his touch. He moved closer, sliding toward her until her curled body was enveloped in the curve of his. He put his arm around her waist.

"Beth," he said hoarsely, "I'm going to teach you to be a woman." On his breath she smelled cigarettes and beer.

She turned her body away and pushed her face into her pillow.

"You've got to know what these young boys are like." He moved his hand up from her waist toward her breast and then felt her through the nightgown. "I've got to show you what to expect."

"Go away, you pervert," she said. "Leave me alone. I hate you."

"Don't you talk like that." His voice was harder now. "The way you dress, you ask for it."

"I do not," she snapped. "I don't ask for anything, you filthy pervert."

"Don't call me that. You know I'm doing this for your own good."

"Like hell you are. Just leave me alone. Go the hell away. I'm going to tell mom. Swear to God, I'm going to tell."

"No, you're not." He grabbed a clump of her hair and yanked it hard.

Beth winced, but bit her lip so she wouldn't cry out.

"You know you'll never tell. You know what will happen."

She knew. He had said it many times, about the scandal, her reputation. And she knew she couldn't tell her mother, not now. It had all grown within her like a terrible lie. She wanted to confess, but the longer she waited, the more difficult it became. And the more it would hurt her mother.

"Goddamn you, you filthy pervert. Leave me the hell alone. Goddamn you. Go pick on someone else. You filthy goddamn pervert."

Her words were deliberate. She knew how he hated to be called a pervert and how he hated hearing her swear. Sometimes she would make him feel so bad that he would leave her alone for a few weeks, and she would begin to think it was over, that her family would be nice and normal again.

But sometimes it made him more angry. Now he moved his hand from her breast, down along her stomach to the insides of her thighs. She pressed her knees together, holding them so tight she groaned. He jammed his hand between her legs and up into her crotch.

"God," she cried. She twisted her body, almost raising herself off the bed.

"I want you to relax, Beth, this is how you learn to be a woman."

"I don't want to learn. I just want you to leave me alone. God, please leave me the fuck alone." She began to cry.

He pulled his hand away, then reached for the hem of her nightgown. He lifted it above her knees, then above her thighs until it was around her waist, leaving her underpants exposed.

She relaxed for a moment, feigning submission. It was her only chance. She closed her eyes and felt him loosen his grip. Suddenly, she bolted toward the side of the bed. But his arm stiffened like a vise across her hips, and he pulled her back hard. He was up on his knees, looking down at her as she lay on her side. He raised his hand and clubbed her on the side of her head.

"Uhh," she cried and tried to lift her hands to protect herself, but he held both of them down with one of his. He poised once again to strike.

"Lie still," he growled.

She squirmed beneath his weight. "Asshole! Pervert! Leave me the fuck alone." She spat the words out. He put his hand to her throat, choking the words off, and struck her heavily just above the ear. The blow thudded against her skull.

He cocked his arm again. This time her body went limp. There was silence as they studied each other in the darkness of the room. He waited a few moments to make certain that their understanding was complete.

She would not resist.

He would not hit her.

CHAPTER 2

Norma Winters arrived home just after 6 P.M. on Tuesday, August 6, a little later than normal and much too late for her husband, Bruce.

"Where the hell have you been?" he growled as she came through the door.

Almost immediately they were arguing. To Norma, it was petty and pointless. He knew very well where she'd been. For the past four months, she'd been working to open up her own business, and as often as not that meant twelve- and fourteen-hour days. Sometimes she got home late. But the argument was typical; they were always quarreling over something. Finally, Bruce, who had already eaten supper, went off to the bedroom in a huff. He customarily slept between 6 and 11 P.M. so he would be rested when he went to the Calexico border station where he worked on the midnight shift as a customs officer. Norma went into the family room where her mother, Virginia Holden, was sitting at the dinette.

Mrs. Holden said nothing until the bedroom door slammed. Then, with Bruce safely out of earshot, she looked at Norma and muttered, "Beth knows enough to put him in jail right now, if she'd only tell you."

Norma narrowed her eyes and glared at her mother. "What do you mean by that?"

"I don't know." She looked away. "I can't tell you. I can't say any more."

"What do you mean you can't say any more? You can't just say something like that and leave it be. What are you talking about?"

But her mother just shrugged.

Norma walked quickly toward the bathroom, where Beth was washing her face, let herself in, and closed the door.

"Your granny just said you know something that could put daddy in jail. Now I want to know, just what does she mean by that?"

"I don't know," Beth replied, avoiding her mother's eyes. "Why don't you ask her?"

"I did ask her. She won't tell me. I'm your mother and I'm asking you, and I expect an answer."

Beth closed her eyes and sighed. Her face seemed pale. "Okay, mom," she said finally. "Let's go for a ride. We got a phone call today from Mr. Peterson to go pick up the letter for the loan. Let's go for a ride and get the letter, and I'll tell you."

The letter was part of Norma's application for a loan from the Small Business Administration to help her get her business—the Reliable Escrow Company—started. Since she'd returned from Europe, Beth had been helping with the final arrangements before the business opened, and Norma was particularly pleased that her daughter was going to stay on and work with her full time.

The two of them walked out to the car. Norma got in on the passenger side, and Beth slipped in behind the wheel. For more than a minute, as she backed the car out of the driveway and headed past the comfortable homes along Andrews Street, neither of them spoke. Finally, Norma broke the silence.

"Come on, Beth. What's this all about?"

"Oh, mom. I don't know. I don't know how to say it."

Norma didn't quite dare to guess what was troubling her daughter. "This isn't like you, Beth. You know you can tell me everything. I'm your mother."

Beth's eyes filled with tears. She glanced over at her mother, then looked back at the road. "Momma," she said finally. "I'm sorry. I think I'm pregnant."

"Oh, Beth, how could you? Are you sure?"

Her daughter nodded, still looking straight ahead. "I'm twelve days late."

"Oh, Beth, who was it?" It must have been someone she met in

Europe, Norma thought. She'd been gone more than a month. And she had no steady boyfriend in Holtville. Who else could it be?

"Momma, I'm sorry. I'm so sorry."

Norma felt the car sway slightly and then lurch back to its path. Her daughter was gripping the wheel so hard her fingers were white. "Who was it, Beth?"

"Oh, momma," she cried, "it was daddy."

The words jolted Norma like a surge of electricity. She sat bolt upright in her seat, and for a moment she was unable to speak. A picture of her husband and her daughter together flashed in her mind—a tangle of flesh. She closed her eyes tightly for a second, as if to wipe the image away. "Oh, God, tell me it was anybody, but not your father. Please. Please, Beth. Not your father!"

"I wish I could, momma. But I can't."

Norma said nothing for a minute and sat in her seat, stunned. She tried to work her mouth, but the words wouldn't come. They arrived at an intersection, stopped, then turned the corner.

"When? When did this happen?" she asked. "I mean—"

"He's been, ah, well, he's been playing with me for a long time, for about six years. Since when I was in the seventh grade, when we lived in the white house across the street from the high school."

"My God. Six *years.* My God. What's he been doing to you? I mean, has he, ah, have you—" She stopped for a moment. "Has he actually—"

"No, momma, he never actually, ah, you know, ah, he never really did it to me, you know, entered me or anything, he just—"

"Well, how can you be pregnant then?"

"—he just, ah, played with . . . he played with me and rubbed me and—" She was speaking very slowly, stumbling on nearly every word. "He put his hands around there, you know, and ah, he, well, he came on me twice between my legs."

Norma shuddered. Was this the man she'd married, the man she'd lived and slept with, the man whose children she'd borne? How could he have done it? A horrible possibility crossed her mind. Had he ever been with Beth and then come into their bedroom wanting to make love? Trees and telephone poles moved past Norma in a blur. The car seemed to be driving itself. She thought she was going to vomit.

"And I douched and everything. I didn't know how close you had to be to, you know, get pregnant—" She broke into tears again. When she could speak, she said she had read that a man didn't actually have to be inside you for you to get pregnant, if it happened close enough. The last time it was close was a couple of weeks before she left for Europe.

"But Beth," Norma said, "you had your period the day you left." She remembered the day because her daughter had seemed unusually happy about the event. Norma had figured she was just happy to get it over with before the vacation. Now she knew better.

"Yes, I know, momma, but you, remember, you told me you had two periods after you became pregnant with me."

Norma slumped back. She knew her daughter's cycle was very regular. Twelve days late was very unusual.

"My God, why didn't you tell me about this? Six years this has been going on? Six years?" She glared at her daughter in anguish. "Why didn't you *say* something?"

Beth told her how her father had said that no one would believe her and that if she said anything, it would turn into a big scandal in a small town like Holtville. "And he said the boys would all know about me and that no boy would have anything to do with me."

"How could he do this to you? How could that man do this to his own daughter, his own flesh and blood!"

"Granny knew, momma, but I made her swear not to tell you. I was afraid. He threatened me, and he hit me in the head, where no one could see the bruises."

Somehow, the car arrived at Mr. Peterson's house. Norma remained in the car and watched as Beth walked slowly to the door. Suddenly, she felt distant from her daughter, as if the girl she had nurtured and raised was somehow a stranger to her; indeed, as if for the past six years, everything she had thought was true had not been true at all.

But as Beth came back toward the car, her face twisted in pain; she seemed so young, so fragile, that Norma wanted to wrap her arms around her.

"No one's home, momma," Beth said as she got back into the car.

They continued to drive around, with no particular destination. Even with air conditioning, the air in the car felt thick and heavy and seemed to press into Norma's face. It was no better with the windows open; at 7 P.M. it was still hot and dry, and there was little breeze. For a while all Norma could feel was horrified and sick. Her chest ached. She wanted to scream. But as they rode around the town, her feelings became more mixed; she felt hurt and betrayed, not only by her husband, but by Beth herself and by her own mother. The two of them had been living in the same house with her all these years, and they had kept this horrible secret from her. Norma thought she and her daughter were close. They talked about a lot of things together. Why couldn't she have talked about this? She could tell her grandmother, why not her mother?

"I don't understand, Beth. Why didn't you say something sooner. Why didn't you tell me?"

"Oh, momma, he told me there would be a big scandal and that he would lose his job and you would lose your job and we would have to move and everything. I didn't want that to happen. And I didn't want to hurt you."

Beth looked more composed now, and she was able to talk more about when it happened.

"Remember the time when dad cracked his ribs and he said he had an accident at work?"

Norma nodded.

"Well, it wasn't at work. He fell over a table chasing me, and he just made that up. And the time just before I went to Europe when I hurt my knee and I told you I fell at school? I made that up. I wrenched it trying to get away from him." Beth explained that the lock on her door, which Norma thought young David had broken, had in fact been jimmied by her father. And once she had asked grandma to stay home from a planned vacation in order to keep her eye on her father and protect her from him.

Norma began to cry again. She remembered a time when Bruce and Beth had been playing on the bed. It had been just innocent roughhousing, she had thought, until she noticed that her husband had an erection. She had hollered at him, wondering what was going on. But he had berated and mocked her and had said it was all in her mind. By the time he had finished with her, Norma hadn't even been sure about what she had seen. He had made her feel so low that she hadn't dared question him or speak to him about it again. Now that scene and the ones Beth was talking about began to haunt her. Maybe she herself was to blame. Six years, she repeated to herself. How could I not have known? Why didn't I notice anything? Why didn't I do something?

"Tell me it isn't true," she pleaded. "Tell me it was somebody you met in Europe, somebody you don't know and don't care about. We can take care of it. But just tell me it isn't your father."

"I'm sorry, momma, but I can't."

They were back on Andrews Street, and Beth turned into their driveway and parked. The two women looked at each other, their eyes red and swollen and their cheeks tracked with tears.

"Momma, I'm going to leave home. I'm eighteen now and out of high school, and I don't have to stay. I'll stay with Walt and Ellen and work for Walt or find some job in San Diego. But I can't stay home anymore, not as long as daddy is there."

Norma nodded. Beth paused a moment at the front door. They embraced, crying.

Inside the house, Bruce was still asleep, and Norma was thankful. She went to the telephone to call Ellen Harris. Although Ellen was Bruce's sister, she was much closer to Norma than to her brother. Norma felt as if they were sisters.

When Ellen answered, Norma wasted no time with small talk. She blurted out what Beth had told her.

There was a brief silence at the other end of the line. "Norma, you don't mean it! Tell me you don't mean it!"

"Yes, yes, I do. Beth just told me the whole story."

Ellen called Walt Lovell, the man she lived with, to the phone and asked Norma to repeat the story.

"It's been going on for six years. Can you imagine that, six years. I'd like to kill the son of a bitch."

"Norma," Lovell said calmly, "why don't you come to San Diego tomorrow and bring Beth. We'll put you both up here at our house."

Lovell, a financial management consultant, had been helping Norma with the arrangements for her new business. Though she wasn't overly fond of him, he had done a lot for her. And now his voice was calm and soothing.

"I'll contact an attorney friend of mine, and you can talk to him about this problem."

"I'm not about to live with Bruce, I can tell you that."

"Well, you can talk to this attorney about what needs to be done."

Norma said nothing for a moment. She was overcome once again with tears. "He got her pregnant," she blurted. "He got his own daughter pregnant."

"How do you know that?" Lovell asked quietly.

"Because Beth missed her period."

"All right. I will make arrangements for her to see a doctor tomorrow. Then we will know for sure. If she is, then we can arrange for her to have an abortion. Don't worry, Norma, everything will be all right. Try to get some sleep, and we can talk this over tomorrow when you get here. Ellen and I will take care of it."

Norma was grateful for the offer. She didn't want to go to a doctor or a lawyer in El Centro. Everybody knew everybody, and the story would spread quickly through the community. If she and Beth could get out of the house for a few days, they would at least avoid the inevitable confrontation with Bruce.

"Okay," she said. "Thank you. One of the men working in the office has to drive to San Diego tomorrow, anyway, to pick up some papers. We'll come with him."

"Very good," Lovell said in a steady, reassuring voice. "Everything will be all right."

Later that night, after Beth was in bed, Norma prepared a light lunch for her husband, and then, instead of going into the room as she often did, she knocked on the bedroom door to awaken him for work. She said nothing to him unless he spoke first, and in the kitchen, as he was about to leave, she stared at him from a distance, but would not allow her eyes to meet his.

Norma went to bed herself at about midnight, but she could not sleep. The anger and resentment welled up within her. It would do no good to confront him. He would only back her down. And he could probably get Beth to admit somehow that it wasn't true, that she was lying. That bastard, she thought. His own flesh and blood. Beth was pregnant. She was going to leave home. All because of him.

Norma didn't know what to do. She wished he were dead. A man like that didn't deserve to live.

CHAPTER 3

Norma and Bruce Winters lived in a brown ranch-style house in a comfortable neighborhood of tree-lined streets and well-landscaped lots off Highway 80, the main road through Holtville. A three-foot brick wall ran along the edge of the front yard, and a large picture window looked out onto the lawn. At eight o'clock the next morning, Wednesday, August 7, Emanuel "Manny" Lopez came by the house in his oversized pickup truck to get Norma and Beth for the trip to San Diego.

They drove first to Norma's office, a modest, single-story office building about ten miles away on the outskirts of the El Centro business district, one of the commercial centers of California's Imperial Valley. As they turned into the parking lot, Norma flinched. Bruce's car was there. He often stopped by on his way home from work, but Norma was hoping he would head straight home that morning. She didn't want to talk to him. She just wanted to escape. She walked in, holding her breath.

He was sitting in the office in his customs uniform, smoking a cigarette. She had always considered him good-looking, especially in uniform, but now, as she looked at his balding head, his long, thick sideburns, and his mustache and goatee, he seemed ugly. She pictured that face, its eyes intense, stalking Beth, and she imagined a look of terror on her daughter's face. He was an animal, she thought. A scream seemed to catch in her throat. She looked away from him.

"Beth and I are going to National City and spend a few days with Walt and Ellie," she said. "We've got some more paperwork to do. We'll be back over the weekend."

He shrugged absently, but said nothing. Norma gathered some papers from the desk and left without saying good-bye.

She said little to Manny as they headed out of El Centro on Interstate 5, which crossed the mountains that separate the desert of Imperial Valley from the temperate climate of San Diego. She'd known him for only a month. He was doing carpentry work at her office in exchange for rent for his own office, which was to be set up in the same building.

She looked over at him. He was about twenty-five and had dark skin, a thick, bushy beard, and serious brown eyes. She tried to talk to him about the business, the weather, anything to take her mind off Beth. But she was unable to concentrate on anything else. She didn't want to say anything to Manny about her personal problems, but finally, after Beth had fallen asleep in the back of the cab, Norma just had to talk.

"I'm going to have to get rid of Bruce," she said.

Manny rubbed his thumbs on the wheel, glanced over at her, then looked straight ahead. He said nothing.

"I'm going to see a lawyer in San Diego, and I'm going to divorce him. Do you know what he did? He's been playing around with Beth. His own daughter." Her eyes filled with tears, and she looked away, out the passenger-side window.

Manny cleared his throat. "Yeah, well, that sounds bad. I don't blame you."

"I wish to God he was dead."

Manny laughed nervously and looked over at Norma. He said nothing.

"Can you imagine that? His own daughter." Eventually, Norma dropped the subject. She felt embarrassed and sorry to have involved him in her troubles. They rode for most of the rest of the two-hour trip in silence.

Manny dropped Norma and Beth off at Walt and Ellen's house, a modest, five-room apartment in National City, a San Diego suburb. Ellen met them at the door, and they all embraced, crying.

For the first time since her talk with her daughter, Norma felt she could relax. Throughout the afternoon, when she could muster the strength, she sat with Walt and Ellen in their living room and told them the whole story.

At ten the next morning the four of them met with Dennis Howe, an attorney for whom Lovell had done some consulting. Lovell had already outlined the problem for the attorney the previous afternoon over the telephone, and he had explained that he was also contacting a doctor to examine Beth. But now Lovell told Howe that the doctor he had found was Roman Catholic and would be unlikely to recommend an abortion if Beth was pregnant. Norma and Beth had already agreed that abortion was their only option. Howe offered to contact another doctor immediately.

Norma was preoccupied with options. The events of the past two days had brought crisis to seemingly every aspect of her life. What effect would all of this have on her new business? Should her husband be prosecuted? How would he react to divorce papers? He might kill her. He had threatened that before. Still, her overriding concern was Beth. It was bad enough that her husband had—had done that to her. But the possibility that she might be pregnant by him affected Norma deeply. Thinking about it left her weak. She was both pleased and anxious when, within an hour of their arrival at the lawyer's office, Howe found a doctor who could examine Beth immediately. Ellen went to the appointment with her. Norma and Lovell remained with the lawyer.

Howe had no immediate answers to the question of prosecuting Bruce. He said he would consult with a lawyer from the district attorney's office without mentioning names and that he would then meet with them again late in the day to talk about that further.

"But my suspicions are that since your daughter is eighteen, it will be up to her to decide to bring charges, and she will have to be a witness and testify in a trial."

"I don't know if she'll want to do that," Norma said softly. "I don't think she would want to go through this in public."

In fact, she couldn't imagine Beth bringing charges under those circumstances. She had gone through enough already, and a trial would just create the scandal her father had threatened her with all along. Norma didn't want her to bring charges, either.

"I'd like to keep all these family problems private," she said. "I don't want to jeopardize my new business. I definitely want a divorce, and I'd like to see them lock Bruce up for what he did and throw away the key." She paused for a moment, wiping away tears. "But I want to hold everything, the serving of papers and everything, until after I get my loan." Bruce would have to sign the application, she said, and he would never sign it if he knew she had started a divorce action.

Howe said he wasn't sure such action could be kept private, and he didn't know how her husband's conduct with Beth would affect the divorce proceedings.

"But if what you say here is true and you can prove it, you could probably send him to Atascadero for six months to a year."

"In six months he'd come back and kill me."

"Well, we can have a restraining order put on him, keeping him out of the house, off the premises and away from you."

"It's just a piece of paper. He can still kill me, and then you can see how good your restraining order is."

Howe shrugged. "Well, the order will guarantee you protection. You can call the police."

"What are they going to do, stay at my house twenty-four hours a day? You don't know the man. He's mean, he's been mean to me. He has beaten me and threatened to kill me. I'd have done this a long time ago, but I'm scared of him, scared of what he'll do." She sighed and sat back in her chair, saying nothing for a moment. Then she looked back at Howe. "Well, I suppose that is the best you can do," she said quietly. She felt helpless.

Shortly after 1 P.M. Howe's secretary called into the office to say that Beth and Ellen had returned. Norma's pulse drummed in her ears. She closed her eyes tightly for a moment. She wanted to know, but didn't want to ask. Then she got up and hurried out into the waiting area.

"She's not pregnant, Norma," Ellen said.

"Oh, thank God," Norma cried. She embraced Beth and broke into tears. Together they walked back into Howe's office.

"Thank God, she's not pregnant," Norma said to the lawyer. Then she collapsed in a chair and cried. She couldn't stop.

For the rest of the week, Norma and Beth remained at Walt and

Ellen's, where Norma continued to work on papers for her own business and to help Lovell with a backlog of paperwork in his consulting practice. She did the work mechanically, and much of the time felt in a daze. She was overwhelmed by the events of Tuesday and Wednesday. And her diet medication, which occasionally left her light headed and distracted, or so Beth had told her, seemed to have affected her, as well. She kept losing track of large chunks of time. She replayed again and again in her mind the story Beth had told her during their long ride in the car. Was her daughter damaged for life? Would she be able to marry? Would she ever be happy? Her own husband had done this to her daughter. He had forced Beth to move away from her. He had broken up the home. He had imperiled her new business. He was an animal. Worse still, something she couldn't bear to think about, the bastard was going to get away with it. She couldn't let that happen. She had to do something.

And on Friday, August 9, 1974, she did.

CHAPTER 4

Norma Winters stepped out of the elevator onto the eleventh floor of the Associates Office Tower in San Diego at precisely 4 P.M. She had called earlier, and the receptionist was expecting her. So was Anthony Pappas, a prominent San Diego businessman for whom Norma had closed an escrow earlier in the year on a restaurant he'd bought in Calexico, near El Centro. She'd been working for another company at the time, and he'd been especially cordial to her, even sending flowers and a letter thanking her for her work on the transaction. It hadn't been his cordiality, however, that had prompted her call. She'd heard things about Pappas, nothing specific, nothing that had ever been pinned down as far as she knew, just rumors about his connections that indicated he might be able to help her.

Pappas's carpeted, expensively paneled office offered a stunning panorama of San Diego. Norma closed the door behind her and sat down without saying hello.

Pappas greeted her with a smile. "Well, what can I do for you?"

"I have a problem," she heard herself say, "and I want you to help me find somebody to kill my husband."

Pappas rose immediately from behind his desk. "I don't want you talking to me about things like that. I think you'd better leave, Mrs. Winters." He began to move toward the door.

"But wait, you don't even know the reason."

Pappas didn't answer. He walked to his door and tersely asked his secretary to show her out.

"That's all right. I'll go by myself," she said. She walked out and hurried to the elevator, looking at no one. She felt stupid.

The next afternoon, a Saturday, she went home to Holtville with her nephew Frank, who had also spent most of the week with her and Beth in National City. Beth however, did not go home; she remained behind with Ellen and Walt. When Norma showed up at home without her, Bruce went into a rage. He told her to send Beth's clothes to her. And he accused Norma of having gone to bed with Lovell and with Frank.

Norma perfunctorily denied sleeping with anyone. He'd made the accusation so often that it had become meaningless and pointless to argue about it. She did not confront him directly with what Beth had told her, but later that evening, hoping to prompt some reaction from him, she told him she'd read a magazine article about a girl whose father had forced her to have sex with him. "Don't you think that's low?" she asked. "Just as low as you can get? If I ever found out you did anything like that to Beth, I'd kill you."

Bruce's facial expression didn't change. He said nothing.

On Sunday, her thirty-seventh birthday, Norma went into her office with some of the papers she had brought back from Lovell's house. Manny was there, continuing with the carpentry work.

Norma thought maybe he knew somebody who could help. He had dual citizenship, Mexican and American, and she thought he might have contacts in Mexico. So, she asked him. At first he laughed. But when she asked him again, he stammered and said it would take some time. Norma thought he was putting her off, and she didn't think Manny would do anything. Once again she felt stupid. She didn't know where else she could turn.

Late Monday afternoon Norma stood on the soft new wall-to-wall carpeting in her office. The smell of freshly cut fabric hung in the air as she scanned the room, planning in her mind where the new office furniture would go. It was now about two weeks before she would open the Reliable Escrow Company. She had lost some valuable time during the past week with Walt and Ellen and it seemed she still had months of work before she would be ready.

Just before 4:30 the telephone rang. Norma's secretary answered, then looked at her. "It's for you," she said. "A guy named Al, from San Diego."

Norma picked up the phone. "This is Norma," she said pleasantly. "May I help you?"

"Norma Winters?"

"Yes, it is."

"Hi. My name is Al, from San Diego." The voice was cool and rough.

"Uh-huh."

"Say, I understand you have a problem."

"On what?"

"Ah, something you want to get rid of."

Norma said nothing for a moment, but pressed the telephone to her ear.

"Mmmm, yeah." She felt uneasy. Who was this? How did he know?

"Well, is there any way we can get together to talk about it?"

"When?"

"You name it. How about tonight?"

Norma couldn't meet anyone tonight. But she agreed to meet the following day at 1 P.M. at Denny's Restaurant in El Centro, just off Interstate 8. The restaurant had a tall sign, easily visible from the highway.

"How will I know you?" the voice asked.

"Let's see, what could I be wearing? Well, I'll have on a pair of white pants and a blue top."

"White pants and a blue top."

"And you?"

"I got long hair, a mustache, and a goatee. I'll be driving a brown Oldsmobile."

"Okay, can you hold on just a moment?"

"All right."

Norma put the telephone on "hold." She walked quickly across the office, where a couple of real-estate brokers, a carpenter, and the secretary were talking, to her own desk, behind a partition that rose about two-thirds of the way from the floor to the ceiling. She picked up the phone on her desk.

"I'm sorry. I didn't have any privacy," she said. "Ah, Manny mean anything to you?"

"Pardon me?"

"Manny."

"Money?"

"Manny. I don't know what, ah, maybe we're not talking about the same thing. I don't know."

"I'm talking about something you want done."

This time the voice was firm and direct, almost demanding. Norma thought for a moment.

"Yes," she finally replied. "Okay."

"What are you prepared to pay?"

"I don't know. I'll have to work that out."

She had not given the price much consideration. She had no idea what the job would cost.

"Okay. Well, there's some things I'll need," he said. "I'll need some pictures."

"Okay."

"I'll need some front money. I have to have five hundred dollars for expenses to start with."

"Okay. I don't think I can have it tomorrow, but we'll talk tomorrow."

"We'll figure it out. I need a list of addresses and locations, where he works, what kind of car he drives."

Norma frowned. "You're not setting me up, are you?"

"Are you serious?"

"I hope you're not setting me up. I swear to God I do."

"Well, it's not my business, lady."

She sighed. "Okay."

"Are you interested or not?"

"I am. Most definitely."

"Okay, get the pictures, the addresses, the vehicle."

"Okay."

"And anything else you can think of."

"Okay, but I can't have the money tomorrow."

"Well, when can you have the money?"

"I don't know. We'll talk about that tomorrow, okay?"

"Okay, but ah—"

"I don't have any privacy here," she interrupted. The visitors and workers lingering in the office made her uncomfortable. Even though the partition separated her from them, and though her voice was soft, she feared being overheard.

"You realize that I want to get this over with as fast as I can," Al from San Diego said.

"You realize I do too?"

"Okay. I'll see you at one o'clock tomorrow."

"Okay," Norma said. "Thank you."

Norma hung up, frightened and not quite sure what she had done. Had she actually talked to this man, this voice, about killing her husband? Was she being set up? Surely, Mr. Pappas had not arranged that call. She hadn't been in his office more than a minute. Or was that the way they operated?

When everyone had left her office, she went back to the telephone to call Manny.

"Hello, Manny. Have you contacted anyone yet?"

"About what?"

"Somebody just called me and asked if I wanted to get rid of someone. Did you talk to anybody?"

"Hell no," Manny replied.

It didn't make sense. She had talked about it to only two people. Neither could have found anyone. Yet, she had just agreed to meet someone the next day who seemed quite ready to do it. W it? How had he found out?

At her home later that evening, after the dinner dishes had been cleared from the table, washed, and put away, and after her husband had gone to sleep to rest before work, Norma gathered the items that Al from San Diego had said he would need before he could do the job. She slipped a tiny snapshot of her husband from one of the plastic windows in his wallet. She took a pen and wrote on a piece of white paper the numbers of the license plates of the family's three cars. And she found a map of Imperial Valley that showed where they lived and where he worked. She placed all three items together in her pocketbook and wondered whether she would go to Denny's the next afternoon and hand them to Al from San Diego.

CHAPTER 5

At 12:45 the next afternoon Norma walked out of her office into the dry mid-August desert heat. It was a hundred and ten degrees, and the inside of her blue Buick with its white vinyl roof was as hot as a furnace. She hardly noticed. Instinctively, she slipped her sunglasses on and pushed the air-conditioning button as she headed out of the small parking lot next to her office, out to South Imperial Avenue and the five-minute drive to Denny's.

She was wearing a blue long-sleeved blouse and white flared slacks, the outfit she'd described to Al from San Diego on the telephone, and she tried to imagine what he would look like. Probably a Hell's Angels type, she figured, mean, tough, and ugly. Who else would do this for money? She shuddered as she recalled stories about such men, stories about murder, drugs, and sex. Her foot shook as she depressed the accelerator. Or maybe he was a cop. She ___ ure which possibility frightened her more.

___ here was no other way. Bruce deserved it. His own daugh-___ very thought made her more determined. She gripped the wheel tighter as she drove down the street, blaming the moisture in her palms on the heat.

Presently, the yellow plastic "Denny's" sign over the restaurant parking lot loomed ahead. She was almost there. She couldn't turn back now. The event had a momentum of its own.

As she pulled into the parking area, she spotted Manny's truck parked among the cars of the lunch-hour customers and breathed a little easier. He had reluctantly agreed that morning to be there during this meeting to keep an eye out for her, although she hadn't told him exactly why. She didn't know what he could do; she just wanted him there.

She drove to the left of the one-story building, to the side parking lot, which Denny's shared with the adjacent Holiday Inn. She parked near the end of the lot, well away from the building and the other cars. Then she clutched her white pocketbook containing the items Al from San Diego had requested, and stepped out of the car. She walked quickly across the parking lot, around the corner of the restaurant, to the entrance, pulled open the glass door, and stopped short. He was standing right in front of her, leaning against the wall.

Norma took a deep breath and removed her sunglasses. She looked at the floor, at the wall, at the man's feet. When she could not wait a moment longer, she looked up. His eyes met hers, and he stepped toward her.

"You must be Norma," he said.

She nodded. "You must be Al."

His eyes seemed to look right through hers to the back of her head. His hair was curly and brown, and his mustache and goatee gave him a tough appearance; but he wasn't ugly. Still, the eyes were cold and mean. Could she trust him?

"You didn't tell me it was hot over here," he said in an almost friendly tone.

"Yeah." She barely heard the remark.

They walked into the dining room, where the hostess greeted them and seated them in the first of a long row of pink-and-tangerine vinyl booths. Norma slid into the first seat, her back toward the door, but avoided looking out over the rest of the booths and tables. She didn't want to see anyone she knew. She didn't even dare look for Manny.

"Care for a drink?" the man asked.

"I don't know if they serve them out here or not. It's lunch time, and you might have to go to the bar to drink. How do I know you're on the level?"

The words seemed to spill out of her mouth. She didn't even pause between the two sentences. This wasn't a time to be social. She wanted to know what she was dealing with.

"Pardon me?"

"How do I know you're on the level?"

"Well, let's just say I owe a friend a favor."

"Can't you explain how—"

"I can't name names. That's how I stay alive and out of jail."

"Can't you give me anything to let me know?"

"Well, I'll tell you this." There was an edge to his voice. "I just drove over a hundred miles. I'm hot, and I don't want to be wasting my time."

"You aren't wasting your time. It's just that I'm afraid anything I say may end up in court against me. I'm afraid you're setting me up."

"*You're* afraid. *I* could be a setup."

"Well, you're not. I wouldn't do that."

"What guarantee do I have?"

She shrugged. "You don't."

"Ah. In my business, you don't take chances."

Norma looked at him quizzically. Who was he kidding? She had to reassure *him*? "I haven't done this before," she said.

He leaned toward her and looked her straight in the eye. "I have."

"Hello, I'm Sherry," a cheerful voice interrupted. Norma jumped, hitting her knee under the table. "I'm your waitress." She placed a glass of water in front of each of them. "Want some coffee?"

"Please," Norma said, feeling almost breathless.

"Yeah, I guess," Al from San Diego added.

The waitress left, and they said nothing for a moment. Norma searched his face, his eyes, for some indication of a cover. She wasn't sure what she was looking for, but whatever it was she couldn't find it.

"I'm serious," she said finally. "I'm dead serious."

"Lady, I'm serious too. It's my business."

The coffee arrived. Norma spooned a couple of ice cubes from her water glass into the coffee to cool it. But she couldn't make her hand stop shaking, and one of the ice cubes rattled out of the spoon and fell onto the table.

"You don't have anything to worry about," he said, soothingly.

"I don't? I'm worried about myself. The less you know about me, the better."

"Well, there are a few things I have to know about whoever it is."

"You don't know who it is?" she snapped. Norma was immediately suspicious.

"Well, I heard it's your husband. Is that right?"

"Um hmm."

"I have to know a few things about him. I have to have some idea of the reasons, so you don't come back on me. Now, once he's dead, he's dead."

"I hope to God he doesn't come back."

"Well, I don't want you to have a change of heart."

"Oh, I won't. You don't have to worry about that."

He asked her why she wanted him dead. She said she was scared of him. She had hoped to avoid the details, but the man pressed her. Norma hated even to think about it, much less to tell a perfect stranger. But as she considered how to phrase it, her fear seemed to abate for the first time in the conversation, and she felt angry instead.

"He has molested my daughter," she said quietly, "my eighteen-year-old daughter, and I found out about it last week."

Al from San Diego smiled faintly. "Are you sure you want him *killed?*"

"Uh-huh. He's been messing around with her since she was twelve years old, and she's his own flesh and blood, his own daughter."

"You just now found this out?"

"I found out last week."

"She told you or what?"

"Yes, she told me."

"Did you say anything to him?"

"He doesn't have any idea that I know."

"How long have you been married?"

"Twenty years this June."

He was silent for a moment, then shook his head. "That's cold. That son of a bitch belongs in the ground. He's rotten."

He sounded almost sympathetic. She still didn't know who he was, but he'd heard the reason. He seemed to understand why she had to do it.

"Well, does he carry a gun?" he asked.

"He carries a gun. He has a federal permit to carry one."

"Ah, a federal officer, huh?"

His tone changed abruptly. He was all business again, Norma thought. She just nodded.

"Did you bring a picture or something?"

"Yeah."

"How much can you pay? How much are you going to get out of the insurance?"

"I haven't even thought about it. I'd have to add it up to see what's there."

"Well, I can't sit around here with my thumb up my ass when it's costing me money and my time. I need something."

"I know there's some money," she said. "I can't recall how much."

"Well, I'd like to have the price of a hotel and some expenses while I'm around here. At least give me enough to get back to the hotel and things until you can get more. It shouldn't take me more than a couple of days if I figure it out, you know, the way. I have to work it over and come up with the best place to—"

"Would five hundred be enough?" She blurted the figure without waiting for him to finish his sentence.

"Five hundred is enough, for the time I'm here."

"That's what I'm talking about."

"Yeah, that's not the total."

"I know it's not. I know that." She thought for a moment. She had no idea what she was committing herself to. "How much will I have to pay?"

"Well, I usually charge five grand," he said. "But a federal officer, ah, with heat like that, it'll cost you ten. Ten grand."

Norma nodded. "Okay. But there's another problem. I can't just pay you in one lump sum. It would be hard to explain where ten thousand dollars went. Can I give it to you in installments?"

"Well, what about the insurance? Aren't you going to get that in a lump sum?"

"I guess. But I don't know just when the payments would come through. And it would still look suspicious if anyone checked."

"Well, let me ask you this," the man said. "If he winds up dead, are they going to suspect you?"

"I don't think so. We've been married for twenty years. We've talked about divorce, but no one knows anything about that—that we've been having trouble. And people do know that I'm setting up the business and I wouldn't do anything to hurt that. I've got loans and an application to the Small Business Administration. I've got to have that loan or I'll lose the deal. People wouldn't suspect me, because they know I wouldn't want to hurt the business."

"Well, I don't want to know anything about your business."

"No, I don't want to know anything about yours, either," she replied. "Except that I'm still sort of curious about who told you about this."

He exhaled loudly, obviously annoyed with the question. "Let's put it this way," he said. "I owe a friend a favor. I got a phone call and this is my way of repaying the favor. I just heard that a woman in El Centro had a problem she wanted taken care of."

"Was it someone from Imperial Valley?"

"No. That I can tell you." He narrowed his eyes. "Ah, maybe you talked to somebody else. I mean, I don't have any competition, do I?"

"Nope," Norma said firmly. "You're the only one."

"I remember hearing you on the phone saying something about Manny."

"I was just testing you. I wanted to know if you knew what you were talking about."

"I don't want some guy named Manny shooting me."

"No. There is no one else involved in this." She kept her voice low-key and steady and looked directly at him as she said it. She considered the question dispensed with.

He asked for more information about Bruce. She told him that he worked the midnight-to-eight shift as a customs guard at Calexico.

"Is there any particular way you want it done?" he asked.

"I want it done good."

"I'll guarantee it will be permanent, but what I mean—"

"Will—will you give him a message for me?"

"Before I kill him?"

"Yes."

"What's the message?"

"That this is from his wife for what he did to his daughter."

"Sounds like you really want him planted."

"I hate his guts," she said, gritting her teeth. "I hate his god-damn guts."

"How are you going to feel when he's dead? Are you still going to hate him?"

"What?"

"Are you going to be pissed off?"

"At who?"

"At me."

"No. I don't even know who you are."

"Okay." He leaned toward her, and his gaze narrowed. "I'll tell you how it is before we go any further. I'll plant you in the desert if you try to burn me."

"Well, you don't have to worry about that."

"Then we understand each other."

"That's fine. I'm glad to hear you talk that way. I'd rather hear you talk that way than any other way."

Norma sipped her coffee and repeated the words to herself, "I'll plant you in the desert."

"Have you told anybody else?" he asked again. "I mean, if you're having me watched or anything while I'm hanging around this town. I don't want anyone spying on me or anything."

"No. You're probably having *me* watched. You're probably a goddamn cop."

"Well, actually I am," he said with a smile. "I do this part time. You know, you have to make a little side money."

Norma did not smile back. "That's probably what's going to happen. I'll probably end up in jail, because you're probably some kind of undercover man, secret agent, or something."

"You've been watching too much television."

"I don't watch television."

"Well, when can you get me the money? I should have the whole thing staked out by Thursday or Friday, and I need some money to get me by for a couple of days. How much do you have?"

"I don't have any with me right now," Norma said. "But I get paid from my job, and I can have some money for you, ah, on the fifteenth, Thursday."

"Well, do you have a credit card or something on your business, so you can give me a hundred bucks today for a hotel room?"

"Yes, I can do that."

"A hundred will get me by. Then you give me the other four on Thursday."

"Fine. I didn't bring anything with me, because I didn't know if I could trust you or not." She felt her pocketbook against her on the seat and was uncertain why she lied to him.

"You think I'm just fucking you around, huh?"

"I don't know."

"You think I drove a hundred goddamn miles just to jive you around?"

"I don't know."

"No, lady. That's not the way I operate. And I don't like to operate on my own money."

"Well, how am I going to pay off the rest of this?"

"Oh, that'll be easy. I'll give you a certain amount of time, and then, whenever you think it's clear, you'll run an ad in the personal column of the San Diego evening paper, and it'll say, uh, 'Al, come home.' Then I'll contact you."

"Is that what those things are used for?"

"Oh, they're used for everything. Then I'll know that you have something for me. If you want to do it in installments, that's okay with me. Ten installments?"

"Uh-huh." She nodded.

"Starting how long after?"

"Well, a month? I don't know how long after. I don't know how long it takes to get the insurance."

"Well, I'm sure you have some money in the bank, don't you? You've been married twenty years, you must have saved something."

"I just sunk it all into my new business."

"Well, can't you scrape a little out of it?"

"I don't know. I don't—"

"I mean, I could go a month. But that's the longest, without getting paid."

"Okay. I'll be sure to get the money for you."

"Then, when I read your thing in the paper, a month after, a month to the day after it makes the headlines."

"Uh-huh."

"A month from that day I'll expect to see something in the personal column. And I'll contact you."

"Okay."

Norma raised her cup and sipped more coffee. Ten thousand dollars, she thought. How would she get the money? She'd worry about that later, she said to herself. All that mattered now was getting rid of Bruce.

They set up a second meeting for later that afternoon at the bar, so Norma could give him the hundred dollars. She asked Al from San Diego when he planned to do the job.

"Before Friday," he said.

"That soon?"

"Yeah. I got something else to do."

"You're going to screw my weekend up." She told him she had plans to be in San Diego Saturday night.

"Well, would you like it done Saturday? If you can get away to San Diego?"

"No, I don't want that. I'm going somewhere Saturday that I don't want to have an alibi for." She hoped he wouldn't press the point.

"Okay. I don't want to mess around too goddamn long. If you do go to San Diego, when will you go?"

"Saturday morning."

"And when will you come back here?"

"Sunday night. I'll probably come back Sunday night."

"Does he work Saturday night?"

"Yes."

"What does he do then?"

"He comes home."

"Can you get me a key to your house?"

Norma said nothing. She didn't want this man in her house.

"I'll kill the son of a bitch while he's sleeping."

"You mean with my mother and son there?"

He scratched his beard and shrugged. "You just move everybody out of the house, and I'll go in and kill him in bed. I'll wake him up and give him your message first."

"Okay, can you do that Sunday?"

He frowned at the suggestion. "You're pushing me for Sunday night."

"I don't want it done Saturday, although I suppose I could call and say I can't make it Saturday night."

"No, that's all right. We'll go ahead with Sunday."

A picture of her husband sprawled on blood-stained sheets in their bed flashed in her mind.

"I don't want it done in my house," she said. "I'm going to stay in my house. Can you do it out in the country?"

"How am I going to get him out in the country?" he asked.

"How about Sunday night when he goes to work?"

He seemed to ponder the suggestion. "That's cool," he said, finally. "How far is it from here to where he works, from Holtville?"

"About seventeen miles, when he goes the back route."

"Okay, I'll tell you what. You give me the route he's going to be taking and the kind of car he's going to be driving, and I'll spend the next couple of days looking it over. And I'll meet you here at . . . what time do you get off?"

"Five o'clock."

"I'll meet you here at about five-fifteen. Give me a hundred bucks, I'll get a room, and we'll do this Sunday." He also asked for a good picture of her husband and for the license-plate number of the car he would drive.

"Okay," she said. "I'll get you everything you need to know." She stammered a moment. "There's no way of you getting caught, is there? I mean, if you're caught, what about me?"

"No way." His voice was stern. "Listen, lady, I've been doing this for a long time, and I haven't been caught yet. If I go down, I don't take anybody else with me. There's people who would zap me from the inside. Do you understand?"

"Uh-huh."

"Okay. Well, best I get to looking around here and finding out if it's safe. What's the local heat around here like? Is there any problem?"

"I have no idea." The question insulted her. "I'm a straight citizen. I don't know how you work."

She sipped more coffee, then stared into her nearly empty cup. "I wish he wouldn't make me do this," she said, "but if you think about it and see—"

"Hey. I have no feelings. I'd kill your mother if you want me to, if the price is right."

She said nothing, then looked up at him again. "I don't want to get caught at this."

"I put my ass on the line all the time. That's why I've been in business so long. I don't fuck up."

Norma swallowed the last mouthful of coffee and shifted in her seat. "I guess I better get back to work," she said.

Norma slipped her sunglasses on and walked with him outside, where the heat shimmered off the blacktop parking lot. He pointed out his car to her, so she would know it in case she had to meet him in it at some point. She showed him her car, the one her husband would probably drive, and she also showed him the side entrance to the bar at Denny's.

Norma stepped toward her car, then heard him speak and looked back.

"The message is good," he said.

"Huh?"

"The message. I can't get over that. I've never been asked to give a message before."

"Well, do that for me, would you?"

"Yeah. You sure she wasn't just bullshitting you?"

"No, I know she wasn't. She's not that kind of girl. She's a good girl."

"He's been balling her since she was twelve years old?"

"Well, he . . . not really. He was playing with her, fooling around, playing with her. I don't know how to put it in nice words."

"You can use any words you want. You're not going to hurt me."

"And he threatened her with scandal in our small community

of Holtville, and he said he would ruin her reputation."

"How long you been thinking of having him killed?"

"Seriously?"

"Yeah."

"Since last week. Off and on, the last ten years."

"Ten years?" His voice showed surprise.

"Off and on."

"Off and on?"

"Yeah. I don't know how I could bear him."

"You realize when he's dead, though, he's dead for a long time."

"I hope so. I hope to God he never comes back."

"That's one thing I can guarantee, unless you have to worry about him in a next life. Okay, I guess we've got everything straight. The money's the main thing."

"Okay."

"I've got to have the bread to operate."

"I've got to get to the bank before three."

"Okay. I'll let you go then. See you at five-fifteen."

Norma turned away and walked quickly toward her car, parked in the far end of the parking lot. Al from San Diego watched her for a moment, then walked toward his car.

A moment later another car, with two people in it, moved out of the lot and eased into the traffic just behind Norma as she headed down the street.

CHAPTER 6

Norma arrived back at her office about 1:45. Manny, who had left Denny's several minutes before she had, was already there, fidgeting with a carpenter's square.

"What did you think, Manny?" she asked. "Does he seem all right to you?"

He shrugged. "Well yeah, I guess so. I don't know."

"Really? Was he really okay, do you think?"

Manny's eyes shifted nervously. Norma knew the question made him uncomfortable, although she had not specifically told him who the man was or why she was meeting him. She did not want to ask him outright whether he thought Al from San Diego was a hit man.

"Yeah, he's fine. He's okay. I don't know what you want me to say."

She decided not to push him further, but she still needed his help. "Can you do one more thing for me?"

He nodded. "Yeah."

"I need you to cash a check for me. I can't tell you why, but I need a hundred dollars." She said she'd write the check to him and put it down in her records for construction work. "We'll make it okay later," she said.

Manny agreed. But even as he left for the bank, Norma was undecided about whether she would give Al from San Diego the money. She still had no assurance that he wasn't a cop, that she wasn't a setup. She still had no explanation for his telephone call. Yet, he seemed to be on her side. He had heard the reason. "That's rotten," he'd said. "That son of a bitch belongs in the ground." Now all she had to do was show up at the meeting, give him the money and the other things he needed, and it would be over. She'd be free. Just the thought brought a sense of relief. It wasn't just the messing with Beth that she would escape, although that was certainly the worst of it. It was nearly twenty years of living in fear of him, of being tormented and sometimes beaten by him.

She couldn't wait. Al from San Diego was right. He was rotten. He belonged in the ground. And there was one other thing the man had said that she mulled over in her mind. "If you burn me, I'll plant you in the desert." She shuddered. If she changed her mind now, she thought, she'd be killed. No, that couldn't happen. If anyone was going to be killed in this, it would be her husband. He made her do this. Why should she suffer any more?

When Manny returned with the hundred dollars, she put it in her pocketbook. She checked to make sure the map and the picture were still there, and she typed the list of license numbers.

It was almost over, she thought. For the rest of the afternoon, she felt almost giddy.

Shortly before 5 P.M., she changed into a pair of green pants and a green tank top, checked the contents of her pocketbook one more time, and bid a cheery good-bye to her secretary.

In the car her anxiety returned. Why couldn't this be over with, she wondered. Should she really see him again? What if she got caught? Then what would happen to the kids? She couldn't think about that. She had to go through with it. Or did she? She seemed to have lost the ability to decide. Her car seemed to drive itself to Denny's.

As she pulled into the parking lot, she spotted an El Centro police car in front of the restaurant. He *was* a cop, dammit, she thought. She was caught. But she couldn't make herself drive away. She watched the policeman carefully as she found a parking space. He wasn't looking at her. As she parked and walked toward the bar entrance, he drove away. She took a deep breath and tried to relax. She felt like a rubber band, one moment taut and the next at ease. She walked quickly toward the bar. Al from San Diego walked out to meet her.

"Hi," he said.

"I saw the police out there, and I thought, 'Oh, shit.' "

"Where?"

"Out in front." She nodded toward the restaurant entrance.

"Well, look, I got a room."

"Oh, you do?" He seemed unruffled, she thought.

"Why don't you go into the coffee shop, wait there five minutes, then come to room 374."

"Where's that?"

He pulled a key from his pocket and showed her the number. "It's in the rear of the hotel." He narrowed his eyes slightly. "You got everything?"

Norma squeezed the handle of her pocketbook. "Yes."

She walked around the corner, back through the glass door and into the restaurant, and took a seat at the counter. She ordered a cup of coffee. After the waitress brought it, she took a couple of sips; then, without checking to see how long she'd been there, she got up, left a quarter by her cup, and walked out. She went around behind the restaurant, under an elevated wooden walkway that went past the swimming pool, and then stepped into the hotel. She blinked her eyes in the darkened corridor until she could see, before walking up two flights to the top floor and wandering down the hallway until she found the door of room 374. She hesitated, then knocked twice. Al from San Diego opened it almost immediately.

"Is everything okay?" he asked.

"Yes." It was dark and very cool in the room. Norma shivered.

"Okay, I'll be in this room for the rest of the time I'm in El Centro," he said. "In case you want to contact me."

"Can I sit down?"

"Sure."

Norma sat on one of the two beds and started to shake. She didn't know whether it was the cold or whether she was just nervous. She felt in a daze.

"You don't mind if I shake, do you?" she asked.

"It is kind of cold in here."

"It really is." He sat across from her on the other bed and looked at her, saying nothing.

Finally, she looked down at her pocketbook and opened it. Her fingers felt numb. Her hands seemed detached from her arms. She pulled out a handful of bills and watched herself give them to Al from San Diego.

"Twenty, forty, sixty, eighty, ninety, one hundred," he said. He folded the money carefully and put it into his pants pocket, then looked at her. "Okay."

She took the map from her pocketbook, spread it out on her lap, and traced with her finger the red line she had marked on it, showing her husband's route to work.

"Well, is this all kind of desolate out there?" Al from San Diego asked, drawing a circle with his finger along the route.

"This is all with no houses, except a little country bar."

"At 11:30 at night, there's no traffic on these streets at all?"

"No."

"Okay, I'll have to case it. I'll have to make sure."

Then she handed him two small pictures of her husband, including the photocopy. It showed him in uniform, with his customs badge.

"Does he still look like this?"

"Well, not exactly. He has grown a goatee and a mustache."

"Is his hair still the same?"

"Yes."

He looked intently at the picture. "He has a mustache now?"

"He's got a mustache."

"How long ago was the picture taken?"

"I don't know."

"Do you want me to keep the picture?"

She shook her head. "No, you take the copy here. I got that out of his wallet last night, and I'm going to have to put it back."

He handed her the picture. She put it back in her pocketbook and gave him the slip of paper with the license numbers on it. It included brief descriptions of the cars and the note, "Leaves home approximately 11:30 P.M. Goes down Orchard Road, over freeway to Calexico." He told her he would memorize the numbers and throw the paper away.

"He might be driving the '62 Comet, white and blue," she said. "It's not registered." She also suggested he would drive the Buick she had driven to the hotel. She just didn't know which car he would take.

"I think he's going to work tonight," she continued, "and I'll have to drive him down, since the other car doesn't work. He couldn't get it started."

"That's cool," he said. He paused. "I'll be there when you bring him down." That way, he said, he'd be able to get a good look at him. It would be better than relying on the picture.

"I'll be down at the border station to see you drop him off tonight. And I'll check it out tomorrow and go over the route, figure out how I'm going to do it. Now, is there any problem as far as anyone being at the house over the weekend?"

"My mother will be there."

"Does she have a house or anything?"

"No. She's old, and we take care of her. She couldn't live alone."

"Well, what are you going to do with her?"

"When?"

"Over the weekend. I thought you wanted everyone out of the house."

"Aren't you going to do it when he's going to work?"

"Yeah."

"Well, I don't want you around the house."

"I was just thinking it would probably be easier to do it the way you say, but if something happens, I'll have to do it another way."

"I don't know if I can get her out of the house. Where will she go? What will I tell her?"

"Well, you understand that if things aren't really right, I can't afford the chance of a mess up."

"I know that, and I don't want you to."

Norma said nothing for a moment. Maybe if he really got a good look at Bruce, he could do it Sunday on his way to work. "Look, if you're up there at eight in the morning, you could see him when I pick him up, too."

"Good. I'll get a good look at him in the daylight, too. Where do you want me to shoot him?"

"Any place you want to. I don't care."

He raised his eyebrows. "No preference?"

She stared at him and looked down. She pictured her husband,

naked and hairy, forcing himself on Beth. "Yes, I've got a preference," she said. She was hardly aware she was answering him.

"You can tell me," he said with a grin. "I'm a big boy."

Norma said nothing.

"You want him to die slow or to go fast?"

"I want him to go fast. I don't want him to suffer. I just want
him dead."

"You thought it all over now and you're sure?"

"I thought it all over, and my secretary said to me, 'You're
happier this afternoon than I've seen you in a long time.' I'm just
really happy that it's going to be over with, that I'm going to be
rid of him."

He grinned again. "Aw, she just thought you snuck away for a
nooner."

"No sir. She said, 'I'm glad to see you smiling again. You look
really happy.' "

"Okay, there are a couple of things I got to know for sure. You
said something back at the coffee shop, and after you left I got to
thinking about it. You asked me if it was from here that I got the
information."

She nodded.

"Have you talked to anybody here?"

"No."

"Are you sure?"

"I'm positive."

"And when are you going to have that other four hundred
dollars?"

"Didn't I say the fifteenth?"

"Yes."

"I'll get it to you then."

"Tell me the real reason you want him killed," he said.

"That's exactly the reason. I hate the son of a bitch."

"That's all?"

"That's about enough. You don't know how mean he is to me."

"I mean, is that the *reason?*"

"Ah, it's not just the thing he did to my daughter, but I'm scared
of him. I want to divorce him, but I'm scared to death of him."

"Has he ever threatened you?"

"Hell, yes, he's threatened me. He's big. He's hit me where you can't see the bruises. He's grabbed ahold of my hair and banged my head against the wall."

"Well, I'm going to be a little pissed off if I find out you're raking in a couple of hundred thousand dollars and I'm only getting ten grand."

"I am getting some insurance money."

"But you're not scoring big?"

"No. I've got a $24,000 policy and a $10,000 policy, and I don't know what he's got at work. And we've got a $3,000 loan on the $24,000 policy. It's not the insurance."

"I know you're going to make some bucks, but I mean, I don't blame you. Ten thousand dollars is ten thousand dollars. But if you're going to collect a couple hundred thousand dollars—"

"It might be more, but I don't think so, and if it is, I'll tell you."

"We'll adjust accordingly?"

"I sure will."

"All right, do we understand each other?"

"Do we?" she asked. She stood up by the bed and looked carefully at him.

"I hope so."

"You're not screwing me, are you? That's what I'm scared of."

He smiled. "Now, that's not part of the deal. That will cost you some more bucks."

Norma laughed halfheartedly. "Oh, that will cost me more, huh? Very good."

"Okay," he said, "now, I'll be looking for you on the fifteenth, right?"

She turned and looked at him. "Four hundred dollars."

"Okay." He accompanied her to the door. She opened it and walked out.

CHAPTER 7

Norma walked quickly back to her car. She did not want to attract attention by running, and she did not look back. She fumbled with the key as she stuck it in the ignition and then moved out of the parking lot, again without looking in the rearview mirror. She was certain she'd see somebody following her.

Not until she was several blocks away from the restaurant, did she dare to relax. If someone had seen her, she thought, he would have stopped her by now. She felt safer, and even a little proud. She'd done it. The matter was now out of her hands. Yes, she still had to get the man the money. And, of course, he still had to *do* the job. But she felt such a sense of relief at having met with Al from San Diego, having made the plan, and having gotten out of there that it seemed the deed itself had already been accomplished. Now, she thought, she could go on with her life.

Back at her office, where her nephew Frank was waiting for her and a ride home, she was immediately preoccupied by the business. She chatted with him as she scanned the waiting room, still without furniture, and looked over at the office itself, where the desks and file cabinets were arranged. Another two weeks and the place would be open for business. She could hardly wait.

They had been talking for only a few minutes when Norma heard the front door open. It was 6 P.M., which was past business hours, but people were always stopping by to see how she was doing. Now two men stepped into the waiting area, and Norma turned to greet them.

"Hello, I'm Norma," she said. She didn't recognize them.

"Norma Winters?" one of them asked.

"Yes, can I help you?"

"Mrs. Winters, I'm Sgt. Mike Ryan of the San Diego Police Department," one of the men said, extending an open hand toward her. She looked at his hand and saw a badge. The other man introduced himself as Lt. Paul Emery, of the Imperial County Sheriff's Office.

"Yes?" Norma replied.

"Mrs. Winters," the one who identified himself as Ryan continued, "we're investigating the possibility of some danger to your husband. We've picked up word that there are some threats on him, that he may be in danger."

"What do you mean, danger?" She was stunned. "What's this about?"

"We'd like to talk to you about it in private, if we could, over at the sheriff's office."

Norma wanted to know immediately. "Can't you tell me right here? This is just my nephew." She nodded to Frank. "No one else is here. Who would want to hurt my husband?"

"We'd like to talk to you about this at the sheriff's office," Ryan repeated. "Would you be willing to come down there with us?"

Norma shrugged. If that's where they wanted to talk, she'd go. "I'll do whatever you say," she said.

It was an eight-minute ride from the Reliable Escrow Company to the sheriff's office, where Norma was escorted into a small, plain room containing a table and three chairs. Ryan motioned for her to sit down, and he himself took a seat behind the table.

"As I told you at your office, Mrs. Winters, we are investigating some threats to your husband. We'd like to talk to you about it, but the law requires that I advise you of your constitutional rights before you can talk to me. Okay?"

She nodded. She heard Ryan tell her that she had the right to remain silent, that anything she said could be used against her in court, and that she could have an attorney present, a court-appointed attorney if she couldn't afford one herself.

"Do you understand each of these rights, Mrs. Winters?"

"Yes, sir."

"Having in mind and understanding your rights as I have told you, are you willing to speak with us?"

"Yes, I will."

"Do you have any information at all or do you know anything at all about any threats to your husband?"

"No, I don't. I don't know of anyone who would want to hurt him. I wish you'd tell me what this is all about."

"Excuse me a moment, Mrs. Winters. I have some more reports and documents in the other room." Norma watched as he pushed himself away from the table, got up, and walked out into the hallway. In a moment he was back.

"Mrs. Winters, there were other officers besides Lieutenant Emery and myself who are investigating the matter, and one of them is Detective Hanscom from the San Diego Police Department." As Ryan spoke, another man walked through the door. He held out his badge and grinned. "Hello, Mrs. Winters," he said.

It was Al from San Diego.

"I knew you were a cop." She glared at him. "I knew all the time you were a cop."

"All right, Norma," Ryan said quietly. "Why don't you tell us what this is all about."

She looked at him for a moment and sighed deeply. Finally she nodded. "Okay."

Then Norma Winters confessed.

Twice.

Over the next few days Sergeant Ryan and four of his detectives wrote their reports and catalogued the evidence. It had been a straightforward case, Ryan thought. After the tip from Pappas, they had set the trap, and Norma Winters had unwittingly stepped right into it. The evidence against her had been assembled into a "book" nearly two inches thick. It included Pappas's statement to Ryan and Hanscom that she had come to him looking for a hired gun; transcripts of the tape recordings that Ryan's unit had made of Hanscom's telephone conversation with Mrs. Winters, of his meetings with her in Denny's and in the hotel room; seventeen photographs another detective had taken from a surveillance van that had been stationed in the restaurant's parking lot, all showing Hanscom and Mrs. Winters standing in front of the restaurant; the one hundred dollars in front money that she had paid Hanscom; the copy of the photograph of Bruce Winters that she had given to Hanscom and the actual photograph that they had later removed from her pocketbook; the map of his route to work; the slip of paper with the descriptions of the family cars; the transcript of Mrs. Winters's first confession to the crime, a taped interview with Manny Lopez, in which he acknowledged his involvement and confirmed Mrs. Winters's intent; and Mrs. Winters's second confession.

In both of her confessions Norma Winters had tried to conceal Manny's role in the crime and to accept full responsibility herself. It was a natural response, born of loyalty and embarrassment, Ryan knew, for her to protect a friend, but if she was trying to protect one person, were others involved as well? In his interrogation he had repeatedly asked her whether she'd contacted anyone else to kill her husband, whether anyone else was involved. Repeatedly, she said no, that it was all her fault, that no one was out on the street with a gun trained on Bruce Winters. Ryan could not be absolutely sure she was telling the truth, but the three days of investigation and interviews had turned up no other leads. He was as sure as he could be that the case was closed. He gathered up the "book" of evidence and took it to the district attorney, who would issue the charges against the suspect.

Ryan handed the stack of material to the DA and gave him a quick rundown of the evidence. "She was Mirandized twice," Ryan added, explaining that he was careful to make sure Mrs. Winters had been advised of her rights. "And she made two confessions to the crime. I don't think we've got any holes in this one."

The two men discussed possible motives—including incest, insurance money, and the fact that the woman had just set up her own business and might have been short of cash. Ryan noted that he had interviewed her husband who had strongly denied ever molesting his daughter. Ryan didn't know what to make of the denial, but none of the motives seemed absolutely clear cut.

"What about insanity or diminished capacity?" the DA asked. "Or the 'didn't mean it' defense? Are we going to run into problems with her state of mind?"

"Nope," Ryan said, shaking his head. "In my opinion, if there's a defense to this one, it hasn't been invented yet."

Indeed, as Ryan left the DA's office, he could think of few cases in his fourteen years of service with the San Diego Police Department in which the evidence he and his unit had gathered against a suspect had been more complete. Any DA would have to appreciate it. Yet, his satisfaction transcended the strength of the case. In an earlier assignment Ryan, a ruddy square-jawed Irishman, had worked in the homicide unit. He'd seen bodies that had been shot, stabbed, burned, hanged, bombed, and mutilated. He'd caught a lot of killers, many of whom were still in jail. But the satisfaction of solving a case had always been compromised by the frustration that no matter how well he'd done the job, it had not changed the fact that somebody had died.

His work with the investigative support unit, which specialized in undercover investigations, especially of underworld figures, was different. It was an area of police work where his skill as a detective could not only solve a crime. It could also save a life. In the case of Norma Winters, he felt good about the evidence he had collected. But he was more pleased about the one piece of evidence he didn't have.

He didn't have a body.

PART II

The Defense

"Simple as the case seems now, there may be something deeper underlying it."

The Sign of the Four

CHAPTER 8

The telephone rang in two short bursts, startling me for an instant as it roused me from sleep. I groped for the receiver on the floor near the bed, and it rang again just before I picked it up.

"Mr. Silverman," the late-night answering-service operator said. "We have a Mr. Lovell on the phone. Do you wish to talk to him?"

I sat up in bed and shook my head to clear out the grogginess. It was nearly midnight, and I had been asleep for an hour.

"Who is it?"

"A Mr. Lovell."

The name wasn't familiar but my answering service would have screened the call to make sure it couldn't wait till morning.

"Yeah, okay," I said. "Put him on."

The switching equipment clicked, and the sound in the receiver changed, indicating an open line.

"Go ahead, sir."

"Hello, Mr. Silverman?"

"Yes, this is Milt Silverman."

"My name is Walter Lovell. I am the brother-in-law of a woman named Norma Winters, and right now she is in the county jail."

"What is she charged with?"

"Conspiracy and solicitation."

"Solicitation to do what?"

"Commit murder."

I was awake now and listened carefully as Lovell summarized Norma Winters's predicament. She had been arrested by San Diego police in El Centro, after having tried to hire an undercover policeman to kill her husband. She had been brought to San Diego, where Lovell had posted $25,000 bail. She would be released shortly.

"We would like to retain you to handle her case," he said.

The man was calm and businesslike, unlike some late-night callers who become hysterical when they or persons close to them are in trouble. He seemed in control of himself. But I could not agree to take a case over the telephone. I would have to meet the defendant first.

"Hiring a defense attorney is kind of a personal thing," I said. "One might be perfect for one client, but just not hit it off with another. And if I take her case she's got to put her problems entirely in my hands. She's the only one who can tell me that."

I suggested I could meet Norma immediately, but when Lovell told me she had already talked to the police and that a detective named Ryan had worked on the case, I figured it would be of little use to meet Norma Winters in the middle of the night.

"Well, whatever damage that's been done is done," I said. "We can't change that now. But between now and tomorrow morning I want you to keep her under wraps. Don't let her say anything to anyone, you understand?"

"Yes, sir. I'll see that she talks to no one. I know the reason she wanted her husband killed."

"We can talk about that tomorrow. Just keep her calm, let her get some sleep. Then come by my office at ten in the morning, 2404 Broadway, it's an old three-story Victorian house on the corner of Twenty-fourth and Broadway. You can't miss it."

"Okay."

"See you at ten, then."

I hung up the phone and without a second thought turned over to a good night's sleep.

Norma Winters was early for her appointment the next morning, August 15. From my office, where I was talking to another client about a bribery case, I saw the car drive up. A man emerged from the driver's side. Two women got out of the front seat, followed by a young boy and a teen-aged girl who were in the back.

When I finished talking with my client, I opened the double doors of my office, ushered him out, and turned back to the large foyer where my new visitors were waiting.

The man was standing in the center of the waiting area. The others were sitting down; their faces seemed to fill the room with gloom.

"Mr. Lovell?"

He nodded, reaching out to shake my hand.

"I'm Milt Silverman."

A short, heavy-set, and partly bald man in his mid-forties, Lovell wore dark-rimmed glasses that gave his eyes an owlish appearance. He wore double-knit trousers with a white belt that matched his shoes, and in his short-sleeved sport shirt were several pens clasped to a plastic pocket liner.

"How do you do, Mr. Silverman." The tone was pleasant but formal.

I turned to one of the women, the one sitting in my oak rocker and neatly dressed in a skirt and blouse. Her hair was cut short around a soft, attractive face that was sullen and withdrawn. When she looked up at me, I was struck by her distinct, penetrating blue eyes. They were so alive and troubled that they seemed separate from her, and they contrasted so sharply with her other features that they didn't seem to belong to her at all. I assumed she was Norma Winters.

"How do you do?" I said, extending my hand to her.

She caught my hand at the fingers, squeezed them without conviction, and nodded. She said nothing.

"How are you?"

"Okay, I guess."

The other woman gripped my hand warmly, but said nothing, and I was left with only a hunch about who was who. I looked to the window seat where the children were sitting, and Lovell introduced them as Beth and David Winters. I nodded and asked them to wait while I met the three adults in my office. The four of us stepped back through the double doors.

The two women took side chairs at my conference table, while

Lovell stood in front of a chair at the head of the table. He belatedly introduced the woman with the troubled eyes as Norma Winters.

"And this is Ellen Harris," he said gesturing to the other woman." "Ah, formerly Ellen Harris," he added quickly, "now Ellen Lovell."

I had read two newspaper accounts of Norma's arrest, and they had done little to flesh out Lovell's report of the night before, except to note that police said money had changed hands, and that they had acted on a tip that she was in San Diego looking for a gunman to kill her husband. The articles made no mention of a possible motive. They did say a man named Emanuel Lopez was being held in El Centro in connection with the case. I asked Norma for her version of what had happened. Slowly, in a quiet, halting voice that was sometimes hard to hear, and with more than a little assistance from Lovell, she related the events of the past week, beginning with her visit to Tony Pappas, then moving on to the phone call from Al from San Diego, the meetings in the restaurant and the hotel, and finally her arrest and confession. It was a formidable series of events, I thought. The police had apparently done some good work.

"The police told me they had all these meetings and stuff down on tape," Norma said. "Is that true?"

"Well, I assume it is," I said. "The police have the equipment to do it."

"Well, that's good."

"Why would you say that?"

"Because that means it's on tape about why I wanted him killed?"

"You told Hanscom why?"

"I sure did. I even asked him if he would give my husband a message when he killed him."

"What was the message?"

"That this is from his wife for what he did to my daughter."

Her face turned bitter. Tears welled in her eyes, and she wiped them away with her fingers.

"What was that?" I asked as gently as possible.

Norma said nothing.

"Well, what did he do?"

"There were some . . . sexual attacks," Lovell said.

"Can you believe that?" Norma added, wiping away tears. "She's his own flesh and blood, his own daughter. His own flesh and blood, and he's been messing with her since she was twelve years old." She broke down crying.

I waited a moment for her to compose herself.

"When did you find out about this?"

"Tuesday night, the Tuesday before last."

"That is the first time you knew of it?"

She nodded.

"Who told you about it?"

"Beth," she said softly.

I gave her some Kleenex, walked over to the door, and called to my secretary. "Sally, get Tucker in here."

Gene Tucker, a private investigator whose office was just upstairs in my building, appeared in my office in less than two minutes. Although he was in business for himself and did work for other attorneys, I used him on all my serious cases. I quickly introduced him.

"Gene, we might become involved in this case, and I want you to interview a witness for me."

I summarized what I had learned and suggested he take Beth, who was still sitting out in the foyer, for a walk up to Golden Hills Park. It was not an easy assignment. I wanted him to ask her whether she had, in fact, been molested by her father, how it had happened, and how she had told her mother about it. Tucker nodded and left.

The interruption had given Norma a few minutes to recover from the ordeal of having to tell a stranger what had happened to her daughter. But it was only the beginning.

"Norma, I'd like to help you," I said.

She looked at me and nodded.

"I've heard a lot of difficult stories in this office. I've defended people accused of murder, robbery, and prostitution, and there's nothing you can say which is any worse than anything I've already heard. The only thing that will hurt you is what I don't know. So you must tell me everything."

She nodded.

"Now, tell me how you found out about this."

Norma sighed, closed her eyes, opened them again, and began to tell her story. She started with the evening of August 6, when she and Beth had gone for the ride, and she talked about her telephone call to Walt and Ellie when they had gotten home, her ride to National City the following day, and her meeting with Dennis Howe. It was a painful, draining experience for Norma. It took nearly three-quarters of an hour and, occasionally, some help from Lovell. When she told me about learning that her daughter wasn't pregnant, she was overcome. She slumped before me, elbows on the table, and rested her head in her hands. Her whole body was limp.

I said nothing for a few minutes, then continued, "Okay, after Beth came back from the doctor's and everything was all right, what did you do next?"

"We left," Lovell replied. "The attorney said he would see us again later in the afternoon, after he talked with the district attorney's office about prosecuting Mr. Winters."

Lovell said he and Norma had returned to Howe's office at 5 P.M. that day and learned that the attorney's initial feelings had been correct: Beth would have to bring charges against her father, and she would most likely need a corroborating witness, since, as an eighteen-year-old, she would have to prove that her father's actions had occurred without her consent.

They had also discussed the divorce process further, Lovell explained, and Howe had been able to give Norma no assurances that she would retain the home or even her own business in a settlement.

"Of course, we also talked about Norma's retaining custody of David," Lovell added. "We would want full custody, without visitation rights, but we also decided we would probably not make an issue of Bruce's conduct with Beth unless we had to at some point down the road."

When they had left, Lovell added, they had agreed that Howe would take no action until Lovell had informed him that the loan application had all the necessary signatures and was approved.

Then Lovell mentioned an incident that had occurred either Wednesday or Thursday night at Imperial Beach. Norma, Beth, Ellen, and Walt were working late in his office when Norma said she wanted to go to the beach. He had often taken her there to relax. They arrived about 10:30 P.M., just as the last evidence of light was fading from the sky. He and Norma walked along the beach together for a while and then separated, with Norma walking barefoot, heading closer to the water.

"I was still in my work clothes, and I stayed along the seawall," Lovell said. "All of a sudden she turned and started to walk directly into the water. I shouted to her, but she did not respond. So I ran onto the beach, and I didn't even stop to take off my shoes or roll up my trousers. I just ran out into the water. By the time I caught her, the water was up to my thighs. I grabbed her, and she turned around and looked dazed. So I shook her, then put my arm around her, and escorted her out of the water, back to the shore."

I turned and looked at Norma. "Why did you do that?"

She glanced at Lovell, then back at me. "I don't remember it," she said quietly.

"You don't remember it?"

She shook her head. "No."

"Are you sure? It happened just a week ago."

Norma thought for a moment, then looked back at me. "No, I just don't remember it."

"Okay," I said with a shrug. I didn't understand that, but it occurred to me that such an unusual lapse of memory might suggest something about Norma's state of mind around the time of the crime. I asked Lovell whether he still had the shoes and pants.

"Of course," he said.

"Good. I'd like to get them and perhaps have them analyzed."

He looked at me quizzically. "Why would you want to do that?"

"It's conceivable that the incident could figure somehow in Norma's defense. I may want to call you to testify, and having the shoes and pants as physical evidence might help corroborate your story."

"I see," Lovell said tentatively.

"So if you've still got them, I'll send Tucker to your house to pick them up."

"Well, I wish I'd known the importance of that before," Lovell remarked. "I just remembered that I washed the trousers and polished the shoes right after the incident. It seemed like a normal thing to do. And I really cleaned the shoes. I guess it's my military background. There just wouldn't be a trace of salt or water left on them. I'm compulsive about things like that."

"Well, that's that, then," I said. "It was a long shot anyway. I'm not sure the criminalist could have really told us much—"

"The what?"

"Criminalist. That's a scientist who analyzes evidence like blood stains, fingerprints, murder weapons, that sort of thing."

Lovell nodded.

"Now, we can't do much about the shoes, but do you know of any other evidence that might have even the slightest significance?"

Neither Norma nor Lovell could think of anything immediately, and I moved to other subjects. Norma said she couldn't remember anything else that had happened the day she had met Howe, but that on Friday, she had called Pappas.

"Did you know Pappas before you called him?" I asked.

"Well, I'd met him last spring, when I closed an escrow for him in El Centro. He was real friendly, and he even sent me some flowers and a letter thanking me afterwards."

"So why did you call him?"

"I don't know, just because of what I'd heard about him, I guess."

"What had you heard about him?"

"Oh, you know, that he might do something like that."

"Who told you that?"

"I don't know. That's pretty well known, isn't it?"

"I'm asking you."

"I don't know." She looked away for a moment. "I guess I just heard it somewhere. It was just my own stupid mind, I guess."

Pappas was part of a prominent business family that owned real estate and interests in race tracks in the Southwest. As far as I knew, law-enforcement agencies had obtained no information linking him to organized crime, but some of the tracks had been under official investigation. Pappas's father had been jailed for income-tax evasion, and Pappas himself had been convicted of a felony—offering a prison official a "gratuity" to treat his father well while he was in jail.

"Well, when did you decide to call him?"

"I called him Friday."

"No, I mean when did you decide you were going to call him. Were you still in El Centro?"

"Oh, no. He wasn't in my mind at all at home."

"Did you talk to Manny about it on the way to San Diego?"

"No."

"Did you mention Pappas to him?"

"No."

"So you just decided to call him on Friday, then, is that it?"

She thought for a moment. "Yes. Just that Friday."

"How is it that you decided to do that? What made you think of Pappas?"

She shrugged. "I don't know, his name just popped into my head."

"Just popped into your head?"

She nodded.

"And where were you when this happened?"

"What do you mean?"

"Where were you when his name 'popped' into your head—in a car, a restaurant, an office, a telephone booth?"

Norma rested her chin in her hand and squinted in thought. The room was silent.

"I don't know," she said finally.

"You don't know?"

"That's right."

"Okay, where did you call him from?"

Again she paused to think about it, cocking her head to one side. Finally, she shrugged. "I don't know."

I knew she might be avoiding the questions, but it seemed that she genuinely couldn't remember these details. I was puzzled. They were significant. A person who makes a call to hire a killer ought to remember precisely why she called and where she called from.

"Okay, Norma, let's go back one more step. How did you get Pappas's telephone number?"

"What do you mean?"

"Well, did you have it memorized? Did you have it in a personal address book? Did you call your office for it?"

"Oh, no, I don't think so." She thought for a moment. "I must have looked it up in the phone book."

"Do you remember looking it up in the phone book?"

"Not really. But where else would I have gotten it? I must have looked it up."

"What name did you look under?"

"Well, Anthony Pappas, I guess."

"Where were you when you looked up the number?"

Norma shook her head. "I just don't remember. I remember what I said. I just can't remember where I was."

"All right," I said with a touch of impatience. "How did you get to his office?"

"She borrowed my car," Lovell interjected.

I wheeled around. In the intensity of questioning Norma, I'd forgotten Lovell was even in the room.

"I saw no harm in letting her use it," he continued.

"She asked if she could borrow it?"

"Yes."

"Did you ask her why she wanted it?"

"No. I let her use the car many times in the past. I didn't see any reason to question it."

"Did you know anything about this meeting with Pappas?"

He shook his head. "No."

I turned back to Norma. "When you talked to Pappas, did he give you directions to his office?"

"No. At least not that I can remember."

"Had you been to his office before?"

"No."

Norma said that she hadn't even known the name of the office building and that she'd never heard of the Associates Office Tower.

She'd nevertheless arrived at his office. She described her visit—her blurting out her request and his asking her to leave and ushering her to the door—in specific detail, but she remembered little of what had happened after that. The rest of the afternoon seemed "hazy" to her.

The following day, she said, she had gone back to Holtville, and she described her confrontation with Bruce, when she had told him she'd kill him if he ever messed around with Beth. Finally, she mentioned her conversation with Manny in her office that Sunday, when she had asked him if he could find someone for her.

"So you had two separate conversations with Manny about this?" I asked. "When you drove over that Wednesday morning and then again on Sunday?"

"Uh-huh."

"But you didn't say anything to him the first time about killing your husband?"

"No. I told him I'd have to divorce him."

"You're absolutely sure of that."

"Yes. It was just on Sunday, after I saw Pappas, that I asked him if he knew anyone. And then on Monday afternoon I got this phone call, from Al from San Diego. And I called Manny to see if he had contacted anyone, and he said no. I didn't know who it was. It seems real dumb, now. I guess I should have suspected. And I did keep asking him if he was a cop. But I just went ahead. And I got all those things he wanted that night and put them in my pocketbook. But I didn't give them to him at Denny's even though I had them."

She said she had really been scared after the first meeting, and she told me about his threat to "plant her in the desert" if she turned on him.

"I thought he meant if I didn't go through with it, he'd kill me," Norma continued. "So I just had to do it. Then I met with him again and gave him all those things, and they came to my office to arrest me."

She paused, and a profound expression seemed to cross her face. "You know, when they came into the office and said there were some threats against Bruce, I didn't even make the connection with the meeting with Hanscom. I thought they were serious."

I hardly had to point out to her now that they were very serious indeed. We had covered the whole week. We had talked about the crime and the arrest and a possible motive—revenge. We turned briefly to the topic of the insurance policies and the likelihood that despite Norma's denials to Hanscom and Ryan the prosecution would raise that issue as a motive.

"And where are the policies?" I asked.

"I have them," Lovell replied. "I have all the financial information that relates to Norma's business, insurance, everything having to do with her business and personal affairs."

"Be sure to keep them in a safe place. We might need them later. And one more thing. This letter from Pappas, do you still have that, Norma?"

"I believe I have that, as well," Lovell answered.

"You have it?"

"Yes. They had some argument over it. Bruce had raised some questions about Pappas's intentions with the letter, and Norma brought it to our house for us to look at it and arbitrate their dispute. It's still there, I think, probably in the files somewhere. I'll look for it."

"Good. That's an example of the kind of evidence we want to get now, not six months down the line, when it may have disappeared. It may not be important, but we should have it just in case."

We had talked for more than two hours. It was time for a change of scene. Tucker and Beth had returned from their walk. I wanted to talk to Beth myself, and, though I knew it would be difficult for Norma, I wanted Tucker to talk with her and Lovell while I was gone.

I explained the next step and excused myself. As I went out the door, I glanced at Lovell's shoes. They hadn't seen a shine in a long time.

Before I headed outside, I asked my secretary to have Tucker come in. Then I reached for the telephone book on her desk and opened it to the P's. There was no listing under "Anthony Pappas." There was none under "Tony Pappas." The Pappas Corporation was there, but it was followed by only a number. The firm's address was not in the book.

CHAPTER 9

Beth Winters, dressed in faded blue denims, torn sneakers, and a checkered shirt with sleeves rolled to just above the elbow, seemed more like a country tomboy of fifteen than a woman of eighteen. She was about five feet four inches tall and slightly overweight, the plumpness not of a heavy eater, but of a girl becoming a woman. When I had greeted her out in the foyer, she had been the only one in the group, other than Lovell, who had looked me straight in the eye, gripped my hand with firmness, and said hello.

An interview with Beth would be particularly sensitive, I figured, and that was one reason I wanted Tucker on it right away. In addition to hearing her version of the story and getting more acquainted with the case himself, Tucker would accomplish two things: determine as best he could whether she was telling the truth and persuade her that she had to tell the truth—no matter what it was. And if Tucker's interview went badly, I'd have a fresh chance to talk to her.

Like the journalist who runs for political office or the union leader who accepts a promotion to management, a policeman who becomes a private investigator jumps to the other side. For Tucker, who had spent eight years with the Maryland state police, it meant working with an attorney tracking down witnesses and information that might acquit a defendant accused of a crime, instead of collecting evidence to convict a suspect, and it was an eye-opening experience. On one of his first cases, while working for another lawyer, he confirmed with a passenger list and an eye witness that a man accused of rape had either been on an airplane or leaving the airport in a taxi cab when the rape had occurred. Confronted with this evidence, the police maintained the charge, holding the man in jail until the attorney finally made so much noise that they were forced to release him. Such experiences taught Tucker that despite vast manpower and financial resources, police departments sometimes conducted superficial investigations and that they sometimes preferred no information to information that exonerated a leading suspect. He learned quickly that the best advantage a defendant in a criminal case could have was an aggressive and thorough defense team. Nevertheless, as he moved from one role to the other, he retained the policeman's skepticism that led him to question and recheck information he had obtained on behalf of a client until he was sure that it was true.

Tucker was prepared not to like Beth. Part of him wondered whether she was a "fast filly" and had made up a story to spite strict parents. Another part of him was uneasy talking to a young woman he'd just met about her having been the victim of incest. He was far more comfortable talking to drunks, rowdies, and small-time hoods.

"Mind if I have a cigarette?" she asked as they walked along Broadway, away from the law office.

"Naw, go ahead."

They walked along in silence for a minute or two. Tucker sensed that she was looking at him out of the corner of her eye, sizing him up, just as he was trying to get an impression of her. Finally, Beth asked a question.

"Do you have any kids?"

Tucker cleared his throat. "Well, yeah, I have a stepdaughter. And I have a son, but he lives on the East Coast. I almost never get to see him."

"Are you very strict with your stepdaughter?"

Tucker smiled. "Well, you know, I suppose I know most of the tricks, and I guess I'm a little strict, but I'm not too tight."

Beth smiled, and he felt the atmosphere between them relax.

"What about you, is your father strict with you?"

She frowned and looked down at the ground, then straight ahead as they walked. "Yeah. He won't let me go out hardly at all with guys. My mother used to cover for me sometimes. But I couldn't go to many school dances; I couldn't even go to the library."

"He wouldn't let you go to the library?"

"No, he doesn't trust me. He doesn't trust me to do anything. He caught me going to the Dairy Queen one day for lunch, and he stopped in the car and just raised hell in front of everyone there. He told me, 'Get your ass back to school.' He's always doing that kind of stuff, right in front of people."

"What was the problem with the Dairy Queen? Why didn't he want you to go there?"

"I don't know, I guess some bad kids hung around there."

"Were these the kids you hung around with when you got the chance?"

"No, not them, but I guess I did hang around with some, well, I don't know, some creeps." She paused for a moment. "To get back at dad, I guess."

"To get back at him for—"

"Yeah, for messing around with me, making me feel, I don't know, like nobody will really want me. Who would want me, you know?" She looked up at Tucker, her eyes glazed with tears.

"Look, Beth, I know this is kind of tough on you, but we've got to know everything about this case, and that includes what happened between you and your father. Now you can—"

"I know." She sighed, as if to summon her strength. "I'll tell you." Then, over the next half hour, she described, at times haltingly, at times bitterly, but always forthrightly, her six-year ordeal at the hands of her father.

Tucker and Beth were sitting on the lawn outside my office when I finished talking to Norma. I smiled at Beth and took Tucker aside.

"How'd it go?" I asked.

"She's an astute girl. And very candid. I was really impressed with her candor. In fact, I didn't have to push her much at all."

He quickly summarized their conversation, pointing out that

she'd insisted that her father had never actually had intercourse with her.

"Do you believe her?" I asked.

Tucker paused just a moment and looked at me. "Yes. Yes, I do, Milt. I think she's telling the truth."

"Okay. Let's see what I come up with."

As Beth and I walked toward the park, she filled me in briefly on what she'd told Tucker. I didn't want her to have to go through the whole story again with me, but I was especially concerned about one thing both Norma and Tucker had said. When we reached the park near my office, we sat under a tree and I went straight to the point.

"Gene says you told him your father never actually had intercourse with you, is that right?"

"Yeah, I didn't know how far you had to go, and it was close, that last time, the one I told Mr. Tucker about was right before I went to Europe. And then when I was in Europe and didn't get my period, I thought maybe I didn't clean myself up good enough. And that's when I finally told my mom. When I got back."

"And you're sure he never penetrated you?"

"He never did. I'm sure of it."

With some hesitation she told me about another incident with her father, while her parents had been separated and she had been visiting him in Arizona. "He got me alone," she said, "and he had a rubber on. But I fought him and moved around before he did anything, and it broke. He got all mad, but he didn't do anything else."

"When was that?"

"Oh, about three years ago."

"Okay, Beth, now this is important. If this case goes to trial and you have to testify to any of this, and you probably will, the district attorney could ask you some tough questions, and maybe even suggest that you sort of seduced your father, that somehow you asked for it—"

"Oh, he always tells me that."

"Your father?"

"Yeah, he says it's all my fault, because I run around the house half-naked and stuff, which isn't true. I dress so I won't be reveal-

ing. You know, I might get up in the morning and put a slip on
and run into the kitchen for something, but I could see nothing
wrong with that. And everyone else in the family ran around in
their underwear. And he would go out and buy me revealing
clothes."

"He went out and bought them?"

She nodded. "Low-cut dresses, an eighth-grader wearing low-
cut dresses. A fat eighth-grader at that." She smiled.

I smiled back. "Okay, Beth," I said gently. "I need to know one
other thing. I know it's hard for you to talk about some of these
intimate things, and I'm not asking you these questions out of idle
curiosity. I hope the answers will help in the defense of your
mother."

She nodded. "I know. It's okay. I know you have to know."

"All right," I said, looking directly at her. "I need to know if
you've ever had sex with anyone. Have you ever had intercourse?"

The half smile disappeared, and she looked away. "Do I have to
answer that?"

"No, but if I take the case, it's something I have to know. The
DA could ask you that, too."

She hesitated again and seemed more reluctant to talk about that
than she had been to discuss her father.

"Well, I always thought, I was always brought up that you
should be a virgin when you got married. I had this boyfriend, and
I thought I was going to marry him. And, well, afterwards, we were
so embarrassed, we broke up about a month later. We were so
ashamed."

"How old were you, when this happened?"

"Sixteen."

"Okay," I said gently. "And there was nobody else?"

She shook her head. "I can't even go out, you know. My dad
won't let me go out, and if I ever do, he always raises hell about
the guy."

She looked away again, more subdued than she had been at any
other point in our conversation. "We were so ashamed." The
words rang clear and true in my ears as I studied her. It was
possible she was lying. But as she answered my questions, her tears,
her gestures, her anguish all seemed natural, not forced. And it

didn't strike me as a story an eighteen-year-old woman could make up. The detail was too painful and too accurate. Beth seemed to speak the truth.

We strolled back to my office, where Tucker was talking to Norma.

It was nearly 2 P.M., four hours after the group had walked into my office. We all needed a break. Norma and Beth were emotionally drained. I'd learned enough for one day. I was caught up in the details of the case, and I agreed to take it.

As they were leaving, Lovell took me aside for a moment. "Doctor, doctor," he said, "I have a pain in my side. Can you fix it?"

I stared at him blankly.

"What's the prognosis?"

"Oh," I said. "Well, I don't have a crystal ball. I can tell you that it seems the police have a pretty formidable case. We're going to investigate every possible avenue of defense Norma might have. That's all I can promise right now."

"Oh. Okay." He paused for a moment. "I guess in a lot of these cases, there's some kind of deal made so the case doesn't go to trial, is that right?"

"That's true. Very few cases actually go to trial. But I can't tell you what we're going to do until we get the case investigated."

I told Lovell I was worried about Norma and the incident at the beach. He said that he was an officer in the air force and had some reserve duty coming up, but that he'd keep an eye on her for me. He also stressed that he would handle all of the financial arrangements. Then he and the women and the children climbed back into their car and left.

CHAPTER 10

I did not see any easy way out for Norma Winters. She had committed a serious crime, and she had confessed. The police investigation had been handled by Mike Ryan, who, I knew from experience, usually put together a strong case, not only accumulating overwhelming evidence, but doing so with investigative techniques that were likely to hold up under defense challenges. I didn't know exactly what he had, but I figured most of it would be admitted into evidence in a trial. And I knew that entrapment was virtually out as a defense. When an undercover officer plays a prominent role in an arrest, a suspect often cries foul, arguing he would not have committed the crime without the policeman's help. But entrapment occurs only when a policeman coaxes a person to commit an offense he or she was not predisposed to commit. Since Norma had gone to Pappas without any prompting from the police, she seemed to have been clearly predisposed to seeking a killer for her husband when she had had coffee that day in Denny's with Al Hanscom.

It was no defense that Norma might have changed her mind or failed to follow through with the crime. In a solicitation for murder case, the words themselves are the crime, and the only intent the DA has to establish is the intent to utter the words. It is no defense, the courts have repeatedly held, to maintain that the defendant wouldn't have gone through with it.

That left insanity. But we would have to establish that Norma had been unable to distinguish right from wrong. Much of her behavior seemed to portray a person who had acted deliberately—and one who didn't want to get caught.

Thus, after the first session with my client, I foresaw no defense that seemed likely to exonerate her. But that was hardly a reason for not defending her. Defense lawyers are stalked by the question, "How can you defend someone you know is guilty?"

The answer is that the defense lawyer has a duty not only to defend the innocent, but to speak for the guilty. America's foremost criminal lawyer, Clarence Darrow, is perhaps best remembered for his defense of Leopold and Loeb, two scions of wealthy Chicago families who had murdered Bobby Franks in an effort to commit the "perfect" crime. Although the media dubbed the case the "trial of the century," it wasn't a trial at all. It was a sentencing. Darrow pled his clients guilty and argued eloquently for their lives. He saved them from the gallows.

But arguing compassion for a "guilty" client often prompts the complaint that lawyers take "guilty" clients to trial in an effort to "get them off." That view, in my experience, is based more on impressions obtained from widely publicized cases than on a fair evaluation of what happens daily in courtrooms around the country. A defense lawyer rarely takes a sure loser to trial. There's just too much incentive to plea-bargain—to plead guilty to lesser charges that carry lesser penalties—before cases get to trial. Thus, most of the cases that do go before a judge and jury involve legitimate disputes over the evidence or over the existence or degree of criminal responsibility.

Our adversary system of justice is based on the premise that an impartial trier of fact—the jury—will best understand a case when the evidence and witnesses are subjected to vigorous presentation, cross-examination, and argument by opposing sides. And the process requires defense lawyers to act as strong advocates for their clients. How long would this system survive if the defense lawyer, and not the jury, were to decide guilt or innocence? Would a jury be bound to accept the defense lawyer's finding? Or should the lawyer defend the "guilty" person, but not so vigorously as to secure the defendant's acquittal? Neither the jury nor the adversary system would survive in such an arrangement. And the basis of American law—that a person is considered innocent until proven guilty—would be undermined, for the "obviously guilty" person would have no advocate, no representation, no access to justice. The system obliges defense lawyers to use their best skills and talents, not only to defend those who are "possibly innocent," but to represent those who are accused of serious crimes, confronted by overwhelming evidence, in the face of which no defense seems available. People who are "obviously guilty." People like Norma Winters.

I wasn't about to give up a search for a legitimate defense for Norma, but even if I couldn't find one, I had something important to say to a judge or jury on her behalf. Incest offered a persuasive motive for her actions, provided it was true. I doubted that a jury would find that she was justified in seeking a killer because of it; a judge would be unlikely to permit such consideration in his instructions to the jury, anyway. But incest did provide mitigating circumstances that a judge might consider in rendering a sentence.

My client's predicament reminded me of a classic criminal case involving a man named Repouille. One evening, he walked to the corner drugstore, bought a lethal dose of chloroform, returned home, and wrapped it in a handkerchief. He went to one of his children's bedrooms, where an infant was sleeping, placed the handkerchief over the baby's face, and held it there, sobbing, until the child was dead. The state of New York tried the man for murder. But the jury convicted him only of fourth-degree man-slaughter and then made a plea to the judge for mercy. Repouille's child had no arms or legs, it couldn't see or hear, and it had no control over its bodily functions.

I told Tucker about Repouille over a couple of steaks at a "cook your own" supper club the following night, when we finally had a chance to discuss the Winters case at length. It was a brainstorming session, a ritual for us whenever I took a new case on, and Tucker helped me to explore all the possibilities and to review the evidence.

"Now, I'm not arguing that Norma Winters is another Repouille," I said, "but she does have a story to tell."

"So is this incest her defense, then?" Tucker asked.

"No, it doesn't rise to the dignity of a defense, but it's certainly something to look at from the mitigation aspect, and it's something we've got to harp on and establish one way or another."

"So you think you're going to have to plead her?"

I shrugged. "Those are the odds."

"But you still want a full-throttle investigation, don't you?"

"Absolutely."

Tucker went over to the grill near our booth and turned the steaks.

"What if this girl is lying?" he asked, on returning. "What if this stuff with her father is just made up?"

I pondered the question for a moment. "Well, we still have a case, I think, because the question then becomes, 'Did Norma believe her?' Even if Beth were lying, as long as Norma believed her, the motive would still hold up. The only other possibility, I guess, is that the whole story is a fabrication, that they are in this together with some other motive for wanting Bruce out of the way."

Norma had told us the day before about her new business venture. Perhaps she and Beth had concocted this tale to mask the real motive—to get enough insurance money to make sure the business would get off the ground. It was an unlikely possibility, I thought, but probable enough for the prosecution to explore and raise in court. That meant it was probable enough for us to take the time to determine whether it was true.

There was one other reason to investigate the incest question thoroughly: it was the only thing we had, the only way we could begin a serious investigation of the case.

"Gene, I want you to get out to El Centro tomorrow and start talking to witnesses. The family, especially Norma's mother. Co-workers, friends, anyone who might know something about Norma and her husband or about this incest business."

"Okay," Tucker said. "Does that include Bruce?"

"I don't know. I'll have to think about that."

We talked for more than an hour about the case as we finished our dinner. When Tucker dropped me off at my small cottage near the beach that night, I had more than just Bruce Winters to think about. Our conversation had raised other difficult questions, as well. Did Norma really go to Pappas's alone that Friday afternoon? Everything she and Lovell had told me in the interviews suggested that they had been together from the moment she had arrived in National City the day after the car ride with Beth until she had left for home late Saturday. They had gone to the lawyer together, to the beach together, to his office together, and to his house together. Ellen had usually been with them. Yet, at 4 P.M. that Friday, they told me, Norma had borrowed Lovell's car and gone to see Pappas without telling either of them where she was going. If she didn't get Pappas's phone number and address out of the telephone book, where did she get it? How did she find the Associates Office Tower if she didn't even know what it was? And was it likely that someone would not remember her own suicide attempt? I didn't expect Norma to level with me immediately, and I didn't need the answers tomorrow; they were simply holes that needed to be filled as the investigation of the case moved forward. But as I went to bed that night, I resolved not to allow Walt and Ellen to participate in further interviews with Norma, and I decided against discussing with them any of my strategy or findings in the case.

CHAPTER 11

It was 2:30 A.M. when the phone rang, rousing me from sleep for the second time in three nights. Once again I groped for the receiver, and once again I expected my answering service. My telephone number is unlisted.

"Hello?"

"Mr. Silverman?"

"Yes."

"This is Walt Lovell."

I closed my eyes and opened them again. What could he want now, I wondered. I had given Lovell my home phone number to use in case of an emergency.

"Yeah, Walt, what is it?"

There was silence for a moment. Then he spoke slowly, in a deliberate, mysterious tone.

"A body has been found in El Centro."

"What?"

"A body has been found in El Centro."

"Oh yeah. So what? Whose body is it?"

"Bruce Winters's."

"What?"

"Bruce Winter's."

"How do you know that?"

"I received a call from Frank Holden, and he told me that the sheriff's office has taken the body of Bruce Winters out of a shack in El Centro."

"Are you sure it's him?"

"Yes."

"How can you be sure?"

"Frank told me."

"How does he know?"

"I don't know."

"Was he drunk when he called?" I asked.

"Not to my knowledge."

Lovell gave me Holden's telephone number, and I told him to stay by the phone and I'd call back. When I called Holden, his sister answered. Frank was down the street, she said, but he'd told her Bruce Winters had been found dead. I dialed Lovell again. I was particularly concerned about Norma.

Lovell said she didn't know anything yet. She was asleep, and he hadn't awakened her.

"Do the police know where she is?" I asked.

"I don't think so."

"Listen carefully. The police might be there any minute to arrest her and charge her with murder. I want you to make sure she makes absolutely no statement to the police, do you understand? Nothing. She is to say nothing."

"Yes. I understand."

"And if the police do show up, you inform them that she is represented by counsel and that I've advised her to make no statements and that they are not to question her. Then call me immediately."

Lovell repeated the instructions back to me.

"I want you and Norma in my office at 9 A.M. sharp."

"We'll be there," he said.

Mike Ryan willing, I thought.

By now, I was wide awake. It seemed likely I had a murder case on my hands. I called another number. Gene Tucker answered with a sleepy, "Hello."

"Gene, we've got some problems. Bruce Winters is dead."

"What?"

"Norma's husband is dead. His body's been found in El Centro."

I winced as I heard myself mimic Lovell.

"Son of a bitch. Was he murdered?"

"I don't know. Lovell got the information from Frank Holden."

"Holden," Tucker said. "Isn't he the guy with the Swiss-cheese brain?"

"That's right," I said, half laughing. Tucker was awake. "I couldn't reach him to confirm anything."

"Norma never said anything about talking to him, did she?"

"No, but he did spend a lot of that week with her in National City with Beth and the Lovells, right after Norma learned about the incest."

"Well, do you think Norma would ask someone in his condition to perform a job like that?"

"I don't know, Gene. There are quite a few things in this case that aren't adding up."

"So what happens now? I guess you won't want me in El Centro in the morning, huh?"

"No, forget the trip for now. Why don't you meet me in the office early, about nine. Lovell is bringing Norma in then."

"Fine. I'll see you then."

I hung up and lay back in bed. I wasn't going to learn much more until morning. This time, however, it was almost impossible to get back to sleep.

By 6:30 I was out of bed and on the telephone with Holden.

"What do you know about Bruce Winters?" I asked.

"He shot himself. In the shack." His voice was nearly hysterical and thick. Holden was obviously drunk.

"How do you know he shot himself?"

"He did. I'm telling you that's what he did."

"Did somebody tell you that?"

"No. But I know he shot himself. He's been over there for a couple of days."

"Over where?"

"In the shack. I just know he shot himself."

"Okay, Frank, just calm down. I want you to just stay at home. Get some rest and relax. I'll talk to you later."

I needed firmer information than Holden could provide. I called a friend in El Centro who had connections with the police and told him I'd heard a rumor I hoped he could check out. He called back in fifteen minutes.

"I can't tell you much, Milt. It's pretty early. He's dead and homicide is investigating. And I did find out where he was found."

"Where was that?"

"In an abandoned shack in Holtville with a bullet in his heart."

One of the crucial principles of criminal defense is the preservation of evidence, especially perishable evidence, as soon as possible. That may include skid marks on a street, bloodstains on a wall, or reluctant witnesses inclined to skip town. The first hours are usually the most important on any case. Six months of tireless investigation can yield less critical information than what is available on the first day, and it can all be wasted if key evidence is destroyed. Bruce Winters, a potential witness in the case of his wife, was already gone, rendering moot Tucker's question of the night before and tossing my client into the middle of a potential murder case. I had little faith in what Frank Holden had told me, and I didn't know whether Norma had withheld something from me when she had said that Pappas, Hanscom, and Lopez were the only people she had approached about killing her husband. But it was possible that Bruce had killed himself. I wanted to make sure any evidence indicating suicide was obtained and evaluated, either as part of the homicide investigation or as part of my own case. I called Western Union and dictated a telegram to Stephen Wolford, the coroner of Imperial County.

"REQUEST NEUTRON ACTIVATION ANALYSIS FOR TRACES OF BARIUM AND ANTIMONY FROM BODY OF BRUCE JACKSON WINTERS TO DETERMINE WHETHER DEATH THE RESULT OF MURDER OR SUICIDE."

The test could determine almost conclusively whether Bruce Winters had fired the gun that killed him. If he had pulled the trigger, invisible traces of barium and antimony, two elements common to all gunpowders, would have collected on his hand. The neutron activation analysis would detect them.

The operator read the telegram back to me.

"That's it," I said. "Please send it immediately."

Then I left for the office.

CHAPTER 12

When I opened the stained-glass doors to meet Norma, she and Beth were standing in the middle of the foyer, weeping, trying to console each other. It was a tender but peculiar scene; only days ago she had wanted her husband dead so badly that she had paid money to have him killed. Now he was dead, and she was mourning him. I felt sorry for Norma, but I couldn't let up now. The next piece of bad news for her could be a murder charge.

I summoned them into the office. Lovell, standing behind them, moved toward the doors as well.

"Walt, I need to talk to them alone."

He stopped short and narrowed his eyes. "Well, all right," he said, clearing his throat. He turned and sat down.

Norma and Beth took seats next to each other at the conference table, their backs to the windows that looked out onto Broadway. They were still sobbing, and I paced around the office as I waited for them to calm down.

"Norma," I said finally, "the penalty for solicitation to commit murder is five years to life. The penalty for murder with a hired killer is the gas chamber."

Her solemn gaze turned tense.

"Now, if you had anything at all to do with this matter, with the death of your husband, then you'd better tell me, and you'd better tell me now. Because that phone could ring any minute, and it could be the police putting a murder rap on you. Do you understand?"

"Milt, other than Hanscom and Mr. Pappas, the only person I even mentioned it to was Manny. That's the truth, the honest truth. And I don't think he contacted anybody."

"What about your nephew Frank?"

"Oh, heck no," she said with a smile. "I wouldn't ask him to do anything."

"Do you think Frank could have done it on his own?"

"Frank couldn't do anything on his own. He's, ah, his mind is messed up."

"But isn't it possible?"

"I really don't think so. Not Frank. He was scared to death of Bruce. I don't think he'd go near him."

"So you don't think it's likely Bruce was murdered?"

She shook her head. "Not by anybody I talked to."

"Okay. Do you think he could have committed suicide?"

She sighed and looked down at the table, pressing her fingers against her brow.

"I don't know, Milt. I don't know." She paused. "He was always looking out for himself, you know. He seemed to think about himself too much, you know, to want to do that." Her eyes filled with tears. "But I remember one time just a little while ago and we were fussing, like we were always fussing, and I just said to him, 'Why are you like this? You are always like this, and you just seem so unhappy.' And he didn't holler at me or anything, like he usually does. He just looked at me and he said, 'I think I'm the unhappiest person in the world.' "

"Norma," I said gently. "I'll be right back."

I wanted to give her a moment to compose herself, but mostly I wanted Tucker with me, and he had just pulled into the driveway. I greeted him at the door, and when we stepped into the office, Norma looked up at me. "I should tell you everything, right, Milt? Because that's the only way you can help me."

"That's exactly right. Everything."

"You know, I trust you."

"Norma, you have to trust me. I know sometimes that's difficult.

And you just came in for the first time two days ago. But we don't have time to waltz around the floor. You're in serious trouble."

"Okay." She swallowed hard and looked away for a moment. "Well, I guess you should know about this," she said tentatively. "Ah, I'm supposed to have dinner tonight with a man named Wayne Connors."

"Who's Wayne Connors?"

"He's a man I had an affair with about four years ago."

I looked at her in disbelief. "A man you had an affair with?"

She nodded.

"And you're seeing him tonight?"

"Yes."

I looked over at Tucker, who was shaking his head. Then I turned back to Norma and stared at her. First a hit man, then a body, and now a lover. Oh, yes, I thought, this case is falling together nicely.

"Well, Norma," I said finally. "Where do you plan to meet him?"

She sighed. "At the Mission Valley Inn."

"And how long ago did you set up this rendezvous?"

"I talked to him on Monday."

"On Monday. That was the day you talked to Al Hanscom about murdering your husband, wasn't it?"

"Yes, but he knew nothing about that."

"On the very day you arranged a meeting with a hit man, you arranged a date with an old lover?"

She looked at me and nodded. "But I'm telling you Wayne knew nothing about this."

"Did you call this fellow Connors before or after you talked to Hanscom?"

"I didn't call him."

"I suppose he called you?"

She nodded again.

"Well, did he call you before or after you talked with Hanscom?"

Norma looked away for a moment, then looked back at me. "He called me in the morning, but I couldn't talk to him right then. So he gave me his home number and asked me to call him collect that evening."

"And did you call him back that night?"

"Yes, I did."

"So you did talk to him after you talked to Hanscom."

"Yes, but I didn't even mention that to him. Wayne doesn't know anything about this." Tears formed in the corner of her eye.

"Don't lie to me, Norma. I told you, I'm going to find out if you're lying, so don't waste my time and don't waste your breath."

"I'm not lying to you. It's the truth."

"When was the last time you talked with him?"

She thought for a moment. "In July of 1971."

"So you're telling me it was just a coincidence then—"

"Yes, it was."

"That on the same day you just happened to talk to an undercover cop about killing your husband, that your old lover, who you haven't heard from in over three years, on that very same day, he just happens to call you out of the blue."

"I know it sounds suspicious, Milt, but that's the way it happened."

"No, Norma, it doesn't sound suspicious. It sounds very logical. It sounds like you're right smack in the middle of a classic lover's triangle murder plot."

"I'm telling you," she said, her voice rising slightly, "that's not the way it happened at all."

"Well, then, suppose you tell me just how it did happen. And you'd better not leave anything out."

It began in January, 1970, when Norma went to Morro Bay, a scenic and romantic setting on the northern California coast, to attend a week-long conference for escrow officers. She had met Wayne at a similar conference the year before, but there had been no special attraction. This time it was different. After enduring several years of an increasingly unhappy marriage, she and Bruce had talked seriously of splitting up. Wayne was on the verge of divorce. They were both empty and longing for affection. And almost immediately, they were struck by their attraction to each other.

They were together almost constantly for the whole week, but they deliberately avoided being alone. If they went out to eat, it was with another couple. If they walked along the beach, there were others with them.

On the final day of the conference, he went to her room to help her carry her luggage out.

"I've had this feeling all week of something wonderful between us," he said. "But it's probably wrong."

She nodded with a sad smile. "I don't think there's anything we can do. I think it's probably best that we don't see each other again."

They shook hands and parted.

But the memories of their time together stayed with her, and on February 26, about six weeks after the seminar, she called from work to wish him a happy birthday. He had mentioned the date to her, and she remembered it because it was the same as Beth's. For the next three months they wrote and called each other often; Norma arranged to have his letters addressed to a friend's house, where she could get them without Bruce's knowledge. Finally, in May they decided to meet for a weekend in San Diego.

Just before she left, Norma told Bruce that she was going shopping for the weekend with one of her friends.

"What are you going to San Diego to shop for? You've been making too many trips to San Diego. I don't want you going to the city. We've got things to do around here."

She just stared at her husband. "Well, I'm going." And she left. It was one of the few times she had stood up to her husband.

She met Wayne at the airport, and they went out to dinner. Then they took a long walk in Balboa Park before going to the City Beach Motel, where Wayne had made reservations for a room with two double beds. Like inexperienced honeymooners, they said little to each other in the motel room, not sure what to expect. When they were finally ready for bed, Wayne got into one and Norma pulled back the covers of the other. Just before they turned the lights out, they looked at each other and grinned sheepishly.

"Well," Wayne said. He paused. "What are we doing here anyway?"

They both laughed, breaking the edge of their nervousness. Norma got up and crawled into bed with him, and they made love.

Norma felt an excitement and passion that weekend that she hadn't known since the first years of her marriage. She was overcome with a giddy, romantic feeling, and she felt as carefree as a kid. When she saw Wayne off at the airport on Sunday noon, they agreed to get together again, and they promised they would each get a divorce, so they could be together whenever they wanted.

After that weekend Norma shut Bruce off sexually. She didn't love him, and she didn't feel right about sleeping with two men at the same time. They fought constantly throughout the summer, and Bruce frequently accused her of having an affair.

Finally, in July they separated. Bruce moved to San Luis, Arizona, where he got a job working for the U.S. Customs Service. He took David with him. Beth stayed with her mother.

It was mid-August before Wayne and Norma saw each other again. Norma took three days, including her birthday, during her vacation to visit him at his home near San Bernardino. The promise of their first weekend held strong, and Norma felt she was in love.

One Saturday morning after her vacation, when Beth was visiting Ellen in San Diego, Norma went to San Luis to help Bruce set up his apartment. He seemed dejected over the separation, and he started drinking early in the day.

"There's someone else, isn't there, Norma?" he said shortly after she arrived. "I know there is."

"What do you mean? Why do you think that?" Her voice was appropriately indignant.

"I just know. There must be."

"Well there isn't." She looked at him with her eyes narrowed. She felt a knot in her stomach. Although she had been especially careful to keep any evidence of her affair away from him, she wondered if something about her presence or her expression was giving her secret away. "Why do you keep bothering me with that question?"

"Because I just know it."

"Well, just drop it. I'm telling you, there isn't anyone else."

"Why do you want a divorce, then?"

Norma sighed in frustration. They had been over this issue a thousand times. They were always fighting. He was often mean to her. There was no love left in their relationship. She just couldn't go on with it.

"Do we have to go into this again? I'm just down here to help you set this place up. And to see David. Can't we just try to make the best of it today?"

"I know there's someone else." He spoke as if he hadn't heard. "If you'll just tell me, I'll give you the divorce, and I won't bother you any more."

"Bruce, how many times can I tell you?" She was on the verge of tears. "There is no one else."

She looked at him. His eyes were heavy and sad. The effect of the alcohol, which she knew often made him violent, had instead made him introspective. He always projected himself as tough and strong, and his voice was loud and demanding, even when he wasn't angry. Now there was a sorrowful tone to his voice, and it hurt her to see him that way.

The argument continued for several hours, off and on. Bruce kept coming back to it, and the more he drank, the more persistent and pitiful the questions became.

"Please, Norma, please." His eyes glistened. "Just tell me who it is, please. I promise, I swear I won't bother you about it again. And you can have the divorce."

Whether it was his persistence or his self-pity, Norma didn't know, but she felt her resistance wearing away; and she was lured by the promise: this will be it, it will be over, and I will be able to live my life as I please. Maybe he really means it this time. She looked back at her husband, and with tears in her eyes she told him.

At first Bruce held his face in his hands, and Norma wanted to run to him, to bury herself in his arms and to promise that it was over, that she would never see Wayne again, and that they would work it out. But she hesitated. Finally, he lifted his face to look back at her, and when his gaze met hers, her eyes opened wide, and a shiver fluttered deep in her spine. His eyes were angry, glazed with a wild look she had never seen before. And his voice turned vicious.

"You miserable fucking whore!" He stood up. "You no-good fucking whore! And you tell me I'm wrecking this marriage. Ha! You fucking goddamned whore!" He stalked toward her.

"Bruce, you said you—"

"Shut up, whore!"

He stood over her, his chest heaving as he breathed. "Why?" He struck her on the head with the heel of his hand. "Why? I'm not good enough?" He hit her again.

She cowered in her chair and covered her head with her arms. "Please stop, Bruce. Please stop."

"Shut up, whore!"

He didn't hit her again. Instead, he walked out of the room. Norma sat trembling in her chair, unable to get up, wondering what would happen next.

A minute later he returned. He had a gun in his hand, and he walked toward her slowly.

"What are you going to do?" She could barely speak.

He kept walking, saying nothing.

Norma started to shake. She felt faint. "Bruce," she said, choking on the word. "What are you doing?"

He just looked at her, his face as hard as stone. When he reached her, he cocked the gun and pointed it at her head, about six inches away.

She closed her eyes, not daring to look at the gun. Tears ran down her cheeks. "I'm sorry, my God, I'm sorry. Please. Please, don't kill me!"

She heard the click of the hammer as Bruce released it, and she opened her eyes, trembling.

"We're going back to Holtville, whore," he said evenly through his teeth. "You've ruined me. You've disgraced me. I want to take you back to Holtville. Then I think I'll kill you." He put the gun in his pocket and walked out of the room.

Norma rode back to Holtville in silence, the presence of David sparing her more of her husband's rage. She heard the click of the gun over and over in her ears. Would he really go through with his threat?

When they arrived in Holtville, he started again. With David outside, Bruce ordered Norma and her mother into the family room and pulled out his gun. He told Mrs. Holden of her daughter's confession, and his rage returned, this time against them both.

"You are not to leave the house," he shouted. "Do you understand? You are not to tell anyone about this. Or I'll kill you both."

He looked at Norma. "I've decided not to kill you, not yet," he said coolly. "First, I'm going to drive you to your friend's house, and I'm going to make you fuck. Then I'm going to kill you both."

"Oh, God, no!" Norma pleaded. "Please. It's my fault. I did it.

Please. Do anything. Kill me if you want. But don't make us—"

"Shut up, whore!" He hit her again. She raised her arms to protect herself, but he pulled them away and hit her once more.

"Whore," he said. "You fucking whore."

Mrs. Holden looked on, helpless, her eyes open wide in fright.

Bruce held them there all afternoon and into the early evening, alternately waving the gun at them and taunting them and then stalking around the house, leaving Norma and her mother shaking in their chairs. Whenever the telephone rang, he would rush to it, order Norma to answer it and then stand over her, keeping the gun pointed at her, making sure she said nothing to indicate her plight.

Throughout the afternoon Norma pleaded with him to leave Wayne out of it, not to make her drive up to his house. Finally, Bruce backed off.

"All right," he said. "Then call him up."

"What?" Her voice was weak. "Call who up?"

"You know goddamn well who. Your fucking friend. You call him up, and I'm going to stand right here, and you tell him this. You tell him you can't stand him, that he's ruined your life and your husband's life, and you tell him that you never want to see him again."

"Oh, Bruce, please—"

"Now." He put his hand on his gun.

Norma dreaded the call. She hoped Wayne would know it was a lie. But she had no choice, and she thought maybe Bruce would finally leave her alone. With tears in her eyes, she walked over to the telephone and dialed the number. Bruce leaned over her and listened as she made the call.

It was a short conversation. She blurted out the message, barely giving Wayne a chance to reply. After she hung up, she burst into tears.

"Shut up, whore!" he bellowed. "You goddamned whore!"

"Please, Bruce. I've done it. I've—"

"Shut up, whore!"

The taunting, the threats, the humiliation continued through the night into Sunday morning. Each time he pointed the gun at her head, she shook uncontrollably, certain that he would pull the trigger. When he put it away and left the room, she remained tense, but she also felt oddly apart from the scene, as if she had walked onto the set of some strange horror picture. Her husband had beaten her before. He had beaten their children and even her mother. But for all the violence she had seen, she could not imagine that he was capable of this. And she could not believe any of it was happening to her.

On Sunday afternoon Norma had planned to go to Ellen's house in San Diego to pick up Beth. He would have to let her out of the house for that, she thought.

"Okay," Bruce said. "We can go. But we have to make one stop on the way."

Norma looked at him skeptically.

"I'm going to drive, and I want you to take me to the hotel you stayed in. I want you to show me where you did it, you whore."

Norma began to tremble again, and she looked at him pleadingly. "My God, Bruce, why are—"

"Shut up." He got the gun out again, making sure Norma could see it, and leered at her. "I want to see where you fucked him."

She was certain that Bruce intended to take her to that hotel room and kill her. When they arrived at the City Beach Motel, she was shaking so badly she could hardly walk.

They finally arrived at the door of room 1162. Bruce glared at it, then at Norma. "This is it, huh?" He shook his head and just looked at it for a long, silent moment. When he turned back to her, he looked at her straight in the eye. "You fucking whore," he said. Then he walked back toward the car.

Norma followed, crying. When they arrived at the car, he put his hands on her shoulders and shook her. "If you say anything to Ellen about any of this, I'll kill you." He put his hand on the gun. "I'll kill you all."

The visit with Bruce's sister passed without incident, and they left with Beth, arriving home late Sunday evening. Once the children were in bed, Bruce confronted Norma once more. "You and your mother better not mention this to anyone, do you understand?"

She nodded.

"If you do, so help me, I'll kill you."

And he left.

Norma, her body quivering with tension, fumbled for a chair. She gripped its arms tightly and listened as a car door slammed and an engine started. She heard the engine whine as the car backed out the driveway and then rev up as it sped down the street. Then there was silence.

For the first time since noon of the day before, she did not have to wonder whether, in the next minute, five minutes, or an hour she would be shot to death. She began to cry.

About three weeks later Bruce returned. His eyes were filled with sincerity and earnestness instead of rage. He did not apologize, but he begged Norma to come back to him.

"I won't bring it up again, I promise," he said. "It's over and done with. We can work this out. We can make it work."

But Norma shook her head. She didn't know how she could bear to live with him. "I think it's better if we just leave it this way," she said.

Bruce's expression changed, and she sensed the rage returning. He stormed out of the room, saying nothing. He returned a few minutes later, with a book in his hand. Norma recognized it immediately—the Bible she had carried at her wedding. It included their marriage certificate and the baptismal records of Beth and David. He held the Bible in front of her.

"You carried this on your wedding day, didn't you, on the day you married me, right?"

Norma nodded stiffly.

"How dare you carry a Bible. You're a fucking whore. Whores don't read the Bible."

Bruce held the book out to her, and as she reached for it, he pulled it back. "Whores don't deserve to have a Bible," he said. Then he opened the book, gripped one side with each hand, and ripped it in half at the binding.

Norma gasped.

Bruce looked at her with a mean smile, then tore out pages and scattered them around the room. "This means a lot to you, huh?" He fumbled through the remaining pages until he found their marriage certificate. He tore it out and shook it in front of her. His eyes were wild.

"Ha," he said. "Ha! And *this* means a lot to you, too, doesn't it. Ha! You know what it means to me?"

He unbuckled his belt and dropped his pants to the floor. Then he turned away from her and bent over deliberately, exposing his buttocks to her. "This is what it means to me!" he said again. He took the certificate in his right hand and wiped himself with it.

He stood up, pulled up his pants, and looked back at Norma. "You miserable whore!" Then he threw the marriage certificate at her and left the room.

Norma watched the piece of paper flutter to the floor, and she looked at it through a blur of tears. She felt nauseated. Her whole body recoiled in a torrent of emotion—shame, disgust, horror, fear —and she broke down, sobbing. Finally, she arose; picked the paper up, and went to the bathroom sink, where she gently tried to wipe the certificate clean.

Meanwhile, Bruce was leaving. He confronted her one more time. "All right. I'll give you the divorce, if that's the way you want it. But let me tell you this. If you ever marry Wayne Connors, I'll kill you both."

Norma resisted going back to Bruce for several weeks, trying to work out in her mind how she could leave him for Wayne without his finding out. But she had no doubt he would carry out his threat, and in the end it seemed hopeless. Finally, she agreed to stay with Bruce. If she couldn't have Wayne, she decided, it wasn't worth the pain of a divorce. Bruce had told her he would get custody of David, and she believed him. At least this way, she reasoned, she would still have both the children.

In early September she talked to Wayne once again. "It's no use," she said. "There's nothing I can do."

Over the next several months, Norma and Bruce worked to rebuild their lives together, and in June of 1971 they started building a new home on a pleasant lot on Andrews Street in Holtville. For Norma, the effort was more resignation than commitment. And Bruce never came through on his promise to forget Wayne Connors. Indeed, whenever they argued, he would bring it up, often in front of the children, taunting her as "the biggest whore in Holtville." Once, after Norma's picture had appeared in the paper with a group of other women, nine-year-old David took a black crayon and wrote, "biggest hore in Holtville," and drew an arrow to his mother.

In addition, Bruce called Norma's boss and informed him that she had been carrying on an affair. Twice he made Beth call Connors, once to tell him to stay out of her mother's life and another time to demand he send back a medallion Norma had given him. Sometimes he held Norma out in his truck, swearing at her so loudly that he was heard easily beyond the truck's closed windows and beating her so that her arms and face became covered with bruises. She had to wear long-sleeved blouses to work. She usually told people she had fallen and was prone to bruising.

In July of 1971 Norma was surprised at work by a telephone call from Wayne, the first word she had heard from him since the preceding September.

"I wish it could have worked out for us," he said, "but I'm starting over. I've remarried, and I'm very happy."

Norma felt a pain in her chest. "Well, we're putting the pieces back together, you know," she said. "We're building a new home now, and everything is going okay." Her voice was flat, and she wondered whether he could detect her lack of enthusiasm. "I hope that everything works out well for you and that you are very happy."

After they had hung up, Norma found a little-used room at work, closed the door behind her, and cried for an hour. She hoped he was as miserable as she was.

In October of the same year Norma and a man named Paul, with whom she worked, decided to attend an escrow-officers seminar in Palm Springs.

"I think I'd like to come along," Bruce told her.

She eyed him suspiciously, but could say nothing. It was as much a social event—it included an evening of dancing and entertainment—as a professional seminar. Bruce had never asked to attend any of her other professional meetings, and she suspected it was not Paul's company that had aroused his interest in this one. He had found a picture of Wayne in her desk one day, and she suspected he would be looking for him.

A few days before the seminar, Norma called Wayne's company in Los Angeles. He had changed jobs, she was told, and was no longer with the company. He had probably moved to the northern part of the state, she figured, and would not attend a conference in Palm Springs.

She was tense as she arrived at the seminar and scanned the crowd of faces for Wayne, hoping that he wasn't there. Slowly, however, she loosened up and began to enjoy herself with her husband in an evening of dancing and drinking.

Near the end of the evening, she spotted him. He was standing near the bar, on the far side of the ballroom.

"I think it's about time we leave, don't you?" she said to Bruce as nonchalantly as possible.

"No. Let's have one more drink." He walked toward the bar, straight toward Wayne Connors.

Norma didn't know whether her husband had seen him. But she didn't wait to find out. She walked quickly towards the ladies room, where she stayed for what seemed to her like an hour. Finally, she went back to the ballroom. She did not see her husband, but she did run into Paul.

"Have you seen Bruce?" she asked.

"No. I think he found someone he knew and went outside with him."

"Oh, God." She made her way across the ballroom, surveying the faces as she headed for the door.

Just outside the entrance a man lay on the ground. It was Wayne, battered and covered with blood. A woman was bending over him.

Norma turned to run back inside, but Bruce saw her.

"Go get Paul and let's go. The police will be here any minute."

Whether out of instinct or fear, she obeyed. "Bruce is a little sick," she said when she found their companion. "He wants to get home."

They went back out the door, and Norma didn't even glance over to where Wayne lay wounded. She just kept walking until they got to the car. Paul knew nothing of what had happened. All the way home she wondered whether Wayne had seen her. The image of his face covered with blood kept running through her mind.

Norma sighed heavily and looked up at me, tears glistening in the corners of her eyes. "Bruce laughed at me all the time about beating Wayne up," she said. "I told him I didn't think it was anything to brag about. He made me say I was sorry hundreds of times about Wayne and me, and I had to tell him. But on the inside I wasn't sorry. I thought at least that I had had something beautiful for a short time and that it was worth everything I went through. But I never heard from Wayne again after that night, not until last week."

I shook my head and said nothing for a moment. "Norma, I want to believe you, I really do. I hope this is the truth. But to insist that Connors's phone call to you last Monday was just a coincidence almost defies logic. What you tell me is compelling and touching. It also suggests that Connors had every reason to want to get at Bruce and would be a willing participant in a plot to get rid of him."

"There was no plot, Milt. He knew nothing of it." She shrugged. "That's the truth."

"Whatever possessed you to call him back after you had talked to Hanscom, then? Didn't you think it might look suspicious?"

"Milt, I got that call, and I couldn't believe what I was hearing. After everything I was going through, with Beth and everything, and here was Wayne on the other end of the phone, telling me that he was split up again and that he wanted to see me. I told him I didn't know if I could arrange it, but I wrote his number down on my notebook. And I didn't even make a connection between the two phone calls. But I just knew that somehow I was going to see him. I just knew it."

"Does he know anything about your arrest?"

She shook her head.

"You haven't been in touch with him since Monday?"

"No."

"Then he still intends to meet you tonight at the Mission Valley Inn?"

"I hope so. As far as I know, he does."

"Well, Norma you're not going to see him tonight, that's for sure."

Her face fell. "Oh—"

"But don't worry. He won't be alone."

CHAPTER 13

The previous night Tucker and I had had only the allegation of incest as a lever for prying into the circumstances of the case. Then, in just a few hours, a body and a boyfriend had added critical new dimensions to Norma Winters's predicament. And the speed with which they developed suggested we could waste no time mulling them over. I asked Tucker to talk to Norma alone, in order to get a description of Connors that would help us identify him in a crowded barroom. Then I turned my attention back to Bruce Winters.

I called Stephen Wolford to confirm that he had received my telegram requesting the neutron-activation analysis and to see what, if anything, I could learn about his findings in Winters's death. As the coroner in charge of the investigation, he had no particular obligation to tell me anything until he had completed his probe, but when I introduced myself as Norma's attorney, he was congenial and helpful. He had received my telegram.

"I think the analysis is a good idea," he said. "Homicide will most likely do it anyway."

"I'm especially concerned that the body not be disturbed, so that this test can be performed."

"I understand. I've already taken steps to make certain that the test is done." He paused. "Did you know that a note was found near the body?"

"A note? A suicide note?"

"That's what it looks like."

Wolford said he wouldn't know for sure until they had investigated the case further. Since his office was treating the death as a homicide, he said the note would be analyzed by a specialist to determine whether it matched Winters's handwriting. He also said he planned a complete autopsy on Monday.

The suicide note was the best news I'd heard about Norma since I'd taken her case, but it was no guarantee that her husband had taken his own life. A substantial amount of circumstantial evidence was already stacked against her, evidence that the medical examiner could consider, along with the autopsy findings, in ruling on the cause of death. The physical evidence is often technical and open to expert interpretation. With Wolford's consent, I arranged to have Dr. Peter Ulrich, one of the most respected pathologists in Southern California, attend the autopsy on behalf of the defense.

I had done what I could to protect Norma's interests in the investigation of her husband's death. Now I hoped we would locate Wayne Connors before the police did.

A sea of lights glistened in the cool evening air as Tucker and I rode along the freeway in his old blue Ford, headed for Mission Valley. The highway splits a succession of expensive restaurants, movie theaters, shopping plazas, and hotels—a kind of upper-class strip that had mushroomed out of what just twenty years before had been a vast pastureland. On this night the lights were a blur, and the signs marking each establishment seemed unreadable. The news of the suicide note had only slightly relieved my anxiety over Norma's predicament. It was consistent with her version of the events, but I wondered whether Wolford would even have mentioned it to me if he had known about Norma's date with Connors. Indeed, if Bruce had been killed by a professional hit man, the note could be just part of the cover. Thus, the relationships of Bruce and of Norma with Connors still posed difficult questions, not only for my client's case, but for my dealings with her. It was quite possible she was lying to me, and I had to question once again each aspect of her story. Was the incest a fabrication? Was Beth involved in a scheme to kill her father? Did Norma contact someone she hadn't told us about to murder her husband? Was Connors involved? Did he help Norma plot the killing, or was he in it even further—was he the hit man?

"All we have is a four-year-old description," Tucker noted, as he pulled into a parking space at the Mission Valley Inn.

"Or so our client tells us."

"Right," he grinned. "I'm not too sure about anything right now."

Tucker had grilled Norma for a description of Connors, searching for some unique feature that might help distinguish him in a crowd. He was six feet tall with a slender build, she'd said, and in his early thirties. He tended to dress conservatively, and he had dark hair, brown eyes, and pockmarks on his face from adolescent acne. Which is to say that he looked like a lot of other men.

Tucker parked inconspicuously in a row of cars, where, if necessary, we could see both the entrance and the exit to the hotel. It was 7:30 P.M.

The lounge was large and dimly lit; it featured a dozen gold vinyl booths and a bar that jutted into the room and was lined with stools on three sides. Three of the booths were filled, with people who didn't appear to match our description. The bar was empty, patrolled only by a single bartender, who was talking quietly with a waitress.

That so few people were in the lounge was to our advantage. We wouldn't have to pick our man out of a crowd. But it was also dark. Brown hair looked black, dark clothes looked alike, and everyone's face was in shadow.

"I think I'll call Norma and see if I can get any more out of her on this guy," Tucker said.

"Okay. I'll check with the front desk on the chance he may have been foolish enough to register."

I approached the reservations desk and nodded to the woman standing behind the counter. "Excuse me, do you have a Mr. Connors registered here?"

She looked quickly through her records.

"No, sir. We don't."

"How about a Mr. Winters."

She checked again and shook her head. "No."

No Mrs. Connors or Mrs. Winters was registered, either, and I toyed with the idea of asking the woman to page Connors. But if he was meeting Norma clandestinely, it might raise his suspicions, I thought, and he might call the desk from a phone or not respond at all. A page seemed a last resort. Tucker and I met back near the entrance as he stepped out of the phone booth.

"Norma's asleep," he said with a frown. "Lovell gave her some sleeping pills or some damn thing, and he says he couldn't wake her."

We had to work with the description we had. Instead of paging him, we headed back to the bar.

We both saw him at the same time. A man sat alone on the far side of the bar, facing the rest of the room. We couldn't see him well in the dim light, but he was the only man at the bar, and he hadn't been there a few minutes before. We stood near the doorway and watched him for a few minutes. He appeared neatly dressed. He had a drink in front of him. And he looked twice at his watch. He seemed to be waiting for somebody.

"Let's go have a drink," Tucker said.

The man was sitting at the bar on a corner stool, and Tucker took the other corner seat, so that he was not sitting directly beside him, but at a right angle to him. I sat next to Tucker, and when I turned my head to talk to him, I could look right into our man's eyes.

"What'll it be, gentlemen," the bartender said.

"CC and water," Tucker replied.

"I'll have a gin and tonic."

The bartender nodded and moved away.

"Well," Tucker said, "what do you want to do, do you want to rent a car?"

"I don't know. How much do they cost down here?"

Tucker shrugged. "I don't know, around eight or ten bucks, I'd say."

"It's probably cheaper than a cab, but I don't know how far we are from downtown."

The bartender set the drinks in front of us. I handed him a ten-dollar bill.

"I don't know, either," Tucker said.

Then he turned to his left and looked at the man sitting at the next stool.

"Excuse me, do you know how far it is to downtown from here?"

The man looked up calmly from his drink. "No, I'm sorry, I don't," he said in a pleasant voice.

I studied him quickly. He had a thin build and wore a dark suit with thin lapels, a white shirt, and a moderately narrow tie, which put his taste in clothes at about 1963. His hair was either black or dark brown, but it was not slicked down. Still, I was convinced we had our man. His face was rough around the chin and cheeks, scarred by acne.

"Well," Tucker was saying, "we just arrived in town on business, and we don't know the area too well. We flew in from LA."

The man's eyes brightened. "Whereabouts in LA are you from?"

"Santa Monica," I interjected. "Near the Barrington Plaza. Do you know where that is?"

"Yes, I do."

"Then you must be from LA too?"

He nodded. "I am."

"This sure is a beautiful town," I continued. "Do you get down here much?"

"No, not very often. The last time was about four years ago, I think."

He sipped his drink until it was about empty and then stretched his arm out casually, exposing his watch from under his shirt sleeve. He glanced at the dial. "What kind of business are you in?" he asked.

"Automobiles," I said. "We're down here for a sales meeting."

He nodded, reached for his drink and put it down again. It was empty.

"What are you drinking?" I asked.

"Well, that won't be—"

"No, that's all right. What is it, gin and tonic?"

He shrugged and nodded.

"Bartender, could we have another gin and tonic down here, please?"

"What kind of business are you in?" Tucker asked.

"Insurance."

As in title insurance, I thought.

"Down here on business?" Tucker continued.

He shook his head. The bartender set the drink in front of him, and he looked at me and smiled. "Thank you very much."

He was our man, I thought, but Tucker was a step ahead of me.

"My name's Gene Tucker," he said, extending his hand.

The man took Tucker's hand and shook it.

"Wayne Connors," he said.

I glanced quickly at Tucker, then at Connors. "Mr. Connors, I'm Milt Silverman, and I'm Norma Winters's lawyer. Gene is a private investigator working with me. Norma is in a lot of trouble, and I want to talk to you about it right now, right in that booth over there."

Connors looked at us agape. He seemed to have had the wind knocked out of him. "Is this a joke?" he asked finally.

"No. This is no joke. This is serious, dead serious."

"Well, what kind of trouble is she in?"

"Let's talk about it over in that booth."

He looked over at the booth, then back at me. Then he shrugged. "Okay," he said softly.

We picked up our drinks and stepped over to the booth. Connors slid in on one side, facing Tucker and me on the other.

"We're sorry we had to play this game with you," Tucker explained.

Connors nodded skeptically. "Have you guys been following me, or what? I mean, how did you know I was here?"

"Norma told us you'd be here," Tucker reached for his wallet, pulled out his business card, and showed Connors his identification. "And she gave us a description."

"But I haven't seen her for four years. Did she show you a picture or something?"

We said nothing.

"Look," he said finally. "I just want to make sure you're not friends of her husband or anything. He almost killed me once. He really beat me up."

"Well, he's not going to beating you up any more, is he," I said.

Connors wrinkled his brow. "What do you mean?"

"He was found last night with a bullet through his heart, just forty-eight hours after Norma was arrested for hiring someone to kill him. We want to know what you know about it."

Connors spoke after a long pause. "I don't know a thing. This is incredible to me."

"Norma said she talked to you on the telephone last Monday."

"Yes, that's when we set up this date tonight."

"I want to know exactly how that conversation happened."

"Sure," he said.

We ordered another round of drinks and waited for them, giving Connors a moment to recover.

"How did this phone call come about?" I asked.

"Last week, I was up in Morro Bay," he said. "And I had fond memories of Norma. And so I just called her."

"Let's get this straight," Tucker interjected. "You called her?"

"Yes."

"What time?"

"It was in the morning. I called her from home. And I called her at her old number at California Title Insurance, where she worked when I met her. The girl that answered told me Norma had started her own business, which was news to me, and she gave me the new number. When I called that number, the girl said Norma wasn't in."

"But you completed that call, is that right?" Tucker asked.

"Yes. She asked if I would like to leave a message, and I said I would call back later."

"Did you?" I asked.

"Yes, I called her from work. We spoke briefly. I think she said she couldn't talk right then and asked if she could call me back. I told her to call me collect at home that evening. And she said fine."

"Did she call you back?"

"Yes. She called me at about five-thirty, I think it was."

"Now, let me tell you something. That same day that you called her, and, in fact, about an hour before she called you back, a hit man from San Diego called her to arrange for the murder of her husband."

Connors swallowed hard.

"Are you telling me that that is a coincidence?"

He looked at me straight in the eyes. "Yes, I am."

"You knew nothing about her conversation with the hit man who turned out to be an undercover police officer?"

"No, I didn't." His eyes didn't waver.

"Did Norma mention anything to you about having her husband killed?" Tucker asked.

"No. She did say that she had just found out something about Bruce and that she had seen a lawyer about a divorce."

"Did she say what those things were?"

"No."

"How was this meeting tonight arranged?" I asked.

"Well, I told her I would like to see her again. And, you know, I was kind of encouraged that she was still having trouble with Bruce, I was kind of hopeful that maybe she would really get a divorce this time. Anyway, we made a dinner date for Saturday, tonight."

"Have you registered at this hotel?"

He shook his head.

"Or any hotel?" Tucker asked.

"No. I just got here."

"When is the last time you spoke with Norma?" I continued.

"Monday."

"You haven't talked to her since then?"

"No."

"What about before last Monday?"

He paused for a moment, looking up as he thought. Then he looked back at me. "About three years ago, the summer of '71."

"You're absolutely sure of that?"

"Yes."

"Okay, let me tell you something else. Tucker here is going to check your phone logs. He's going to know everything there is to know about you before we're through with this, do you understand?"

Connors nodded.

"So if you're lying to us, we're going to find out. I promise you that. And if you're lying to us, you're hurting Norma, not helping her. My only interest is in helping Norma, and the only way I can do that is to know the truth."

"I told you the truth."

"Well, hear me out a minute. If you are involved in this, if you know any more about Bruce's death, or if you had even an inkling about the possibility of Bruce's death, I want to make this deal with you. I don't want you to tell me that you are involved. I just want you to tell me that you will not give me any information. I'd rather have no information than erroneous information. So if any part of what you have told me is untrue, I want you to tell me that you withdraw what you have told me. Do you understand?"

"Yes," he said evenly. "And everything I've told you is true. I don't know what else I can say to make you believe it, but I swear, I'm telling you the truth."

"Will you take a lie-detector test?"

"Yes," he replied, without hesitation.

We were unable to shake his story, and by now he was at ease with us, talking quietly but forthrightly. He seemed to be telling the truth. But I wanted to check further and see whether his account of their relationship matched what Norma had told me.

"What are those fond memories you have about Morro Bay?" I asked.

"Well, we spent a week there at a conference, you know, and we just were very attracted to each other. I guess we were both having tough times at home, and, well, it was nice. But nothing happened between us, and when we said good-bye, I figured we'd never see each other again. Then she called me a few weeks later to wish me a happy birthday."

Connors confirmed the weekend in San Diego and the weekend in August of 1970 in his apartment, as well as his own phone call to her the following summer during which he told her he had remarried.

"She wished me luck and everything, you know, but it didn't sound like she meant it."

"Well, what about that beating from Bruce?"

Connors swallowed hard. "It was about three years ago, in Palm Springs, at another convention. I was there with my wife. I guess Bruce came with Norma. He came up to me late in the evening and said he wanted to speak to me outside. He seemed polite and nice; it didn't sound like a threat. So I walked outside with him. He was a little behind me as we went out the door, and when I turned around, I got clobbered. His fist was right there, and he just slugged me. My face and clothes were covered with blood." He paused, looking away for a moment. "He beat the shit out of me."

"Had you ever seen or heard from Bruce before that?"

"Well, he did call me once."

"When?"

"Before the Palm Springs incident. And Beth called me, too, around the same time. Bruce just swore at me in a terrible voice. Beth told me I was destroying her mother's marriage and demanded that I never see her again. I didn't think I was destroying anything, you know. There didn't seem to be much of a marriage there. Anyway, I told her I wouldn't see her. And she also asked me to send back a medallion that Beth had given me." His voice was soft and somber. "I sent it back."

Tucker and I glanced at each other, saying nothing for a moment. He had confirmed just about every part of Norma's story, and he hadn't contradicted her on one single point.

"What's going to happen to Norma?" he finally asked, setting his drink down after a last sip.

"I don't know," I said. "It doesn't look good. She's in a lot of trouble. It's hard to say anything until we know why Bruce Winters is dead."

He nodded solemnly. "I'll do anything I can to help, but I'd like to know one thing, is there any chance of seeing her?"

"Not right now. If you really want to help, then the best thing you can do is go out to the parking lot, get in your car, and drive home. You can send me the copies of your telephone records for this month. And if Norma tries to reach you, you can refuse to speak to her until I give her permission. We've got to get this case sorted out."

"Anything you say. What should I do if the police contact me?"

"I can't advise you on that. If you are involved in this matter in any way, I suggest you speak with a lawyer."

"I've already told you what my involvement is," he replied with conviction.

"Then, if the police contact you, my advice is that you tell them the truth."

He nodded. We all shook hands. I put a ten-dollar bill on the table, and Tucker and I left. We walked quickly to the car and waited. Within five minutes Connors emerged from the Mission Valley Inn and got into a baby-blue Chrysler with California license plates.

Tucker wrote down the license number and the make of the car. "I'll check it," he said.

CHAPTER 14

By Monday morning, August 19, the police had not yet charged Norma with murder, which suggested that they still lacked hard evidence that her husband had been murdered. But when I called Wolford to check on the status of the autopsy and the neutron-activation analysis, he did not have good news.

"Mr. Silverman, I informed homicide of your request for the test," he said, "and homicide gave specific instructions to the mortuary that Mr. Winters's body was not to be moved, studied, or tampered with until we gave official approval."

"Yes?"

"But someone didn't get the word. The body was washed."

"So the test is useless then, isn't it?" I said. I knew any traces of the chemicals would have been washed away.

"I'm afraid you're right. I'm very sorry this happened. But I want to assure you once again that this investigation will be thorough and impartial. I'm very sorry for the mix-up."

I said nothing for a moment, absorbing the shock of yet another twist in the case.

"Well, I guess there's nothing we can do about that," I said finally. "Did Dr. Ulrich get in touch with you?"

"Yes, sir. And we have scheduled the autopsy for late this afternoon, after he gets here."

"So he will be able to observe the autopsy?"

"Absolutely. I promise you, it will not begin until Dr. Ulrich arrives."

Perhaps out of embarrassment over the washing of Bruce's body, or perhaps out of his natural openness, Wolford volunteered a few pertinent details of the investigation before we hung up. There had been no signs of a struggle in the house where Bruce had been found, and the point of entry of the bullet was definitely a contact wound—the muzzle of the gun had been pressed against his chest when the gun had been fired—an indication that Bruce had pulled the trigger.

"What caliber was it?" I asked.

"It was a .38-caliber revolver. And there's one more thing. He unbuttoned his shirt before the gun went off. That's not uncommon in suicides when people shoot themselves in the chest. Naturally, we might find other factors that we don't know about yet, and I'm not telling you this is definitely a suicide, but that's what we've found out so far."

I was pleased and somewhat relieved by Wolford's cooperation and by his description of the investigation. And I sensed, both from what he told me and from the tone of his voice, that he would be surprised if the full investigation, including the autopsy, did not confirm his initial suspicion—that Bruce Winters had taken his own life.

During the visit to my office on Saturday morning, Walt Lovell had told me about a confrontation he said he had had with Sergeant Ryan, who had gone out to National City to interview Beth. She had been at the beach, and Ryan, Lovell said, had become upset and demanded to talk to her "before the defense lawyer does," or any statement from her would be "useless, because the defense lawyer would tell her what to say."

I didn't want any misunderstandings between me and the police, especially Ryan, whom I'd grown to respect, and I was not trying to keep Beth away from the police. She was a witness in the case. I decided to call Ryan to see what the problem was.

Ryan assured me that he hadn't accused me of protecting a witness and told me about an incident at the police station when Norma had been arrested in which Lovell had created a scene in a corridor.

"That guy's a pain in the ass," Ryan remarked. "I didn't accuse you of tampering with the daughter at all. We just like to get to our witnesses when the case is fresh in their minds and before they tell the world about it."

"Right, Mike. I understand."

"I'm sure you do," he said with a chuckle. "I understand you like to hang out at the Mission Valley Inn on Saturday nights."

For a second the comment didn't register. Then I realized he was talking about Wayne Connors. They had found him.

"Yeah, I guess I do," I said, laughing. "But just remember, we got to him first."

"Yeah, you did. What did he tell you?"

"Oh, probably the same thing he told you."

"Yeah, probably. Then he must have told you about the three guys in San Jose that she hired a couple of years ago to do the job on her old man."

My hand tightened its grip on the telephone, and I felt a pounding in my chest. Norma had lied. Beth had lied. Connors had lied. All of them. The case was finished. And I had bought every line.

"Are you kidding me?" I shouted.

Ryan remained silent for a moment. Then he laughed. "Yeah," he said.

When I recovered, Ryan offered some more information about Lovell: his mug shot was on file at the police station.

"What was he arrested for?" I asked.

"Nothing serious, just a minor jam."

"Come on, is this another sucker punch?"

"No, no. I'm not pulling your leg. Lovell's picture is here with some numbers on it."

Ryan refused to tell me what the arrest was for. We hung up cordially, but the call left me with an uneasy feeling about Walter Lovell. I called Tucker, told him about the conversation with Ryan and then gave him another task: to find out why Lovell had been arrested.

The next day, the twentieth, Norma was arraigned in San Diego Municipal Court on two charges—conspiracy to commit murder and solicitation for murder. They had an ominous sound to them, but they could have been worse. And I was happy that the charges were before the court, because once Norma was formally charged, the process of discovery would begin, and the defense could see the evidence the police had amassed against her. Under a U.S. Supreme Court decision known as *Brady* v. *Maryland,* and the liberal application of that ruling by California courts, the prosecution is required to provide to the defense all evidence—both harmful and helpful to the defendant's case—that it accumulates in its investigation. A trial is not a game, the courts have reasoned, and justice is best served when both sides can prepare a case fully informed of its basic facts. Thus, I anticipated that Norma's entering a "not guilty" plea to the charges would open up her case file to us. But the deputy district attorney had other intentions.

"Your Honor," he said, "we intend to proceed by indictment on this case. We ask that the matter be set for arraignment in superior court on August twenty-sixth, for bind over to the grand jury."

"Very well," the judge replied. He ordered Norma to appear in court again on the charges the following week.

I glared at the DA. His request meant much more than an inconvenient second trip to the courthouse. It would hold up discovery, since Norma would not be considered "formally charged" until an indictment was handed down. That could take several weeks. The DA could have opted for the more common method of bringing a case to trial in California—simply filing a criminal complaint. Such action entitles the defendant to a preliminary hearing, a kind of mini-trial in which the prosecution calls witnesses and presents its evidence before a judge, who rules whether the evidence is strong enough to bring the case to trial. Since the defense may also question and call witnesses in a preliminary hearing, it needs access to the police-investigation file in order to prepare its case. Discovery begins almost immediately. The grand jury, however, is secret. The defense does not participate and therefore is denied an early look at the evidence against the accused. From a theoretical standpoint the preliminary hearing is a much stronger guarantee of a defendant's rights than is the grand jury at this critical stage of the judicial process. A judge, after hearing testimony and arguments from both prosecution and defense, is more likely to make an impartial ruling than is a grand jury, which hears only from the district attorney and which is therefore more inclined to affirm the DA's presentation of events. On a practical level, defense attorneys consider the preliminary hearing an important opportunity to evaluate both the hard evidence against a client, and the credibility of the witnesses, and how they might withstand cross-examination.

But it was the impact of the DA's position on discovery that concerned me most in this case. After the arraignment I asked whether he would consent informally to our looking at the evidence. Not until after the indictment, he said. Although legally proper, his stand impeded the progress of our own investigation of the case. The police files, complete with crime reports, tape recordings, photographs, and witness interviews, could provide important leads for Tucker and me. We wanted to talk to the people the police had interviewed, perhaps fleshing out their reports in order to open up new questions and new leads, and we wanted to do that before their memories faded. We knew the police had interviewed Bruce Winters. What had he said? His death had already eliminated one potential witness; the washing of his body had eliminated potential crucial evidence. Other perishable evidence might disappear before we could get to it, I feared, unless we could see the police reports right away. Otherwise, discovery, when we got it, might be a hollow right. I decided to file a motion, asking the judge to order the DA to grant immediate discovery in the case.

When I returned to my office that afternoon, however, I had no time to draw up a legal motion. I had an urgent telephone call from Sam Blake, the bail bondsman in El Centro. The $2,500 check—the ten percent premium to the bail bondsman—had bounced. The check was drawn on a trust account managed by Walt Lovell, and it bore his signature.

I called Lovell immediately. "There must be some mistake," I said to him. "The bondsman just called and said your trust account for Norma's bail has bounced. Is that possible?"

Lovell said nothing for a moment, then replied nonchalantly, "Well, just have him redeposit the check. It will go through all right."

"Listen, Walt, things are not that simple. The bondsman is obligated to inform the court immediately that his company is withdrawing its bond. That means Norma goes back to jail. I need a lot more than just your assurance that the money is there."

"I've already talked to Madeline Peters, and she's willing to put up the bail money. It will be in the account."

Madeline Peters, a chiropractor in Holtville, was a close friend of Norma and her husband, and Tucker had already arranged to meet her the next day at Lovell's office.

"Is she still coming to your office tomorrow?" I asked.

"Yes, she will be here."

"Good. I'll be by with Tucker, and I'll talk to her about loaning the money then."

I hung up, shaking my head in disbelief. Lovell's voice had been disturbingly casual. He hadn't even seemed surprised by the bad check. That should never happen to a trust-account check, I thought, especially not to one written by a financial consultant. And he'd seemed unconcerned about the check's potential impact on Norma's freedom.

I called Blake back and explained that it would take me a day or two to get the money together.

"Well, okay, but no longer," he replied. "I shouldn't let this go, but Norma and I got back a long ways, you know. We've been friends for many years."

Blake and Norma had known each other for more than fifteen years in El Centro, a community where everyone appeared to have at least some information about everybody else.

"I appreciate this," I said. "I won't let it go. You'll hear from me by Thursday."

Late the next morning, I filed a thirteen-page motion in superior court, seeking an immediate opening of the discovery process and access to the police evidence against Norma. A hearing on the motion was scheduled for Friday. Tucker and I then drove to National City, to see Lovell.

Lovell's business was in a small, single-story office building that was occupied by about a half dozen other tenants, including a real-estate agent, an insurance agent, and a lawyer. Lovell arrived with Norma, Madeline Peters, and Norma's sister just as Tucker and I were stepping out of his car. Lovell's own office was a large paneled room nearly filled with a massive desk piled with papers, a brown swivel chair, and a long table. Numerous certificates, credentials, and photographs hung in narrow black frames on the wall behind his desk. Another small room off the far end of the office housed a small computer that had spewed a long readout onto the floor. It was a modestly appointed office, certainly not in the style of the large consulting firms in the city, but it was pleasant and clean.

We wasted little time with formalities. I was preoccupied with the bounced check. Tucker would talk to Madeline and Norma's sister about the details of the case, about their knowledge of the relationship between Bruce and Norma.

Madeline Peters was a warm, pleasant, and well-educated woman who told me she had met Norma and Bruce at the Southern Baptist Church, where she was a more active member than either of them. She was fond of both of them and had treated Bruce for tension.

"I would like to help Norma," she said. "And I understand she might be getting some insurance money."

"I guess that's likely," I said. Bruce had about $50,000 worth of insurance policies that, like most policies, contained a suicide exclusion, but only if the suicide occurred within six months of the date of the policy. Bruce had taken all the policies out several years before. Of course, if the police concluded that Norma had murdered her husband and if she was convicted, she would get nothing.

Madeline said she understood that risk, but was confident Norma had not committed murder. "I understand from Mr. Lovell that she needs $2,500."

I nodded.

"Well, I have some money saved for my children's education. It amounts to about three thousand dollars. I can loan her enough for the bail. Can you write me some kind of paper that would say that I would be paid back as soon as Norma gets the money from the insurance?"

It was a generous and reasonable offer, I thought. "I'm sure it won't be a problem. Walt is handling the financial matters, as you probably know. Let me go talk to him about it and see what we can arrange."

She nodded and I went out to the reception area, where Lovell was sitting in one of the two chairs. I suggested we talk outside, where I explained Madeline's proposal.

"It sounds like a good idea," I said. But I sensed something was wrong. Lovell's body stiffened, and he leaned away from me as I spoke.

"That would create some problems, a legal document like that," he said. "Norma's financial picture is very delicate."

"Well," I said in a normal tone of voice. "Her legal picture is very delicate, too. She could be sent back to jail. This money is important. Why would this proposal present a problem?"

Lovell explained that Norma had a $15,000 bank loan outstanding, which she had taken out to start her business as an advance against an anticipated $30,000 loan from the federal Small Business Administration. But with her arrest the SBA had immediately reneged on its commitment to the loan.

"Now, I have contacted the bank officer and the SBA," he said. "And I gave them a lecture about the right of a person to be considered innocent until proven guilty. They reversed their position. She'll get the loan. But her position is still delicate, and it is likely to be that way for a few weeks. This is a very complex matter, but I have everything under control, and I'll handle it. Madeline can loan her the money, and you tell her that I will see that she gets it back within a week."

I felt frustrated, but I said nothing more to Lovell about the money. He was handling my client's financial matters, and I didn't want to breach that relationship without consulting Norma. But he had bounced a trust-account check; he had suggested the check be redeposited, apparently knowing that the account still had insufficient money to cover it. Why would he need a loan from Madeline Peters if the bounced check was just a problem of cash flow? And now he was saying no to a perfectly reasonable request for an assignment to repay Madeline out of Norma's insurance money. I wasn't about to tell her that, based on Lovell's word, she would have her money back in a week.

I returned to Lovell's office, where Tucker was talking to Madeline, and interrupted to inform her that I could not give her the assurance she wanted, and I advised her not to give money to anyone on Norma's behalf until she was certain of being repaid.

While Tucker completed his interviews, I spoke briefly with Norma and told her of Lovell's decision.

"We need another way of coming up with $2,500," I said. "Why don't you meet Tucker and me for lunch tomorrow. We can talk this over then."

Norma nodded. She understood that she was to come alone, without Lovell.

Tucker spent several more minutes finishing his interview with Madeline, and in the course of the hour that we had been in Lovell's office, he had also spoken with Norma's sister and Lovell. As we drove out of the parking lot, he filled me in on one item of good news for the case: Bruce had admitted to Madeline that he had made sexual advances toward Beth, but he had insisted that he had never actually had intercourse with her. It was our first outside confirmation of the incest story, perhaps the best we would get, and it was a welcome reassurance that that part of the story was true. Then Tucker went on to relate another disturbing story about Lovell.

"While you were talking to Madeline, he kind of sidled up to me, conspiratorially, and said some nice things about me to the effect that I would make a good attorney someday. I'd told him I've been going to law school. Then he said I had a knack for communicating with people, unlike some attorneys. And he said, almost in a whisper, 'I hope you'll keep an eye on Silverman and keep things under control. I hope he doesn't turn this case into a family circus. I don't think it's necessary. I imagine we'll have to make some deal with the prosecutor, and plea-bargain this case.' "

"A family circus, huh?"

"Yeah, and then he said that when Norma had been arrested that first day in San Diego and the police came to pick up Ellen to take her to the station, he couldn't go because he wasn't part of the family. He married Ellen the next day, and he said he now can help Norma manage her affairs, since he is now part of the family."

"Well, a guy who bounces trust-account checks doesn't seem to me to be so capable of managing Norma's financial affairs, I don't care whether he's family or not."

The next day I called Mr. Peterson to verify Lovell's story about the status of Norma's SBA loan.

"No, it isn't that way at all," Peterson said after I summarized Lovell's story. "The SBA was absolutely adamant that they would not loan the money to Mrs. Winters while she was awaiting trial. As you can understand, the criminal charge severely affects her credit standing. After I explained that to Lovell, I went back to the SBA and asked if they might change their position if our bank guaranteed the loan. The most they could say was that they might consider it."

"That's hardly the glowing picture Lovell painted."

"Hardly. I'd be very cautious about what he tells you," the banker said. "Do you know how Mrs. Winters's insurance money is going to be paid?"

"No. At this point I don't know."

"Well, you might check that. As you know, we do have a note due, the $15,000 loan, and we are expecting payment from the insurance money. Lovell already promised that, but—"

"I understand."

"I'd appreciate it, Mr. Silverman, if you would make sure that the insurance money is going into an account controlled by Mrs. Winters."

I decided against telling Mr. Peterson that no insurance money would be paid to Norma under any account if the police decided to charge her with murder and she was convicted. It wasn't necessary at that point to jeopardize her financial status any further. I had talked with Dr. Ulrich the night before. The results of his autopsy, although not absolutely conclusive, were consistent with suicide. I began to trust an assumption that, overwhelming odds aside, Bruce's death and the meeting with Wayne Connors were a bizarre set of circumstances that ganged up on my client. It seemed highly unlikely that she would be charged with murder. That did little to suggest a possible defense on the still serious charge of solicitation to commit murder. And I had no way of knowing how a jury might react to those circumstances if we ever got to trial. But, for the moment, I put their significance in the back of my mind. By now I was preoccupied with another problem, the puzzling character of Walt Lovell.

CHAPTER 15

Tucker and I met Norma for lunch the next day at a restaurant where the tables, booths, and counter stools were crowded with lawyers and businessmen. The clatter of dishes and the din of the chatter inside made almost any conversation a private one. We ordered sandwiches and coffee and heard one piece of good news from Norma: Madeline Peters had decided to lend her the $2,500 she needed for her bail premium.

"I told her not to give that money to you unless she were certain of getting it back. That money is for her kids' education, and with Lovell controlling your funds I'm not sure she'll get it back."

"I know, Milt, but she insisted. I'll find a way to pay her back."

"Well, that's between the two of you. But a financial consultant just doesn't bounce a check from an account he manages for his clients."

"How well do you know him?" Tucker asked. "What is your relationship with him?"

"He just got married to Ellie, and he's been going with her for over a year, and Ellie's my best friend." She paused, as if to continue, but said nothing.

"Listen, Norma," I said finally. "I don't want to keep harping on this, but—"

"I know, Milt. I'm supposed to tell you everything. But I'm basically a shy person, and it's hard for me to talk about some of these things."

"Well, we've got to know about this guy. He says he has your interests in mind, but some strange things are happening that are affecting you and this case."

She nodded.

"And I don't want to alarm you, but we have some information that Lovell was arrested for something once. Do you know what that was?"

"No, I don't, but it doesn't surprise me. I've never trusted him."

I stared at Norma. "This guy is managing your money and watching over you while you are involved in a criminal case, and you don't even trust him?"

She shrugged and looked down at the table.

"Why are you letting him do all of this if you don't trust him?"

"I don't know. I don't really like him. He's been good to Ellie. And he was helping me set up the escrow business. I just wanted to get that going, and I figured I wouldn't need him around any more once I got the business open."

"How long has he been helping you with this business?"

"Since about April, I guess."

"Why is it that you don't trust him?"

"I don't know," she said, putting her head in her hands. "It's a long story."

"Well," I replied, "we've got lots of time."

For several months beginning in late 1973, Norma had been gaining confidence in herself as an escrow officer, and she was noting with increasing curiosity and mild frustration how much money she was making for her company. If she went into business for herself, she reasoned, she would share in the profits of the business rather than just draw a salary. At the same time some of her regular real-estate customers volunteered that they would do business with her if she went out on her own.

In February, 1974, she began discussing such a move with her secretary, and by the end of March they had tentatively decided to go into business together. Norma wrote to the California Division of Corporations for information on how to set up a business, and in mid-April she retained a corporate attorney in El Centro to do the legal work. She made plans to rent and furnish an office, obtain bank financing, and apply to the federal Small Business

Administration for a loan.

It was also in April, one weekend when she was visiting Lovell and Ellie in National City, that she first mentioned her plans to them. Lovell offered to take care of the books and other financial duties, including preparation of the applications for the SBA loan and the escrow license, for nothing. After all, he told Norma, he was practically part of the family.

"No, I won't have it that way," Norma told him. "You can do the books, but only if I pay you what anyone else would charge."

An accountant in El Centro told her the services she needed would cost from $250 to $500, in addition to a retainer fee of $50 per month.

"Okay," Lovell told her. "I'll do it for $250, plus the retainer."

Over the next few months it became clear that it was more than his feeling himself part of the family that had prompted Lovell's generous offer.

During April and May, Norma continued to work at her regular job and thus had to devote weekends to the preparations for her own business. She spent most of them visiting Lovell and Ellie, partly to make her business arrangements and partly to get out of the house and away from Bruce. While she was in National City, she and Lovell developed background information for her loan and license applications and priced office equipment and furniture. When she stayed in Holtville for the weekend, she scouted for available office space.

On May 3 Norma's attorney officially reserved the name "Reliable Escrow Company, Inc." with the California secretary of state's office. It was the first formal step toward opening the business, and Norma felt a surge of excitement; this was no oddball dream—it was going to happen.

To complete her file at the secretary of state's office, Norma had to post a $10,000 cash bond as a guarantee against deposits she accepted from clients as part of her business transactions. She determined through her shopping trips that she would need about $5,000 worth of equipment, and through a variety of financial computations that Lovell had worked out with her, she decided that another $15,000 would provide enough working capital to get the business established before it started making enough money to meet the monthly bills. That meant she would need a $30,000 loan from the SBA. Lovell, however, had another idea.

"Look, this is the federal government," he told her. "And the SBA doesn't even look at loan applications for less than $20,000 or $25,000. It's not worth it to them. This $30,000 might cover your expenses, but it's nice to have adequate operating cash on hand. You ought to ask for all you can get, you know. Why don't we try for $40,000?"

Norma wasn't wild about the idea, but he was a financial consultant, and the money would give her an extra cushion. If Lovell thought she could get the money, she had no objection. On May 20 they filed the application, for $41,773. Included in the backup material was an item under "management services" for $250, the amount Norma was to pay Lovell for preparation of the application.

Meanwhile, Norma had found two potential offices in El Centro by the weekend of May 18–19, when Lovell and Ellie came to Holtville, and at Lovell's request she showed them to him. They decided on Norma's first choice, a single-story cement-block building just outside of the downtown area; it provided five rooms, including a small separate office in the front of the building, just to the right of the main entrance.

A lawyer handling the lease for the building's owner drew up an agreement a few days later, but when Norma showed it to Lovell in National City the following weekend, he balked.

"I think we need some changes in it," he suggested. "I've been thinking, with that small office in front, I could sublease it from you and open up a second office in El Centro. I could work there a couple of days a week and in National City the remaining days." He grinned. "We'd sort of be in business together."

Norma paid little attention to the suggestion. She didn't think Lovell would ever go through with such a plan. But she didn't object to it, either. "As long as the owners go along, it's okay with me," she said.

During the following week, Lovell traveled to El Centro once again to meet with Norma and the lawyer handling the lease. It was amended, giving her the option to sublet the smaller office.

On June 6 Ellie and Lovell came to Holtville for Beth's high-school graduation, and they attended to some business matters, as well. Norma had asked Ellie to serve as an officer of Reliable Escrow, and that was the day they signed the articles of incorporation. Bruce was listed as president, Ellie as vice-president, and Norma as secretary-treasurer and manager. Although she was listed third, Norma considered the presidency and vice-presidency figurehead positions. It was the secretary-treasurer who knew where the money was and how the business was running.

Later in June, Lovell mentioned to Norma offhandedly that she probably wouldn't need the entire $41,773 that she had applied for from the SBA.

"Well, I told you I thought I only needed $30,000," she reminded him.

"Well, I thought I would take the extra money and use it to set up my second office in your building. I'll pay you back in installments, as you need the money to repay the loan."

"Is that the proper thing to do?"

"Of course. What difference does it make to them? They'll get their money back."

It didn't sound just right to Norma, but she trusted Lovell's judgment. She guessed that as long as the loan was paid back properly, it wouldn't matter.

By mid-July, however, Norma's doubts were moot. The SBA denied the loan, because the amount requested was too high. A few days after the notification, she and Lovell met in San Diego with the loan officer who had ruled on the application. He suggested that a lower amount would be more appropriate and would stand a much better chance of approval. Norma decided to resubmit her application with her original request of $30,000.

As they left the SBA office, Lovell appeared agitated. "That's the same officer that turned down my application," he muttered under his breath.

"What do you mean, *your* application?" Norma asked. "Have you applied for one of these loans before?"

"Yeah, I asked for some money to buy a new computer. They turned it down because I wouldn't disclose the source of some of my financing."

He seemed almost proud of the reason, Norma thought. She

didn't press the point, but Lovell told her the extra financing was money that Ellie had received as part of a settlement in her separation from her husband. Norma was mildly surprised. It was none of her business, but that money belonged to Ellie. Lovell was not part of the family, not yet anyway, and she wondered why Ellie would turn it over to him.

By early summer Lovell's behavior seemed headed beyond what Norma considered proper in a business relationship, or even between friends. When she and Lovell were riding alone together in a car, he would hold her hand. If someone else was riding with them, he would arrange to sit next to her and move his leg against hers. It seemed harmless at first, but the advances quickly became more deliberate, and Norma felt uncomfortable. During the hours when they worked in his office, he often came over to her, rubbed her neck, and told her that he loved her. She stiffened and, for the most part, tried to ignore him, hoping he would understand that she wasn't interested and would stop. He didn't.

One day in early July, during a shopping trip in which she had purchased a safe and a copy machine, Lovell clasped Norma's hand in the car and said, "Norm, I sure hope this venture is a success. I feel in a way that we've worked together on this, and that it is something we've both given birth to. Just like it's our child."

Norma pulled her hand from his and looked at him. "Walt, don't talk like that. I don't like all that mush. It's corny."

But he persisted. He named his computer "Norm," which was what he called her when they were alone. And on several occasions, he mentioned how nice it would be when he opened his office in El Centro.

"Maybe Ellen and I will move to El Centro, and we can all live in the same house. She can do the housework and the cooking. I know you don't like to do that. And we can work together and spend time together during the days. It will be like one big happy family."

Norma didn't expect to have any time to spend with Lovell while she was working. And on those weekend days and nights when she worked in his office—often on *his* work, not hers—his innocent I-love-yous and neck rubbing turned into hard kisses on the mouth.

Norma firmly resisted those moves. She was troubled by what

Ellie might think if she learned about them. But she didn't know how to put him off without causing a scene or a family spat, and she figured it would end once her business was underway. Ellie would never move to El Centro, she thought, and she herself would be too busy to deal with Lovell. He would just slide out of the picture.

"Well, Norma," I said. "I'd say he's still in the picture, wouldn't you?"

I told Norma about my conversation with Mr. Peterson, noting that Lovell had lied to me about the SBA loan. It would be difficult to run the case, I said, with Lovell in control of her money. If I had to call in an expert, such as the doctor who flew in to do the autopsy, I'd need a check, and I could no longer count on Lovell to have that check. Norma thought for a few seconds and finally suggested we open up a new trust account, in which she would deposit the proceeds from Bruce's life-insurance policies. Both of our signatures would be required to write checks or to withdraw money from it. If that's what she wanted, I said, that would be fine with me.

"Find out the names of the insurance companies where Bruce had policies in effect and get the proper forms for the claims," I said. "My office will fill out the forms and direct that the proceeds be deposited into the trust account."

A worried look spread across Norma's face. "I don't think I can do that, Milt."

"Why not?"

"Walt already had me sign the forms. Right after Bruce's death, he went to Civil Service, Prudential, and everything. The checks are going to be mailed in care of him to deposit in his account."

CHAPTER 16

The next morning, Friday the twenty-third, I appeared in court to argue for my motion to open up the police files in Norma's case immediately, before any formal indictment was brought against her. It was an unusual request; I couldn't find any case law to support my position. But with the constantly changing and vanishing evidence I had already confronted, I considered my argument strong. The judge seemed to think so, too, as he listened to both sides of the question during the hearing, but in the end, having no similar case as a precedent, he ruled against me. I decided to appeal.

After the hearing I met again with Norma in my office, just before her scheduled afternoon visit with Dr. Charles Nyquist, a psychologist to whom I had referred her and her children after their first visit to my office. To make certain she made the appointment, I told her that sessions with him might yield information that would help the case. Although he rarely testifies in my cases, I often use Nyquist as a kind of psychological consultant, to evaluate the mental status of my client and to offer a private opinion regarding the possibility of "state of mind" defenses. But I had other reasons, as well, for wanting Norma to see him. Both she and the children were going through a difficult period, and I thought any counseling they could get from him might make it easier. I was troubled by Lovell's report of that night at the beach when she had walked into the water. I wasn't certain it had been a suicide attempt, but I knew lawyers whose clients had killed themselves in the course of a criminal case, and I wanted to be on the safe side.

While she was in my office, I made a telephone call to Wayne Connors. Norma had asked me when she might see him, and now that the investigation of Bruce's death was all but wrapped up, I could see no reason why she and Wayne could not meet. He filled me in on the details of his interview with the San Diego police; he said there wasn't the slightest indication to him that he was considered a suspect in Bruce's death or in the solicitation-for-murder charges against Norma. I handed the phone to Norma, and after they talked briefly, they made a date for lunch on September 9. Then Norma left for her appointment with Dr. Nyquist.

Late that afternoon I received a telephone call from Gene Tucker, who was in El Centro and Holtville, talking to Bruce's and Norma's friends, relatives, and co-workers. It was the trip he had intended to take the previous Saturday, but which had been abruptly canceled when we had learned that Bruce was dead. He told me he had some interesting information, so we decided to meet at my office at nine o'clock that night.

It had been a busy nine days since Norma had first walked into my office. The case had consumed virtually every waking minute. So when Tucker arrived, we relaxed in a couple of big leather chairs in the office of one of my law partners, where I poured Tucker a drink and asked him what he'd found.

He reached inside his briefcase, took out a snapshot, and handed it to me. I glanced at it and waited for an explanation. Tucker said nothing.

"What's this?" I asked finally.

"An important witness."

It was a picture of a woman who looked to be in her mid-forties. Her hair was clipped short, and she wore a simple blouse and slacks. There was nothing extraordinary about the picture, except for one detail: she was fat. Enormous, in fact. She appeared to weigh close to two hundred pounds. It was a classic "before" picture for an ad layout for a weight-losing scheme.

"Who is she?" I asked Tucker.

Tucker paused a moment for dramatic effect.

"Norma Winters."

I leaned over the picture for a closer look.

"You're kidding."

"Nope. It was taken five months ago."

"Five months ago?"

Tucker nodded. "Norma's sister gave it to me this afternoon."

"And she told you it was taken five months ago?"

"That's right."

I looked at the picture again. Norma's current weight, I guessed, was about 135 pounds. In five months she had lost at least 60 pounds.

"How did she lose all that weight?"

Tucker sifted through some papers in his file, picked one out, and read from it. "On February 28 Norma went to the offices of one Dr. Alfred Richard, who has an office in El Centro. He's a diet-pill doctor. Norma has been seeing him regularly since then."

"Has he been giving her pills?"

"I guess so."

"What kind of pills?"

"I don't know, Milt."

I wondered whether such a weight loss could have affected Norma's behavior.

Tucker shuffled some more notes around and broke the silence. "Do you want to hear some more?"

I looked up and smiled. "Sure. Go ahead."

Tucker had left for El Centro early that morning. He arrived about mid-morning and headed directly for the sheriff's office, where he had two assignments. First, Norma wanted him to get back her car which the officers involved in the investigation of the crime had impounded. Tucker was unable to obtain its release, however, because it was registered in the names of Bruce Winters and Beth Winters; it was not legally Norma's car. Beth would have to claim it, he was told.

Tucker then identified himself as a private investigator working on Norma's case and asked to speak to Sheriff Carl Hardy. After a brief wait he was ushered into the sheriff's office. Tucker went straight to the point.

"I wondered if you could fill me in on the status of the Bruce Winters investigation. Have you determined if it was a suicide?"

"As far as I know," the sheriff replied, "my officers are sure that his death was a suicide. The autopsy indicated it was a contact gunshot wound. There was a suicide note, and handwriting analysis indicated the note to be written by Mr. Winters."

"So you have ruled it is a suicide."

"I don't know that the case is closed, but we are virtually certain those were the circumstances. We've found nothing else to suggest otherwise."

At Tucker's request, Hardy had a copy of the suicide note made. Tucker put the copy in his brief case, chatted a few more minutes, thanked the sheriff, and left. The trip had already been productive, he thought. Law-enforcement officials are not always so cooperative, especially with someone who works for the defendant in a criminal case. Tucker knew. He had once been on that side himself.

Tucker's chief aim on this visit to El Centro was to gather as much information as he could about Bruce Winters. Nearly all the details uncovered thus far had come directly from Norma and Beth, and while they had offered compelling and plausible information, he wanted to confirm, develop, or impugn it through witnesses who had a little less at stake. With Bruce dead, Tucker had to rely on a collage of co-workers, family, and friends. He knew from experience that some information would be helpful to Norma's case and that some might be harmful. But his job was not to weigh the relative worth of what he came up with. The private investigator's task was to collect as much pertinent evidence as he could, Tucker felt, and to let the defense attorney evaluate it.

Tucker's next stop was Norma's house on Andrews Street, where he met Norma's mother and other members of her family. He spoke briefly with the three of them and then with Mrs. Holden alone. She told him she had read a note that Bruce had written before he had left on the morning he had killed himself.

"He read it to me," she said, "and I think it began, 'To whom it may concern: I'm sick and can't go on. My daughter is eighteen years old.'" She thought for a moment and shook her head. "It went something like that, and it said he had made advances on Beth, but never actually had intercourse. That's all I can remember."

"The note said he had made the advances?" Tucker asked.

She nodded. "He asked me to sign it, but I didn't. I mean, I knew about what he did to Beth, but I told him not to think like that, about killing himself, and that he was needed around here."

Tucker was puzzled. The note he had picked up at the sheriff's office was different.

"Is a copy of that note around here, by any chance?"

Mrs. Holden shook her head. "I don't know, I thought the police had a note. But you're welcome to look around as you please."

Tucker searched the house as thoroughly as he could over the next half hour, wandering through it and spending considerable time in the living room and in the master bedroom. He did not find another suicide note, but the search was far from fruitless.

In one of the bedrooms he found four guns between the mattress and boxspring of a bed—a 30-30 lever-action rifle, a Browning .22, a Savage combination shotgun-rifle, and a Savage twenty-gauge double-barreled shotgun.

In the back bedroom, under the bed where Bruce and Norma had slept, Tucker found a shirt box full of pornographic magazines, some in English, some in Spanish. They were not "over-the-counter" magazines like *Playboy,* but hard-core pornography, including a comic book that depicted the savage murder of a young couple who were having intercourse, as well as a publication that included a story about a father involved in an incestuous relationship with his daughter.

In the living room Tucker found a half-dozen volumes of the *World Book Encyclopedia* out on a table, each stacked upon the other, their pages opened to a subject related to criminal law. And he found a copy of the California penal code, a manual Bruce had undoubtedly used in his position as a border guard. It was open also, to the section explaining the penalties for "child molesting."

"He was reading that book there the day Norma was arrested," Mrs. Holden said.

Tucker shrugged. "Do you mind if I take some of these things back to San Diego? I think they might help Norma's case."

"Take whatever you need."

Tucker gathered the shirt box, the penal-code manual, the encyclopedia volumes, and a collection of Bruce's military papers that he had found in one of the bedrooms, told Mrs. Holden he would return later, and headed out for his next interview, with Rebecca Hoyt.

Rebecca, an attractive woman in her mid-thirties, was a real-estate broker whom both Norma and Bruce had met through social functions at Norma's place of work. The two women had become close friends during the past two years.

She told Tucker about a time about a year ago when Norma had had a black eye. At first, Norma had told her she had run into a refrigerator door, but later she had talked about a fight she and Bruce had had over a girl in a bar in San Luis.

"I guess I don't know who was jealous of whom in that one," Rebecca said. "But I think she hit him over the head with a bottle, or something, and he slugged her. Then Bruce used to get mad at me a lot, especially one time a few weeks ago after Norma and I got back from a shopping trip to San Diego."

"What was he mad at you about?"

"I don't know. The trip was a really big deal for us, because we both looked good, and I guess he suspected that something was up, that we were running around in the city or something."

"You 'looked good'?"

"Well, we had lost weight. Norma was really losing weight."

"A lot of weight? I mean, was Norma ever heavy?"

Rebecca smiled. "Was she *heavy?* She weighed about 190 pounds."

"What kind of pills was Norma taking?"

"I don't know. At least, I don't always know what they are. The bottles don't always have labels on them."

She also said Mrs. Holden had told her that Norma had begun acting differently after she had started the diet.

"Why was that?"

"I don't know that, either. She was taking a lot of Valium. But there was more than Valium involved."

"So you and Norma lost all this weight in just a few months, then," Tucker remarked.

"Yeah, and, you know, we started to look pretty good." She winked. "So, between you and me, we started, you know, going out on the town a little, out to have a couple of drinks, once in a while, and we took a trip to San Diego. And I think Bruce was jealous.

It sure made him mad."

"What, you going out?"

She nodded.

"He didn't want Norma out on the town, huh? He thought—"

"I guess he thought we were out looking for men, or something. We were just out for a good time, you know. Showing off a little. Bruce really didn't like me, I guess. But Norma told me he didn't like many of her friends."

Tucker thanked Rebecca for her time and help, and left. His next stop was the border station in Calexico, a nine-mile ride from El Centro. On the way out he smiled to himself, thinking about Rebecca and Norma, the classic fat housewives losing weight together and testing their wings at some bar.

It was just after 5 P.M. when Tucker arrived at the Immigration and Naturalization Service in Calexico. He deliberately waited until after four, since Bruce's co-workers rotated to the four-to-midnight shift that week.

Don Walton, who had shared a car pool with Bruce when they both worked at the fire station in El Centro several years before, told Tucker that Bruce had seemed very close to his son David, but that he couldn't recall his having talked much about Norma or troubles in the marriage.

"He did tell me once about an affair that Norma had or something with some guy she met in San Diego," Walton offered. "But that was a while ago. He hasn't said much since."

"Did he ever talk to you about his relationship with his family?"

"Well, he did say his in-laws didn't like him much. But he was always nice to me and my family. He was the kind of guy I liked to invite to my home."

Walton also said he knew little about any drinking Bruce might have done, and he had never known him to be rough with anyone.

Walton was friendly enough, but not much help, Tucker thought. He introduced himself to another man on the shift, Tom Rathbone.

"I'm looking for some information about Bruce Winters, and I wonder if you could help me out?" Tucker said.

Rathbone looked at him skeptically. "Are you with law enforcement?"

"No, sir. I'm a private investigator." He showed the man his ID. "I'm working for his wife's attorney."

Rathbone scowled. "Naw, I don't want to talk about it."

"Look, I won't take up much of your time. But I need a little information—"

"I don't know how you can take money for doing work like that. Working for his wife."

Tucker said nothing for a moment. He had been in similar situations, trying to get reluctant witnesses to talk. As a private investigator, he had only his personality and his finesse at hand in order to get someone to talk to him. His identification, issued by the state, gave him some legitimacy, but far less than a policeman's badge imparted. This guy was going to take some work, Tucker thought.

"Well, if you were in her position, you'd want somebody working for you, wouldn't you?"

"I don't know how you can take money for it," he said again.

"I was a policeman once," Tucker added. "And I understand how you feel. You know, you want to see bad guys in jail. So do I. But you're not talking to me, and that makes me wonder about Bruce, like maybe there's something bad about him, something you don't want me to know about."

"Bruce was a good guy," Rathbone insisted, "and he always treated me right. I don't really want to talk about it." He said nothing for a moment. Then he added, "He was tired a lot, you know. He said he would go home and his old lady was always on his ass."

"Everyone's old lady is on his ass."

"Not like this."

"What made this different?"

"I don't know." Rathbone shrugged. "Bruce didn't say."

"What did he tell you about his family?"

"Well, I never met his wife, but my wife knew her from where she worked, and said she was a smart lady."

"What about his kids?"

"He talked a lot about his boy. He really loved his boy, but he said his daughter never talked to him except when she wanted something."

"Did he ever play around any, do you know?"

Rathbone paused again, then shrugged. "Yeah, Bruce played around. I'm not going to say he didn't. But from what I hear, the family was really on him. Like I said, he loved his son, but everybody else really gave him a lot of trouble. I don't want to say any more. I've already said enough. I feel sorry for his wife, I guess, but she got herself into the position she's in. And I'll never believe he killed himself. Never."

None of Bruce's other co-workers were on duty, so Tucker went to his car, made some notes, and headed back to Holtville.

"And that's where I got that picture," Tucker said. "When I got back to Norma's house, I asked about it, and her sister got it from somewhere."

I looked at the picture and shook my head. "A hundred and ninety pounds."

"Amazing, isn't it?"

"Did you talk to that doctor?"

"I tried to reach him, but he wasn't in. He didn't have any office hours in El Centro that day. I guess he has an office in Los Angeles, too, and he flies in from LA a couple of times a week to give out his pills."

"Is Norma still seeing this guy?"

"As far as I know, she is."

"We better find out what's in those pills."

Finally, Tucker pulled the copy of the suicide note from his stack of papers and handed it to me. It was dated "16 Aug. AM."

To whom it may concern:

This is where our lives together started & a fitting place for mine to end. I am sick physically & this stuff thats happened has driven me out of my mind. I am innocent of sexually molesting my daughter & may God forgive both Beth and Norma for what they have done. I have known of both of their dislikes for me since Norma's affair with Wayne Connors which Beth knew about & kept from me.

It is my wish and desire that David Henry be allowed to live with my father. . . . I don't want him to live with my sister Ellen . . . who is living with Walter N. Lovell without benefit of wedlock.

It is also my will & desire that all my personal belongings go to my son David Henry Winters and that my estate if any be divided equally between Beth Winters and David Henry Winters both of whom I dearly love.

I am sorry to have to go this way, but I can't bear to subject my family to the pain and anguish of a trial of this nature & go through bankruptcy & all. I am too old and tired to start all over again. May God forgive me.

David, you have been my life son and I can hardly bear to leave you but its best, I think. Always be a good boy, don't harbor any hard feelings toward your mom & sister and go to school, do good and make something of yourself. I love you David.

Bruce Jackson Winters

I said nothing for a moment. "Well, Gene, that's a side of Bruce Winters we haven't seen yet."

CHAPTER 17

Bruce Winters's childhood was filled with violence and poverty. His mother died when he was five, and his father was a heavy drinker. He, his older sister, and two younger brothers, one of whom was three months old, went to live with Bruce's aunt, a school teacher who lived comfortably on a big farm. The children were happy with her, but in a few years Bruce's father married an eighteen-year-old woman and took Bruce, then eight, and his younger brother Joey back to live with him.

Bruce's father lived in a run-down farmhouse that had drafty windows and peeling paint and lacked indoor plumbing. The two boys cut wood, tended the garden, and did most of the hard work on the farm. Mr. Winters spent much of his time and what little money he had getting drunk.

Indeed, the family was so poor that Bruce went without shoes during the summers and lived through the harsh Appalachian winters with just one pair of shoes and one pair of overalls. He had so little to eat, he had told Norma, that for a while he looked like a war orphan.

When his father got drunk, he often picked up a buggy whip and ordered Bruce and Joey to fight. If they didn't beat each other up, he whipped them until they bled. Sometimes he fought them himself. Bruce often missed school for weeks at a time because of the welts and bruises he suffered from the beatings. But he did learn to use his fists. One day, when he was about twelve, his uncle visited at the house, got drunk, and started teasing Joey. Bruce became enraged, went to his brother's defense, and started fighting his uncle. When the battle was over, he had so severely damaged his uncle's left eye that it had to be removed.

As he grew older, he became part of a tough crowd, and he was constantly in trouble with the police. But at fourteen he ran away from the hunger and pain and joined the army, having no trouble convincing the recruiter that he was old enough. Eight months after signing up, however, he broke his leg during training maneuvers, and a check of medical records blew Bruce's cover. He was sent back home. Two years later, when he turned sixteen, he joined the navy.

The patterns of violence that marked his childhood followed Bruce into the service. By the time he met Norma, he had been disciplined eight times, for fighting, for drunkenness, or for being absent without leave. He was court-martialed again shortly after she met him.

By contrast, Norma's childhood was tranquil and comfortable. She was the youngest of four children, but because her brother and two sisters were so much older than she—the youngest one was thirteen when Norma was born—she was raised as an only child. Her family lived on a small farm that her mother worked while her father worked in town. She had few playmates in her preschool years, but she had her father, and that was enough. He adored her and spent hours reading fairy tales and, especially, taking her fishing in a small rowboat. Norma usually took a book along, because she didn't have the patience her father had. If he got one bite in a morning, it would keep him going another couple of hours. And he'd always tell her half seriously, half teasingly, "Now if you make any noise, the fish won't bite," or, "Those fish will know you're reading and not paying attention, so don't expect to catch one."

Mrs. Holden almost never went fishing. She did the farm chores with the steadiness and sweat of a man, Norma thought. And it was because she wanted to. Norma often heard her mother complain about being a woman. She was a domineering mother, who, it seemed to Norma, spanked her just about every day for something. Norma always ran to her father when she was punished, and he would go yell at his wife for touching his daughter. Later Norma learned that he usually winked at her mother while he was telling her off. No matter. The effect on Norma was the same. Mother was the boss who meted out punishment. Daddy was fun. And he never spanked her, not once.

Her father died suddenly of a brain tumor two months after her sixteenth birthday, and Norma's childhood was over. Three months later she met Bruce.

It was a sunny Sunday morning two days after Christmas in 1953 when Bruce came by the house with a friend of hers while they were on a weekend pass from the naval base in San Diego. She was wearing red pedal pushers and a white sweater when she answered the door. He'd always remembered the outfit and her "cute little ass." During the visit Norma's friend Peter told her that Bruce was twenty-one. Bruce admitted later that he had asked him to tell her that. Actually he was twenty-four.

Norma was attracted to him, especially by his big brown eyes. But when she told her mother she'd probably see him again, her mother said she hoped she wouldn't. She thought he had mean eyes.

In March, three months after they met, he proposed, but not exactly in storybook fashion. Two friends told them they were getting married, and Bruce didn't even congratulate them. He just said, "Norma and I are getting married, too."

He and Norma hadn't even discussed the possibility, but she did not turn him down. By May he'd bought her a diamond and their engagement was formally announced. There was just one hitch before they could marry: Bruce's divorce would not be final until mid-August. The previous summer, he told her, he'd gone out with a barmaid whom he'd married on a ten-dollar bet with a friend. Norma never questioned the story and never gave a second thought to Bruce's cavalier attitude toward marriage.

Norma had dated only two other men before she met Bruce and had hardly even kissed another boy before she accepted a ring from him. As their wedding day grew closer, Norma's mother told her that sexual intercourse was something a woman had to put up with, and that she should never deny her husband "his wants and desires."

Two weeks before their wedding, when Bruce and Norma were in the cottage they were to live in, Bruce demanded that they make love. She tried to persuade him to wait just a few more days, until their wedding night, but he persisted and finally wore her down. It was a painful, unpleasant experience for her, but not nearly so unpleasant as what followed. For the next fifteen years, anytime they had an argument, he would berate her "because you weren't a virgin when we got married."

They had a church wedding on September 4, 1954, three weeks after Norma's seventeenth birthday and a week before she started her senior year in high school.

Norma lived in Holtville during the first five years of their marriage, while Bruce was stationed aboard a ship based in San Diego and was frequently at sea. She had little trouble enduring the long separations. Beth was born in February, 1956, and Norma's mother being available as a baby-sitter, Norma got a job as a secretary. When Bruce was in port, he commuted home on weekends. Occasionally, if he could get off early, he would take a bus out in the middle of the week, spend an evening with her and the baby, and then hop on a 2 A.M. bus back to the naval base.

The weekend visits kept their relationship young and full of romance, Norma thought, and she came to think of those years as an extended honeymoon. Although they enjoyed their moments together, they learned very little about each other. When Bruce was transferred in 1959 to a navy electronics school near Memphis, Tennessee, Norma began to understand that the honeymoon was over.

It happened gradually. First Bruce began to swear in front of her, something he had never done before. Then it was his drinking with friends. He had told her when they were married that he would quit drinking and stay out of trouble.

In 1960 Bruce was transferred back to San Diego, and the decline in the marriage became much more rapid. He frequently brought home car loads of friends for unannounced drinking parties, and when he was out with the boys, he would always come home drunk. Their fights became more frequent, and they often left Norma in tears.

They might have ended their marriage then, but early in 1961 Norma learned she was pregnant again. Neither of them had wanted another child, but Bruce had been so much against it that he insisted that she try to end the pregnancy, first with some old wives' ginger-tea remedy, and then with a kind of morning-after pills that he had bought in Mexico. Neither method worked, and Bruce even talked of selling the baby. But both of them were happy when the child, David, was born. Bruce seemed particularly pleased to have a son.

David's birth did little to alleviate the strain on their marriage. In 1965, when Beth was nine and David was four, Norma and Bruce broached the subject of divorce. It was an especially difficult topic for Norma, who had strong convictions against it, but there was another reason why they couldn't agree to split up—custody of the children. They both wanted David.

The following year Bruce retired from the navy, and the whole family moved back to California. Bruce was hired as a fireman at the naval air station in El Centro, and Norma went to work for a title-insurance company, a job that introduced her to the escrow business. Their two incomes and Bruce's navy retirement pension provided them with enough money for a comfortable living. Indeed, they moved into a nice home with ample room for the two children and Norma's mother, who had lived with them since they were married. And the children themselves never lacked for anything.

But it was not a happy home; it was filled with anger, tension, and, on occasion, violence. Bruce himself seemed to change dramatically. He had retired from the navy as a chief, a rank that had given him some authority to give orders to those under him. At the fire station he was back at the bottom. Stripped of his authority at work, he assumed even more control at home. But Norma was changing, as well. Her nine-to-five job didn't coincide with Bruce's shifts at the fire station, and they were home together less frequently. She put more and more energy into her job, from which she received more and more personal satisfaction, and before long she was working extra hours, bringing work home with her, and attending lectures, meetings, and conferences that sometimes kept her away from home for days at a time. Bruce wanted her to work, for the extra income, but he resented the out-of-town trips and the longer hours. For Norma, they represented independence, from home and, even more, from Bruce. It wasn't long, however, before Norma was making more money than her husband.

For the most part, the decline of their relationship was a matter kept within the family. During the first years after Bruce's navy retirement, it didn't hinder their social life. Norma noticed, however, that Bruce seemed to be drinking more and more at parties, almost always getting very drunk and often turning mean. After one such party Norma suggested that he not drink so much.

"It's not worth drinking if you're not going to get drunk," he retorted. "If you're going to drink, get drunk. If you're going to be a son of a bitch, be a son of a bitch."

When David was seven, Bruce told him about the tea and the pills and the plans to sell him after he was born. "Your mother didn't want you," he told him. "She wanted to get rid of you."

The accusation left Norma helpless. Bruce hadn't wanted him, either. He had bought the pills. He had suggested selling him. But she could never explain that to David, not without causing Bruce to taunt and ridicule her and without increasing the damage to David. The more she tried to explain it, the guiltier she felt and the worse she looked. Bruce always did that to her. He twisted everything around on her and made all the troubles in their marriage seem like her fault. When their sex life deteriorated, he blamed her. But David slept between them almost every night, at Bruce's insistence. He told Norma that he had always been cold and lonely as a kid and that he didn't want David to feel that way.

He also beat the children, sometimes so hard they were forced to stay home from school in order to recover. One day, after a neighbor complained that David had thrown rocks at some ducks, Bruce whipped him with a fishing pole until the back of his legs were a bloody mess. On another occasion he beat Norma's poodle so badly that it had to be put away.

After hitting the children, Bruce would become remorseful; the next day he would apologize to them and bring them a special present. He bought pretty clothes for Beth and eventually a motorbike for David. He told Norma he worked at *not* getting mad at the children because he knew that once he started hitting them, he couldn't stop. He rarely apologized to Norma, however, and he never bought her anything.

In 1970 Norma and Bruce finally agreed to divorce, and they separated, with Bruce and David moving to San Luis, Arizona. It was then that Norma enjoyed her tender, but brief, affair with Wayne Connors. When Bruce's forcing her to confess to it ended her hopes of divorce, she started putting on weight. It was partly a measure of her lack of self-respect, partly a calculated show of contempt for her husband. Within a year her weight jumped from 135 pounds to over 160, and by 1973 it exceeded 180.

She continued to plead with Bruce for a divorce, and each time he told her the door was open. But he said he would use the affair to prove in court that she was an unfit mother. "I'll get custody of the children," he said. She believed him. He had always managed to lay the blame on her somehow. Finally, she decided she would hold out until their twenty-fifth wedding anniversary. David would be eighteen by then and on his own. Custody would not be an issue. On that day, September 4, 1979, she would have him served with divorce papers at work and leave town before he could get home.

Early in 1974 Norma started thinking about opening her own business; it was the first step toward ending the marriage, she thought, for it would provide her with the financial independence she needed to live without her husband. One prerequisite to success in the business venture, Norma decided, was a substantial loss of weight. She wanted to lose at least fifty pounds. She made her first visit to a weight-loss clinic in El Centro on February 28, and the next week she picked up her first packages of pills. She began losing weight immediately.

Starting in April she made frequent trips to San Diego and National City to work on her applications with Walt and Ellie. And in mid-May, at her regular job, she closed an escrow for a man named Anthony Pappas. In return for her work on that job, Pappas sent her flowers and the following note on his letterhead:

Dear Norma:
   I just want to thank you for all you did last Thursday. I appreciate how trying it must have been for you, and you are to be complimented on the tremendous way you handled everything.

Please be my guest with another couple for cocktails and dinner.
Just call Ed Cronin and let him know when you can come. Again,
thanks for a great job.

Sincerely,
s/Tony

Norma thought little about the gesture. She had no intention of
taking Pappas up on the invitation. She had just done her job. But
when she brought the flowers and the letter home, Bruce went into
a rage.

"This is more than just a business relationship, isn't it?" he
shouted. Pappas was inviting *her* to dinner, Bruce insisted.

"Don't be silly. He's inviting both of us and another couple,"
Norma said.

"Bullshit. He wants to see you. What, have you been to bed with
him, or something?"

"No, I haven't been to bed with him."

"Then why'd he send you flowers?"

The argument was heated and quickly reached an impasse.
Norma suggested she could take the letter to Ellie and Walt's the
next evening and let them arbitrate.

Ellie read the note and agreed with Norma. She called her
brother and tried to talk to him about it. Lovell wasn't so sure
about the letter's intent. But he didn't care. He just thought it was
"really neat" that Norma had received flowers and a personal letter
from a man of Pappas's stature.

By the time Bruce had gotten over the implication of the letter,
he was accusing Norma of sleeping with Lovell himself. She went
to see him and Ellie nearly every weekend, and when she returned
to El Centro, Bruce always had a snide remark for her.

Meanwhile, Beth was leaving for Europe during the last week in
June, and the whole family gathered at the airport in San Diego
to see her off. Bruce promised to write to her while she was gone.
Two and a half weeks later, the family had received just one post
card from her, and Bruce was hurt. On July 13 he wrote to her,

Dearest Beth,
Sorry I didn't have a letter for you in Belgium, Germany and
Switzerland, but I was kinda upset w/you for not letting us hear

from you. We finally got a card from you mailed in London. Everyone around had heard from you long before we did and it was hard to realize that you would put friends ahead of family, but guess that's the way things are, huh? I imagine you'd have written if your Mom had been doing the corresponding w/you so maybe that makes it easier to understand knowing how you dislike me, huh? I love you regardless & miss you very much & you know everyone else does too, huh?

He told Beth about a fishing trip he had taken with David and then he concluded,

Well, I guess I'd better shower and go to bed. I've been working in the yard, planting more grass, fertilizing watering, etc. Looks pretty good. Got it edged and everything. David is still up as usual watching T.V. Granny is up also, worrying about Norma. You be sweet & let us hear more from you if possible. I meet the mail man every day & am disappointed about everyday. Was in S.D. when he brought the card. Love you anyway & will sure be glad when 1 Aug arrives.

All our love,
Bruce, Norma, David, Granny

When August 1 did arrive, the whole family welcomed Beth home at the airport. David brought his sister some flowers, and for a while, at least, the tension that seemed to be part of the family eased. It was a happy reunion. It was also the last happy time they were to enjoy as a family. Six days later Beth revealed to her mother the secret of her father's incest. One week after that, Norma was in jail, under arrest for hiring a man to kill her husband.

The night of Norma's arrest, after the policemen had left the house, Bruce hurried almost aimlessly around the house for a while, not sure what to do. Finally, he gathered a change of clothes, some cosmetics, and other personal items for Norma and headed to the Imperial County Sheriff's Office. He wanted to see his wife, he said. He wanted to help her.

But the police would not permit Bruce to see her. They promised to give her the items he had brought with him and sent him away.

Bruce was distraught. He wanted to arrange bail. He wanted his wife out of jail. He wanted to see her. But he was powerless to do anything.

The next morning he wrote a note, a confession of sorts, which he read to Norma's mother. In it he confessed his sexual relationship with Beth, but denied ever having intercourse with her. He asked Mrs. Holden to sign it. She refused, but she sensed that Bruce was having thoughts of taking his own life. He had also learned that morning that Lovell was arranging for Norma's bail. Lovell surely knew about him and Beth, he figured, and he told Mrs. Holden that Lovell would have him arrested for playing with Beth.

Later that evening Madeline Peters, the chiropractor, called Bruce to inquire whether she could help.

"I don't know what to do," he said. "I don't understand. I don't want her to suffer. I don't want her to go to jail." He paused a moment and cleared his throat. "I didn't know Norma hated me so much."

Two days later, on August 16, Bruce Winters went out to the abandoned shack where he and Norma had first lived, "where our lives together started," as his note said. According to the autopsy report of August 26, and the investigation of the Imperial County sheriff, he then put a .38-caliber revolver against his chest and shot himself through the heart.

CHAPTER 18

The issue of Bruce's death was now behind me, but I had new information to consider. Norma's loss of more than sixty pounds in five months seemed like critical information, although I had no clear idea of what it meant. All I did know was that Norma was almost unrecognizable in a photograph taken just a short time ago. All that weight loss had to have some side effects, I figured. I called Norma early the following week and asked her about the pills.

"I see this doctor once a month, and he gives them to me," she said. "I don't know what they all are, but, you know, I've lost a lot of weight."

"How do you feel after losing all this weight so rapidly?"

"Well, I feel really good about it, Milt." She laughed. "I was terribly fat."

That was an understatement. "Yeah, Norma. I mean besides that. How do you feel emotionally and physically?"

"I don't know. I feel all right, I guess. Beth says I seem kind of goofy sometimes. Some mornings I wake up dizzy, and they said I've walked into the walls a few times. I've been really tired some days. And, you know, sometimes I feel a little high. I feel fine right now."

"Do you get these pills at a pharmacy with a prescription, or what?"

"No. The nurse gives them to me when I go for my appointment."

"What about the doctor?"

"Well, he's only there about half the time. And when he is, he just asks you how you feel, and that's about it."

"And then you pick up these pills?"

"Right."

"And you say you don't know what they are?"

"Not exactly. They're just diet pills. They come in these packages, you know. They don't have any labels on them, at least most of them don't. Just a few numbers."

She seemed to just shrug these details off.

"When's your next appointment?"

"Sometime this week. Wednesday, I think."

I thought for a moment and then asked Norma to talk to Dr. Nyquist about the pills on her next visit with him. He was doing a battery of psychological tests on her, and that sounded to me like something he should know. She agreed. Just to be sure, I called Nyquist myself.

"That's very interesting," he said. "I'll check that aspect carefully."

Within a week he had referred Norma to a physician, and both of them told her to stop taking the medication. She was already down to 125 pounds. But I suggested that she keep going to the doctor, get the pills, and save them. We might need them for evidence.

Exactly what the pills meant was one of dozens of questions that two weeks of investigating the case had raised, and it was one of the few that suggested the possibility of a defense. The presence of drugs can change the whole complexion of a case, depending on the dosage and on the length of time a defendant has taken them. It suggested several potential defenses, including diminished capacity, unconsciousness, and even insanity. Whether the pills had significantly affected Norma was a complicated question. I hoped we could find an answer. But it could take weeks of investigation and analysis. While I awaited more information from Dr. Nyquist and from Tucker, I turned my attention back to some of the legal details, particularly the question of discovery.

I prepared a seventeen-page writ to the Court of Appeal, seeking access to the evidence against my client before the indictment. On August 30, however, after having considered my appeal, the court turned it down. I drafted another writ, this time to the California Supreme Court. My secretary was typing it up on September 11, the day the San Diego County grand jury indicted Norma on two counts of solicitation to commit murder.

The indictment made my writ moot, since the prosecution no longer had a rationale for denying me access to the police file, or so I thought. It also confirmed that charges against Manny Lopez, the man who had cashed Norma's $100 check the day she had met Hanscom, had been dropped. Otherwise, Norma would most likely have faced a third count, and perhaps another charge—conspiracy to commit murder.

Norma was arraigned on September 13, but partly because of the disagreement over the discovery issue, I had Norma waive her plea on the indictment for ten days. When we returned to court on September 23, the discovery matter was still not settled. But rather than delay the process further, we reserved the right to challenge the court's jurisdiction on the second count, and Norma pleaded "not guilty." Trial was set for November 5.

California law guarantees a speedy trial to any person charged with committing a crime, but despite the good intentions of that law to insure that justice is meted out quickly, delays are often inevitable. Norma's immediate future was uncertain. While she knew she ultimately could end up in jail, she couldn't afford to hibernate until the judicial process had run its long and tedious course. She had a business to manage and a family to support. Gradually, she began to lead a new life, one apart from my law office, the courthouse, and the constant preoccupation with the charges pending against her.

Norma's license to operate an escrow business became effective on August 22, and she opened for business almost immediately. She had been in her office since the first of August, making the renovations necessary for the opening, and although the SBA had withdrawn its approval for a loan on the day she had been arrested, interim bank financing in anticipation of that loan was providing enough operating cash to keep her going. She expected to pay off the loan with proceeds from Bruce's insurance policies.

The local newspaper and radio stations had covered the details of her case quite prominently, but, judging by the first weeks after her opening, the publicity did little to hurt her business. In fact, friends stopped by to offer encouragement and support. She made no plans for the possibility that she would be in jail before the end of the year. While she was in her office, she was delightfully consumed by her new business, seemingly untroubled by the criminal charges she faced.

She did think about Wayne Connors. She looked forward to seeing him again and hoped to renew their romance. There would be little grieving over her husband's death. That relationship had been over years before. She wanted to get on with a new life.

But she was interrupted at least once a week, and usually more often, by developments surrounding her court case, by appointments with Dr. Nyquist, and by dealings with Ellie and Walt Lovell, all of which required trips to San Diego. Those visits were part of Norma's second life, which was constantly enveloped in emotional turmoil, particularly as it involved Lovell.

On September 9 Norma came alone to the city to meet Connors for lunch. She had planned to visit Lovell briefly at his office on the way, but when she arrived in San Diego shortly before noon, she decided she didn't want to see him at all. She stopped to call him.

"I just want to be by myself today," she told him.

"You have to come over to the apartment," he said. "We have a lot of bills on your account that must be paid."

"Go ahead and pay them. I'm not coming over. I want to be by myself, and I'm going to the park." Her voice was sharp and direct. Lovell said nothing. Norma hung up and went to meet Connors.

It was their first meeting since late in 1970 and the first time Norma had seen him since Bruce had nearly killed him that night in Palm Springs. But almost immediately it seemed as if they had seen each other only the week before. They had a pleasant lunch, took a walk in Balboa Park in the city, and agreed to meet again, for dinner on Saturday night, the fourteenth.

On the thirteenth, after her court appearance, Norma went

shopping with Beth, David, and Ellie at the Navy Exchange on the amphibious base at Coronado, about twenty minutes from Lovell's home in National City. As a military dependent, Norma still enjoyed shopping privileges at the exchange, and she was looking for clothes and other items for David, who was entering the San Diego Military Academy. But she had left her military ID card at Lovell's house. She asked Beth and Ellie to get it for her while she finished shopping with David. When the women returned, they had a message for Norma: Walt wanted her to call.

They went through the cashier, and Ellie accompanied Norma to a telephone booth, dialed the number, and handed the phone to her.

"Hello, Walt," she said when he answered.

There was a short pause.

"I have 25,000 one-dollar bills on my desk in front of me. Why don't you come over and pick them up?" His voice had a condescending tone to it.

Norma could say nothing. She handed the telephone back to Ellie and began to cry.

When Norma regained her composure, she called to tell me about Lovell's remark. The money, she knew, was from Bruce's insurance policies, and she had yet to inform Lovell that she was retaining and accounting firm to handle her money.

"If you don't want him managing your finances, Norma," I said, "he's got to be told. If you do want—"

"No. I absolutely don't. I don't trust him."

"Do you want me to tell him, then?"

"No. No. I want to tell him myself."

Later that day Norma, Ellie, and Beth went to Lovell's office. When they arrived, Lovell was sitting at his desk. There were no stacks of dollar bills in front of him. He held a check for $25,000 in his hand.

"Here, Norma. Sign this," he said. He put the check face down on the edge of his desk in front of her.

"I can't, Walt. I'm sorry."

Lovell seemed stunned. "What do you mean, you can't sign it? Of course you can sign it. You have to sign it."

She could no longer avoid the confrontation.

"I've set up a separate trust account with Milt Silverman. I'm sorry."

Lovell stood up abruptly and glowered at Norma. "I'm telling you to sign that check," he said, almost shouting. "You've told me to pay your bills. You've authorized these checks to be mailed to me. I'm overdrawn on your account."

"I'm sorry."

"I see. You're letting your young attorney take control of your money. And you're putting me on the spot. I've already written checks on your behalf. You're going to leave me high and dry. You must sign this check."

Norma just stood at his desk and said nothing.

"The hell with it!" He threw the check at her. It fluttered to the floor.

She maintained her composure, stooped to pick up the check, and put it in her pocketbook.

"How much do I owe you for those bills?" she asked.

"Three thousand dollars. I need it by Monday morning at the latest."

"I don't have my checkbook with me, but I'll go back to El Centro over the weekend. You'll have the money by Monday morning."

Lovell narrowed his eyes. "And that's not all. You owe me more money as well."

"For what?"

"Services rendered."

Norma stared at him, partly in anger, partly in bewilderment. "Well then, send me a bill."

She turned, nodded to Ellie and Beth, and walked out.

Two days later, having had dinner together the night before, Norma and Wayne drove to El Centro to pick up her checkbook, then made the two-hour trip right back to National City so that Norma could pay Lovell the $3,000. When she handed the check to Lovell, she announced deliberately that she was spending the night with Wayne. Lovell stared at her for a second, then turned his back, blew his nose loudly, and feigned a fit of clearing his throat and coughing. Norma and Wayne smiled at each other and walked out.

The next day, Monday the sixteenth, Wayne headed back to Los Angeles to work, and Norma met Ellie for lunch.

"What did Walt say when Wayne and I left?" Norma asked.

"What the hell could he say?" Ellie replied. "We lived together almost two years and weren't married."

"Well, I was just curious." A wry smile spread across her face. "When Walt and I were alone in August, after Bruce died, he said he was concerned about men taking advantage of me."

Before their lunch ended, Ellie handed Norma a white sealed envelope with Lovell's letterhead on it.

"Walt said that's the bill you asked for," she said.

Norma opened the envelope, unfolded two pages and looked at the bottom line. She gasped. "Net now due and payable to this office," it read, "$9,034.81."

Norma scanned the front page of the bill, anger building in her chest. It was an itemized list of checks and deposits, listed by date, check number, and payee. It seemed reasonable. Then, on the second page, the next to the last item told the story: "Professional services 225 hours @ $30 per hour. $6,750."

Lovell had never mentioned anything about thirty dollars an hour. And she knew it was not possible that he had spent that much time on her books. There weren't even any books to keep yet.

"That bastard," she said aloud, to no one in particular. She looked at Ellie. "That's impossible. You tell him I want an itemized list of those hours."

Lovell finally provided that on September 30. It included sixty-six hours for the preparation of the SBA loan applications and the selection of furniture, equipment, and other items and thirteen hours for preparing an audit of Norma's finances in June and July for her escrow-license application. Those were the services Norma had understood Lovell to have originally offered to provide free of charge until they had agreed, at her insistence, on a fee of $250. Lovell's view of the price: $2,370, nearly ten times as much. Then he listed seventy-seven hours for setting up insurance claims, filing for federal benefits, obtaining copies of vital records, and performing other similar services after Bruce's death—$2,310. And he charged her for sixty-nine hours for making the arrangements for Bruce's funeral—$2,070.

Norma seethed as she read the bill. Is it usual, she wondered, to bill your sister-in-law for making the arrangements for a family funeral? Then she looked carefully at the final two items. Lovell had done almost all the work on the insurance claims and other benefits, as well as on the funeral arrangements, between August 17 and the day Bruce's body was flown to Tennessee, August 21, less than five full days. She did the figures. If he had worked twenty-four hours a day, he could have put in only 120 hours on those items. He was charging her for 146.

When Lovell called her a week later, on October 8, to inquire about payment, she scoffed at him.

"The bill is bullshit, Walt. I'm not paying another cent."

That conversation sent Lovell back to the typewriter.

> Dear Norma:
>
> This office extended considerable time and effort on your behalf, over a long period of time. Most recently this office experienced considerable cost as well. If you will review our September 14th billing you will find that funds have been ADVANCED for you personally. We have been very patient in the matter of no money. . . . I feel that I have been taken advantage of. . . .
>
> You were discharged as a client of this office as of September 14th last and your records were picked up by you and others on your behalf. None of your records are in this office, having been removed as indicated.
>
> The records of this office indicate an unpaid balance of $6,034.81 still remaining. This office can ill afford carrying a client with such a large balance, much less one that has been discharged by this office. My conclusion based upon our telecon of this date is that I must now seek other remedies for collection. I am sorry that this is now necessary, but it appears that I have no choice.
>
> > With respect,
> > s/W. N. Lovell

If Lovell wanted to sue her, Norma thought, let him try it.

On October 11 she made plans to meet Ellie at a Sambo's restaurant in San Diego at 11 A.M. for a board meeting of Reliable Escrow. The main item of business was the appointment of a president to fill the vacancy left by Bruce's death. When Ellie didn't show up by 11:30, Norma became concerned and went to the telephone booth to call her. Just as she heard the ringing in the receiver, she spotted Lovell coming through the door.

"That son of a bitch," she said aloud. She hung up, walked back to her table, picked up her records, and walked over to Lovell.

"My meeting is with Ellie, not you," she said through her teeth. "I have nothing to say to you."

She left.

Later in the day, when Lovell was apparently in his office, Norma met Ellie at their home, and they appointed Beth president of Reliable Escrow.

Although they were close friends, Norma and Ellie rarely discussed Norma's problems with Lovell. Ellie was not in the best of health, and Norma thought that Lovell was at least providing for her. If Ellie became involved in their dispute, Norma feared, it could put a strain on her marriage. Norma didn't want to do anything to hurt her. And she was convinced that despite her silence on the issue, Ellie supported her.

On October 14 Norma received yet another letter from Lovell. This one was not on letterhead, and it did not bear the signature "W. N. Lovell." Signed simply "Walt," it was a rambling effort that sought a reconciliation. He said he had come to the Sambo's instead of Ellie because she hadn't wanted to get involved in their spat. He continued,

> For whatever reason you made the 180° turn away from me and the work I was performing for you, I don't know. What I do know is that this foolish in-family quarrel is beginning to tear the family apart. . . . In our new home, Ellie and I work and plan so very many things, but never is there a word about Norma and the kids visiting. It hurts me to think that I have come between two people's twenty year closeness. It hurts to think that something in our business relations has now caused a breakdown in the personal family relations.
>
> All that I am asking, I guess, is, whatever the reason or reasons, can't we stop feuding and be family? I hope that isn't too much to ask. I may not always be right in the things I say and do, or the way I say and do things, but when I have errored, I do try to apologize and make amends. For whatever I did to cause this split, I AM

SORRY. I guess it's up to you and me to solve the problem and keep the family together.

Won't you give it some thought?

Norma had already given it plenty of thought. She loved Ellie, and she dearly wished they could maintain their friendship. But Lovell had gone too far: the outrageous bill, which included his services for the funeral arrangements, his apparent insistence on controlling her money, and now the threat of legal action. Yes, she thought, it was too much to ask.

Two weeks later the rift escalated when Lovell called Norma late in the afternoon of October 29.

"I have three more checks from Prudential, representing additional proceeds from Bruce's life insurance," he announced loftily.

"Yes."

"Two are for $5,210.32, and the third is for $21,926.51. What is your pleasure?"

Norma thought for a moment. "Why don't you leave them at home with Ellie. I'll come by to pick them up Friday when I'm in San Diego." She said she'd be by late in the morning and confirmed the time with Ellie herself.

But when Norma arrived at their home three days later, Ellie wasn't home. Thinking that her sister-in-law might have been avoiding her and just didn't want to come to the door, she went to a pay phone and called her. There was no answer. She called Lovell at his office. He was at lunch with a client, she was told. Norma was perturbed by the misconnection. She thought she and Ellie had been very explicit about the time. But she could do nothing about it now. She headed for her 2 P.M. to 5 P.M. appointment with Dr. Nyquist. After leaving his office, she reached Lovell at his office.

"Do you have the checks with you?" she asked.

"Yes. I have them here."

"Can I meet you at your house and pick them up? I'd like to get to the bank to deposit them before it closes at six."

"Fine. I'll see you at home, then."

Norma didn't like the tone of his voice; he seemed cool, yet almost mischievous. About thirty minutes later she met him at the house, and he invited her in.

"I just want the checks, Walt, and I need them now. The bank closes in a half hour."

"Please come in first."

"No. I'm in a hurry."

"Well, if you want the checks, I insist that you come in."

Norma sighed and stepped into the house. She followed Lovell into the kitchen, a spacious L-shaped room connected to the dining room. Large cabinets contrasted with the off-white walls and appliances. It was a nice new house, Norma thought. Walt was indeed providing for Ellie.

Lovell sat down at the dining room table and motioned for Norma to take a seat, as well. He pulled three checks from his pocket and laid them out on the table.

"Norma, you still owe me a lot of money. More than $6,000."

Norma bristled. "I don't owe you a cent."

He ignored the statement. "I want to make a deal with you. I will give you these two checks, one for $21,000 and one for $5,200. You endorse this check for $5,200 over to me. And we will call it even."

Norma stood up immediately, barely able to control her anger. She looked him straight in the eye.

"I won't endorse anything over to you."

She turned and walked out. The checks remained on the table.

The next day Norma met Wayne again in San Diego and asked him to take her back to see Lovell, so that she could try one more time to get the checks. They found him working in his office on that Saturday afternoon. Lovell stiffened as she entered.

"Walt, I want those checks. They are mine, payable to me, and I don't think you can hold onto them."

"Fine. All you have to do is endorse one of them to me."

"You have no right to ask me to do that. They are my checks."

"Then I will not release them to you."

"You're a no-good son of a bitch."

Later that day she met Tucker and me in my office to see what she could do about getting the money. On the following Monday I called the two insurance companies that were involved and asked them to stop payment on the checks. By the end of the day, Lovell had relented. He left a message with Norma's secretary that he had turned the checks over to his lawyer to be returned to the companies' home offices in Florida. On November 12 Norma received them herself and put them in the trust account.

But she had not heard the last from Lovell. On November 27, the day before Thanksgiving, he sued her.

CHAPTER 19

It was the Saturday after Thanksgiving when Norma met me at my office to tell me about the lawsuit. She seemed not the least concerned about the consequences of the suit itself. Lovell couldn't possibly win it, she figured. She was just angry. She was already in enough trouble, and yet here came Walt Lovell, her friend, her best friend's husband, and her brother-in-law, and he sued her.

It was disturbing, but not necessarily surprising, news. Tucker had done some checking on him after the bail check bounced and after Ryan had mentioned that the police had his mug shot. Although Lovell had led us to believe he was an officer in the air force Tucker learned that he was actually a commander in the Sea Scouts. A lawsuit had been filed against him, which caused me to question his practices. His involvement with the law had been over his failure to pay child support to his former wife.

But whether or not the suit was justified, it could not be ignored. Under state law Norma had thirty days to file a response to it, or she'd be considered in default and automatically lose the case. She needed a lawyer.

My hands were already full with the criminal case. Indeed, I had spent much of the past two months battling the district attorney's office over the discovery issue. At the end of September I had received most of the police reports, witness interviews, and transcripts of Norma's conversations with Hanscom and confessions to

Ryan, but I had not obtained everything. The transcripts suggested that some of what Norma had said to the policemen had not been picked up by the tape recorder. I wanted to hear the tapes myself. I also wondered whether the DA's office or the police had a copy of what I thought might be a second suicide note, the one Bruce had shown to Norma's mother, and I assumed they had photographs taken outside Denny's restaurant on the day of the arrest and a report of an interview the police had had with Wayne Connors. None of those items were among the documents I had received. On October 1, I wrote a letter to the DA requesting the missing items, and for the next three weeks I followed the letter with telephone calls, which went unreturned. By October 23, the day of the "readiness conference," in which lawyers from both sides in a case meet with the judge to make sure everyone is prepared for trial, we still lacked essential evidence. The judge, at my request, continued the trial to January 20. The district attorney assigned to handle the Winters case, Edward Morrison, said he would review my letter of October 1 and get back to me. But by November 13 I had received neither the items I had requested nor a satisfactory explanation for the DA's failure or refusal to produce them.

On that day I filed a motion in court, seeking a judicial order compelling the district attorney to provide full discovery. The motion was heard on November 27, the day Lovell's suit was filed, and after more than an hour of argument the judge ruled in my favor. He issued a sweeping order, granting me access to virtually every piece of evidence the DA had acquired in the case. I needed time to look it over.

I told Norma she should have another attorney handle the matter with Lovell and suggested one of the last men I'd want to have against me in the courtroom—Don Rushmore.

I called his office, and although it was a Saturday, he was in. Rushmore seemed interested, but he was tied up in other litigation. However, he offered to set Norma up with another lawyer in his firm and to follow the case as it evolved. If the case went to trial, he said he'd handle it personally. I said Norma would call to make an appointment the first of the week.

But it was more than the legal maneuvers in Norma's criminal case that were occupying my time. Our investigation was picking up again, as well. In early November Dr. Nyquist sent me a note summarizing his observations of Norma during ten weeks of therapy and examination. In it he stated, "(1) Ever since I have known her she has been consistently depressed, (2) she has shown indications of irritability, i.e., she tends to flare up rather easily with the slightest provocation, (3) she appears to have a mild to moderate degree of mental confusion as well as an inability to make decisions, (4) she also appears to be quite anxious, a kind of anxiety I would characterize as free-floating, and (5) she appears to have some memory deficits in that at times she has a difficult time recalling specific events. Overall, I have a hunch that some of these behaviors could be a by-product of her drug use."

I was particularly struck by two statements in the letter—the possible relationship between her psychological profile and her diet-pill regimen and the finding that Norma suffered "memory deficits." I was well aware of those myself, and I had constantly been frustrated by them. Norma came to my office almost every time she came to San Diego, and either Tucker or I would always talk with her about some aspect of the case. Each time she would have difficulty recalling some specific and seemingly important events. Under persistent questioning she still didn't remember the night she'd walked into the water at the beach when Lovell had had to rescue her; she didn't remember exactly where she'd called Pappas from or how she'd gotten his phone number; and she still insisted that she didn't know why she'd thought of Pappas, that his name had just "popped" into her head. The police reports I had obtained through discovery indicated that Norma had made two phone calls to Pappas before meeting him; she remembered only one.

Three months of investigation had also turned up puzzling questions about Norma's conduct with Hanscom. On the day of their meeting, she had told him she didn't have $500 to pay him and had finally bargained with him to pay $100 that day and $400 two days later. Tucker checked her bank records, however, and found that she had had over $1,400 in her checking account. Why had she lied to Hanscom? She insisted that she didn't know. It was possible she figured $500 was enough to implicate her and that she'd get caught.

But she still would have had to cover up $400 two days later. If she hadn't wanted to arouse suspicion, she could easily have hidden the payment in remodeling costs for her office by asking Manny to cash a bigger check or several smaller ones.

In addition, she had pushed Hanscom to kill Bruce on Sunday night. Tucker checked work records, however, and discovered that Bruce hadn't been working that Sunday night. Without telling Norma what we knew, we asked her about it. To our surprise, she knew it. She and Bruce had discussed his taking that Friday and Saturday off and changing his schedule to days beginning that Sunday.

"Then you knew when you talked to Hanscom that Bruce would not be working Sunday night?" I'd asked her.

"Uh-huh."

"Why did you want it done that night, then?"

"I don't know," she'd answered. "Maybe because of Wayne."

"Yeah, but that doesn't have anything to do with the fact that Bruce wasn't working the night he was supposed to be killed going to work, does it?"

Norma had shrugged. "I just never connected the two, I suppose."

Beth later told Tucker that her father had never driven to work along the route that her mother had traced for Hanscom. When we confronted Norma with that, she shrugged again. "I never knew him to take that route, either," she said.

Tucker also learned that the unregistered car she'd told Hanscom Bruce might be driving wasn't even running. And the small photograph bore little resemblance to her husband; she'd had several better pictures that she could have given him.

As Tucker and I developed this information, we questioned and requestioned Norma about it. She had no explanation for her actions. She insisted that she had not connected in her mind the possibility of getting caught with her providing the map, money, descriptions, and the date to the man she'd considered a killer for hire. She simply didn't know why she'd acted the way she had.

Norma had no reason to deceive us. In fact, she had insisted from the beginning that she was guilty and had indicated that she expected and deserved to go to jail. Yet, she seemed to be holding something back. How was it that she could describe in minute detail her meeting with Pappas and not remember how she had gotten there? How was it that she could remember gathering all the items she was to have given Hanscom and not recall her rationale for giving him so much misleading information? Occasional lapses in memory are not unusual, especially in people who have endured severe emotional trauma, but the inconsistencies in Norma's memory seemed to go beyond that. They had baffled me. Now Dr. Nyquist's evaluation suggested that the drugs she'd taken might offer some explanation.

His observations made me decide that Norma should see a psychiatrist—one who would evaluate her with the expectation that he might testify in court about his findings and defend them under cross-examination.

I called Dr. Stanley Ellison a highly respected psychiatrist in San Diego with a special expertise in forensic psychiatry. He frequently appeared in the courtroom to testify in criminal cases, but was regarded in the legal community as a "prosecution doctor" because he usually testified on behalf of the district attorney. That hardly meant, however, that he couldn't render an objective judgment in his examination of a client for the defense. And by including him on that side of the case, I was taking one of the prosecution's best potential weapons against me and turning it back on them. If Dr. Ellison examined Norma and found helpful evidence, the prosecution would have a difficult time discrediting a doctor who had consistently been one of their own best witnesses on the stand.

Ellison listened to the details of Norma's case when I called, and he agreed to see her. An appointment was set for December 10.

At Dr. Nyquist's suggestion Norma had undergone a physical examination in mid-November and had admitted to the doctor that she was continuing to take her diet medication. The doctor determined that the pills were causing hypermetabolism—an excessive functioning of the body's chemical processes—which was indicated in her agitated state of mind, dry and warm skin, and high pulse rate of ninety-nine beats per minute. The doctor ordered her to stop taking the pills.

Meanwhile, I wanted to find out just what was in the pills. I called Dr. Richard to obtain the records of Norma's visits to his office. Despite my having Norma's authorization for their release and despite my informing Dr. Richard that the records could figure in the defense of a woman charged with a serious crime, he refused to send them to me. I assumed that he preferred to release such records only to other doctors, and I therefore asked Dr. Ellison to get them.

On December 3 the judge officially signed the order granting me access to the tapes and other documents I'd been seeking for four months, and a few days later Morrison permitted me to make copies of the tapes of Hanscom's phone call to Norma, the meetings in the restaurant and hotel room, and Norma's two conversations with Ryan.

When I listened to them back at the office, it was apparent to me that there were problems with them. Although the telephone call was clear, the tapes of the two confessions were difficult to understand without straining the ear, because of the low, plaintive tone in which Norma spoke. They were clear enough to be admissible evidence, however, and the prosecution could prepare a transcript to aid the jury in following what was said. But the other tapes were almost unintelligible. Much of the conversation in Denny's was lost in a clatter of dishes, and the meeting in the hotel room was obscured by the whine of air conditioners. Neither tape could be played for a jury. But that was more of a hindrance than a help to the case. Enough of the conversation had been retrieved, according to transcripts I'd already gotten, so that the officers could use the transcripts to refresh their recollections and recount the conversations for a jury almost verbatim. The "almost" troubled me. If Norma had said anything to help her case, something buried in the background noise, I couldn't hear it. I contacted an acoustical expert and sent the tapes to an electronics firm in San Diego that had equipment designed to "clean up" distorted or garbled tapes. Then I hired a transcriber to go over and over the tapes, listening to them with a special headset, and to transcribe every possible word. I wanted to know at least as much about what was on those tapes as the DA did.

Norma's first appointment with Dr. Ellison was on December 10, when she underwent a battery of psychological tests administered by him and by a psychologist who worked with him. A few days later the associate called to tell me they were having trouble getting Norma's diet records. Dr. Richard had sent them a letter saying that Norma had been a patient at his clinic several years ago and that her records were in storage. Norma had been to his office within the past two weeks. It was clear now that Richard's brush-off of me was more than a matter of professional formalities.

For the first time since Tucker had dropped Norma's photograph on the desk in my office four months before, the issue of the drugs and weight loss took on some urgency. While the pills and Norma's memory problems had puzzled me, it hadn't occurred to me that a licensed physician would give a patient drugs that might cause harm. I didn't know much about medical weight-reduction clinics such as the one Dr. Richard operated. If this had been a civil case, I could have subpoenaed the doctor and his records under discovery procedures permitted in civil matters. But because it was a criminal case, I could get that information only by subpoenaing him as a witness in the trial. That would be too late. Dr. Ellison and I agreed that it was now imperative that he have those records as part of his psychiatric evaluation of Norma. I had no choice but to suggest that he ask Dr. Richard for them once again. And I decided to do a little research on my own.

Early the following week, on December 18, I called the office of the Food and Drug Administration and described to an official there the weight-loss program in which Norma had participated.

"My problem is that I can't find out what kind of pills my client was taking."

"I'm not surprised," the official said. "Some of these diet-pill doctors are reluctant to share this information even with their patients. It is a serious problem."

"Well, what kinds of drugs are involved?"

"Usually, you can expect a diuretic, which is something to help you lose water, some thyroid, and some amphetamines."

"Amphetamines?"

"Yes, sir."

"You mean speed?"

"That's right. It's a widely abused drug, and it can pose a serious health hazard."

By the time I got back to Dr. Ellison with that information, he had some news for me: Dr. Richard had found Norma's records and mailed them to him.

"But there's one problem," he said.

"What's that?"

"They're all in code. The whole chart is a bunch of numbers, and I have no idea what they mean."

I drove over to Ellison's office to look at the records myself, made a copy of them, and headed back to my office. I decided to try to get through to Richard one more time. It took three days before he would come to the phone, but I decided against complaining about that. I thanked him for sending the records.

"Now, doctor, we need to know just what Mrs. Winters was taking," I said. "I wonder if you could tell me what these numbers mean."

"I'm sorry," he said. "I don't give away my time for nothing."

"Oh, how much do you charge?"

"One hundred dollars an hour."

"Fine. I'll send you a check for a hundred dollars. Now, tell me what these codes mean. What kind of pills is my client taking?"

"I can't talk to you. I don't have the time."

"Dr. Richard, my client is facing very serious charges, and you have information that might be important to her defense. I can subpoena you to come to court if I have to, but I'd appreciate it if you could help me now."

"Now, you listen to me, sonny boy," the doctor said. "I have very good connections. I think you ought to know that. And I know some very important lawyers."

He mentioned a name. It was not familiar to me.

"I can make a lot of trouble for you," he continued.

"There's no need for trouble for either of us. I just need this information. I just need you to tell me what these numbers mean, so another doctor can read your chart."

"He's a doctor. Let him figure it out." He hung up.

Clearly, I was going to have to subpoena him in order to get the information I needed. But I had to find out what was in the pills before then. After Dr. Ellison tried one more time to get the information from Richard himself, I decided it was time to call Dave Harper.

Harper was a forensic scientist who evaluated physical evidence
—everything from murder weapons to blood stains and seat belts
—and testified about his findings in both civil and criminal cases.
He had done work for me on other cases, and although he was
barely in his thirties, it could take several minutes to state his
credentials to a jury. I explained the case to him briefly, and he
agreed to try to identify the pills.

At my request Norma had saved more than thirty packages of
pills of various shapes and colors; none of them were clearly
marked with the contents, although nearly all of them included a
slip of paper on which there was either a number—such as 1660,
1499, or ACR–2—or a dosage instruction. The numbers corre-
sponded to codes written on the medical records.

When Harper saw the pile of pills and the records, he asked the
obvious question. "Why don't you just call up the doctor and ask
him what this means?"

"We've tried that, several times. He won't tell us."

Harper looked at me skeptically, walked over to his bookshelf,
removed a large, thick volume, and carried it back to his desk. It
was the *Physicians' Desk Reference,* known by those who use it as
the *PDR.* It is a drug encyclopedia, containing lists, photographs,
uses, and side effects of hundreds of drugs produced by the country's major drug companies. He opened one of the small packages
I had dumped on his desk, picked out a pill, and flipped through
the pages of the book, trying to match the shape of the pill with
a picture in the book. He shook his head, picked up another pill,
and repeated the process. After checking more than half a dozen
pills, he looked back to me.

"Well, this isn't going to be very easy. None of these pills are in
here."

"None of them?"

"Nope. My guess is that most of them were manufactured by
marginal drug companies, maybe even some companies in Mexico,
where the doctor can purchase them at a lower price. Those pills
wouldn't be listed in here."

"So what can you do?"

"Well, one of the pills says 'Ardel' on it, and a couple of others
have markings that probably indicate what companies manufac-

tured them. I'll try to track down these companies and see what they can tell me. If that doesn't work, then we'll have to do a complete screen for dangerous drugs on all the pills with some of the equipment in the lab here."

I looked around the room, where men and women in white smocks were bent over microscopes or standing next to intricate machines with dials and lights and digital readouts on them. It was a sophisticated setup.

"Will you have any trouble testing the pills for amphetamines?"

"No. I can do that right now."

Harper walked over to an elaborate machine and fiddled with it for a moment. Then he scraped away part of one of the pills and reduced it to a powder.

"This isn't a definitive test," he said. "I just want to give you an idea of whether it's an amphetamine."

"What does the machine do?" I asked.

"Ultraviolet spectrophotometry."

"Oh. Okay." I smiled. In a few minutes Harper read a curve on a graph attached to the machine.

"Its definitely an amphetaminelike substance," he said. "Probably phendimetrazine."

"What's that?"

"Essentially, a synthetic amphetamine." He pulled out another book and started to explain the intricate chemical bonding of the substance.

"Okay, Dave," I said. "I'll leave the chemistry to you. When can I have a definitive answer?"

"How about in a day or two?"

"Fine. Can you give me a quantitative analysis, too?"

"Sure. If there's enough of it here, you might have some kind of psychiatric defense. There's a lot of recent data on the effects of amphetamines on the personality structure. If you take large doses, it can even create a form of psychosis called amphetamine psychosis."

I knew a little about that, but from what I could see, Norma hadn't been crazy when she'd contacted Pappas and Hanscom. But perhaps the drugs had somehow affected her personality. "Well, it sounds worth following up," I said. And I noted that the FDA man had suggested Norma might be taking thyroid, as well. Harper said he'd check, but that unless he got help from the drug companies, it would take at least a week before he could determine which, if any, of the pills contained thyroid and how much.

Up to this point I had been able to think of no possible defense for Norma Winters. With the trial set for January 20, one month away, it seemed that all I had to present to a jury were the mitigating aspects of her predicament: the incest and her violent marriage. That might establish that Norma was not a cold, hardened criminal, but a troubled, desperate woman who had no other place to turn. That was not self-defense, however, and none of the circumstances could convince a judge or jury that she had somehow been justified in hiring a man to kill her husband. All the evidence could do was lighten her sentence. There was no need to present it to a jury. Juries decide facts. Judges render sentences.

But now these drugs were taking on more significance. Amphetamine psychosis seemed highly unlikely, since nothing in the evidence suggested that Norma had gone crazy and been unable to distinguish right from wrong. But was it possible that the pills had reduced Norma's capacity to form the intent to commit the crime? Even that seemed like desperate speculation, but when I mentioned the notion and the preliminary indications of Harper's findings to Dr. Ellison, he didn't flinch.

"It would not surprise me to find that these drugs played an important role in this crime," he said.

"What makes you think that?"

"Well, from what I learned so far through the psychological testing, Norma's actions in this crime were what I would call 'ego alien,' which is to say that they were not consistent at all with her personality."

Norma, he explained, was a passive-dependent, a personality type that not only did not resort to violence, but that avoided violence and confrontation at almost any cost.

"And you think these pills might have changed her personality?"

"I don't want to speculate about that until I know exactly what was in those pills. And I haven't completed other aspects of my evaluation."

He said he wanted to interview Norma again and to talk to her children and possibly her mother, as well.

"I need to settle some apparent conflicts in the information and tests I have to date. She seems to have suffered some memory lapses."

We were scheduled to go to trial in about four weeks, but Dr. Ellison said he'd need probably another thirty days to complete his evaluation. We would have to have another delay in the trial. On January 3 I went back to court, armed with a letter from Dr. Ellison to help justify the need for another postponement of the trial. The judge granted a continuance, to February 18.

The next day Harper called with a report on his investigation. Many of the pills, he said, had been manufactured by fly-by-night drug companies whose phones were disconnected. But he had deciphered much of Dr. Richard's code. The package labeled "1499" was not phendimetrazine, as he had thought at first. It was dextroamphetamine, he said, five milligrams per tablet.

"What do you think about that dosage?" I asked.

"I'd say it's light to moderate, but you'd better have a psychiatrist tell you about that. There might be some other factors."

He also identified "PC" on the doctor's records as potassium chloride, "ACR–2" as ammonium chloride, and "mepro" as meprobamate.

"The others are vitamins," he said. "Do you want me to tell you what kind? It's pretty complicated."

"No, I don't think I'll need that. What about the thyroid?"

"I still haven't been able to determine that. But I'm still working on it."

I telephoned Dr. Ellison and gave him the new information.

Meanwhile, Tucker had picked up the tapes from the audio experts, and we had had them transcribed independently of the police version. The process had filled in a few holes in the police transcript, but it hardly yielded results comparable to the amount of time and frustration that had gone into battling the DA for them and getting them "cleaned." We had turned up little new information and nothing that was critical to the case. But we sent the tapes, both versions of the transcript, and all the police reports to Dr. Ellison as part of the evidence he would use to determine Norma's state of mind at the time of the crime.

He completed his evaluation of Norma on January 10 and called me with his report. He had interviewed Norma, her mother, and her children. He had given Norma twelve and one-half hours of psychiatric tests. He had reviewed the police reports, including the transcripts of her conversations with Hanscom and Ryan. He had reviewed the reports and health records that he had received from five doctors who had examined Norma within the past six months. He had considered a fourteen-page autobiography Norma had written, detailing her relationship with her parents and her husband and explaining her work and health histories. And he had examined Harper's reports on the amphetamines.

The final evaluation, he said, confirmed his earlier view that Norma was passive-dependent and that the act of murder for hire was completely out of character for her.

"And I believe that had she not taken those pills, she would not have committed these crimes."

He said Norma's change in character coincided with her first visits to the diet doctor. It was at that time that she had decided to start her own business after having worked for eighteen years as a service representative, department clerk, escrow secretary, and the like.

"This in itself seems significant, though not necessarily conclusive. But members of her family and others I have talked to all note similar changes. Norma was shy, introverted. She avoided controversy, followed directions—never led, but always followed. Then, in recent months, her personality seemed to change dramatically. She became jumpy, irritable, quick to scold, easy to anger. She worked constantly. She spanked David, something which she never did, she bumped into doors and walls from time to time, and she cried a lot."

He compared that information, he said, with the data from the battery of psychological tests, and found the contrast dramatic. The tests showed that Norma's passive-dependency was a long-standing personality characteristic—it had clearly existed long before the crime and her visit to the diet-pill doctor.

"It is a personality marked by withdrawal, dependency on others, and nonassertiveness," he explained. "Essentially, such a person uses meekness and helplessness in relationships with others. It is a character totally inconsistent with a person who would make a move to have her husband killed."

Ellison's evaluation went a long way toward establishing a possible defense for Norma, but it didn't solve the whole case. The mere fact that she'd become more assertive didn't mean she had been unable to distinguish right from wrong or to weigh the consequences and appreciate the seriousness of her actions. We had to do more than show that the drugs had contributed to Norma's conduct. We had to prove they had been responsible for it.

At Dr. Ellison's suggestion I consulted with a couple of specialists in San Diego who were familiar with the effects of amphetamines. They agreed that the pills may have had some impact, but the dosage seemed low. They couldn't say for sure. So I called Dr. Michael Truro, a nationally recognized authority on drug toxicity, from Denver, Colorado. I made arrangements for him to fly to San Diego on January 15 to meet and consult with Dr. Ellison, Harper, and me.

Truro was impressed with our information and intrigued by the case. But though he didn't dispute Ellison's opinion that the drugs had contributed to Norma's committing the crime, he could not make the connection I was looking for.

"Fifteen milligrams of speed a day is a light to moderate amount," he said. "It is nowhere near enough for amphetamine psychosis. She would have had to take at least one hundred milligrams a day over the same period for that to occur."

"So you don't see any way in which her use of this drug might have confused her mentally to an extent that she was not legally responsible for her actions?"

"No, I don't. The drug, in the dosage that your client was taking, would not have such an effect on the user."

Truro's analysis left me discouraged. I had known that the drug connection was a long shot, but as it had grown in importance, and as the evidence from Harper had begun to fall in place, I had gotten caught up in its possibilities. Now I was let down.

After the meeting I spoke briefly with Ellison. A tall, silver-haired man in his late fifties, Ellison rarely spoke, and when he did, it was with few words. But he was animated by this case. He didn't directly dispute Truro's findings, but he stood firm on his own. He puffed slowly on his pipe, and said, "It's just too improbable that a woman with her psychological makeup would become involved in something like this. If those drugs alone weren't enough to do it, there's something else there. Something else is there."

If that was the case, we had to find it quickly. The trial was just a month away, and we still had no defense, only mitigating circumstances. I asked my law clerk, Eric Miller, to check out every possible precedent he could find in the case law that might turn Ellison's findings into a defense for Norma. Then I told Tucker to type up his witness-interview reports and a chronology that we'd been keeping on the case. And I asked Harper and Ellison for final written reports to make sure I had all the key evidence at hand. I would review all the reports and hope that Miller would find something in the law that would fit our facts. Failing that, there would be little point in going to trial. I'd have to call the prosecutor and feel him out for a deal.

But two days later, on January 17, I learned that Dr. Ellison was right: something else *was* there.

CHAPTER 20

On the afternoon of January 17 Norma, Beth, and David stopped by at my office after their weekly visit with Dr. Nyquist. The three of them seemed to have responded well to the counseling sessions, especially recently. Both Beth and David had resented their mother's dating Connors so soon after their father's death, above all because they remembered the effect that her earlier affair with him had had on the family. And David, who was twelve, had blamed his mother and sister for Bruce's suicide.

Indeed, while Beth seemed somehow well adjusted despite the years of sexual assaults from her father, David had suffered the most from the years of tension and violence in his family. He was thin and tall for his age and had a mop of blond hair that had never seen a comb. He looked like Dennis the Menace, but unlike that impish character, he seemed serious and troubled. He had been a problem in school since the first grade; on at least two occasions he had assaulted teachers who had reprimanded him. His grades were well below average, and even further below what tests indicated as his potential. Lately, he had become involved in some fights with other kids that resulted in complaints to the police. Although no charges were brought against him, he was gaining a reputation as a troublemaker.

I had never talked directly with David about the events surrounding Norma's arrest and his father's death, partly because he was so young and partly because I knew from Norma how close he had been to his father. I wasn't sure he needed to go through it all again. But as we got closer to trial, I wanted to make sure we had covered everything, and I decided that if David knew anything we didn't, we'd better find out about it.

As the three of them milled around my office, I asked Norma and Beth to step outside. Then I motioned David to the head of the conference table, and he told me what he remembered about the day his mother was arrested.

David answered the door when the police arrived at his home on the evening of August 13. They took his father out on the patio and closed the door. David couldn't hear their conversation, but he could see that his father was very upset—not angry, but distraught. When the police left, his father showed them to the door. He said nothing to David, but went into the bedroom. He came out a while later with a small suitcase. He looked at his son.

"Your mother has been arrested and is in jail. I've got some of her things, and I'm going to see her. I'll be back later."

"Why is she in jail? What did she do?"

"I'm not sure, son. I'm going to find out."

When he returned later, he looked in on David, who was still awake in bed and told him the story. David cried himself to sleep.

The next morning David had a football game, and his father offered to drive him to the field. David was surprised, because his father didn't want him playing football and had never driven him to a game, much less come to watch him play.

At the game Bruce got out of the car and walked David to the field. Before he turned to leave, he put his arms around his son and squeezed him.

"Be a good boy and be careful, Dave."

Later that day his father returned to pick him up. David thought he seemed particularly sad and troubled. That night his father was unusually affectionate, and while they often slept in the same bed, his father was now particularly insistent about that.

The next morning Bruce got up about six and went to the kitchen to make a pot of coffee. He looked back into the bedroom to check on David, went over to the bed and hugged him, then walked toward the door. David got out of bed and followed him.

"Where're you going, dad?"

"I'm going away, son."

David put his arms around his father and hugged him. He felt something hard in his father's back pocket. It was his service revolver.

"Why do you have the gun, daddy?"

"David, your sister made some charges that I had relations with her. What she says is partially true. I never actually completed the act all the way, but I did play around with her. And I shouldn't have done that."

David looked into his father's eyes, then down to the floor. He didn't know what to say.

"David, I love you," Bruce said softly, "and I want you to be good to your mom and your sister. I want you to love them. Don't have any hard feelings against them."

"But where are you going, dad? What are you going to do?"

"I'm going away, and when the police come to get me, I'm going to shoot myself."

"No, no. No, dad." He hugged his father tightly, holding on so he couldn't leave.

"Dave, it's only a matter of time before they come to arrest me. I can't put you all through a trial. It would tear us apart. I would go to jail for what I did, and when the other prisoners found out I was a policeman, well, they would kill me."

"No, please, dad. Please stay here. Please."

"I've got to go." He embraced his son for the last time. "And when they come to get me, I will be gone. I love you, Dave."

He carefully pulled his son's hands apart from behind his back and looked him in the eye.

"Good-bye, Dave."

He turned and walked out the door.

Tears had formed in David's eyes as he had told his story. I said nothing for a moment. Then I told him that Beth had once mentioned a telephone call that Bruce had made to Norma at Lovell's house the night after her arrest.

"Do you know anything about that call?" I asked.

He nodded. "Dad called from the living room. I was in the bedroom and without dad knowing it, I picked up the other phone."

"So you heard the conversation?"

"Yeah."

"What happened?"

"Well, my dad called Lovell's house."

"Who answered the phone?"

"Lovell. My dad hated Lovell."

"Do you remember the conversation?"

"Well, yeah. Dad says, 'This is Bruce.' And before he could say anything else, Lovell says, 'Oh no. You're not talking to anybody, not after what you did to Beth. You've screwed up your own family, and you're not going to screw up this one.' "

"Lovell said that right off the bat?"

"Yup. And then my dad asks if he could talk with Beth, and she gets on the line. She was crying."

"Okay," I said.

"And she says, 'Daddy.' And he says, 'Beth, they're going to come and get me. They're going to take me off.' And she says, 'No, daddy. Don't let them. Get out of there. Run away. I'm not going to say anything about it. I won't press charges.' And then he says that he thinks someone will. And then he says, 'Why did you tell them I completed the act with you?' She says, 'I didn't say that, daddy.' And he says, 'I didn't do it all the way, you know.' And she says, 'I know, daddy. I didn't say you did. Honest. I never said that. Get out of there, go to Arizona so they can't get you.' "

"Then what happened?" I asked.

"Then my dad calls out to me and says, 'Dave, do you want to talk with Beth?' So I put the receiver down on the table and go into the living room, and my dad hands me the phone."

"What did you say to her?"

"I don't remember."

"Okay. Was that it?"

"No. Then mom comes to the phone, and I talk with her."

"What did she say?"

"Well, she gets on the line, and my dad is right there, and he says to tell her that he loved her."

"Did you do that?" I asked.

"Yes. I said that to mom."

"Did she say anything?"

"Yes. She says to tell him that she loved him too."

I got up from my chair, walked over to the stained-glass doors, and beckoned Norma and Beth to come back into the office. I wanted to ask them about this telephone call. As David told the story again, Beth's eyes grew puffy with tears. And when he talked about his mother's coming to the telephone, Norma gasped and looked at her son in disbelief.

"I talked to you?" she asked.

"Yes."

"What did I say?"

When David said that she had asked him to tell Bruce that she loved him, Norma stared blankly at him for a moment, then covered her face with her hands and cried uncontrollably.

I called to my secretary to get Norma and Beth some Kleenex and coffee. Then I asked them to step outside again to compose themselves while I talked further with David.

Within five minutes the door opened slightly, and someone reached inside, holding a note. I walked over and took it, returned to the table, and sat down as David continued to talk. I unfolded the note. It was in Norma's handwriting, and it read; "Walt Lovell drove Beth and me to Tony Pappas's. Lovell knew why, Beth didn't."

I glanced at the note, first in disbelief, then in anger. I bolted into the reception area.

"Norma, get yourself into that office. Beth, you get in there, too. Now."

I told my secretary to call Tucker down to my office immediately.

"Thank you very much, David. I need to talk with your mother again." I asked him to go into the other room and sit down.

By the time he had settled into a chair, Tucker was downstairs and in my office. I closed the doors. Beth was sitting at the far end of the table on the same side as her mother, her back to the windows. I was standing, glowering at Norma across the table.

I had never been fully satisfied with Lovell's claim on the first day he and Norma had come to my office that he had let Norma borrow his car without knowing where she was going. He had hardly let her out of his sight for the five days she had stayed in El Centro after learning of the incest. I had repeatedly asked Norma to explain that, and she had always shrugged and said it had just happened that way. Now it turned out that she had lied.

"You've been lying to me for four months, Norma, on this very question, and who knows how many others."

Norma looked away sheepishly and said nothing.

"Why didn't you tell me this?"

"Lovell said it was my responsibility and that I shouldn't get anyone in the family involved."

"Oh. Is Walt Lovell still running your life? Maybe you should ask him if he'll represent you."

She said nothing.

"Damn it, Norma, I'm running this case. Either you accept that and tell me the truth or forget it."

"Do you remember the first day I was in here, and you asked me how I'd gotten to Pappas's, and he interrupted and said he loaned me his car?"

"Yeah."

"Well, afterwards, he said that if I just told everyone that I had gone alone, it wouldn't get Beth involved."

"Did he know why you were going to Pappas's?"

"Yes."

"Then didn't it occur to you that maybe it was Walt Lovell that he didn't want to get involved?"

Norma bowed her head. I turned to her daughter.

"Beth, did you know why your mother was going to Pappas's?"

"No." Her body shifted slightly as she answered.

"Beth," I said, looking her straight in the eye. "Did you know why your mother was going to Pappas's?" She twirled her hair with her fingers.

"Beth, . . ."

She slumped in her chair and nodded. "Yes," she said softly.

"How did you know?"

"When we drove there, Walt said I should go with him to the

coffee shop downstairs while mom went to see Mr. Pappas."

"Uh-huh."

"When mom came back down in the elevator—she was only there for a few minutes—and when she came down the elevator, Walt said, 'Down so soon?' And mom said, 'He kicked me out of his office.' "

"But how did you know what your mother was seeing Pappas about?"

"Well, after mom said that, Lovell said, 'Hmmm, maybe he thought you were trying to set him up.' "

"So you put it together from that?"

"Yes." She nodded again.

"But you didn't know when you got in the car with your mother and Lovell that she was going to see Mr. Pappas about killing your father?"

"No. I didn't, Milt."

That meant she was not a participant in the crime, not a conspirator. Barring other evidence that suggested she was lying, she was safe from prosecution.

But the implication of what she and Norma had said was staggering. If what they were telling me was true, Norma had confessed to her involvement in a *conspiracy* to commit murder, and the coconspirator was Walt Lovell.

"All right, Norma, who drove to Pappas's office?"

"I don't know." She shrugged.

"Lovell did," Beth volunteered.

"Where did you sit?"

"In the back seat."

"And your mother was in the front?"

She nodded.

"Where did you park?" I thought perhaps Lovell might keep the parking stub as a business expense or tax deduction.

"On the street, at the corner, I think."

"Not in a parking lot?"

"No, on the street."

"What street?"

"I don't know. I don't know the street names."

"Do you know what building you went to?"

"Yes, the Associates Office Tower."

"Where did you get the idea to call Pappas?"

"I've told you several times. It just popped into my head."

"It just popped into your head." I paced the room. "Are we going to go through this again? I don't want any more lies, Norma, I want answers. Now how did you happen to think to call Pappas?"

"I don't know, Milt. His name just popped into my head. I don't know how else to tell you."

"Well when did you call him, then?"

"Friday morning."

"Did you call him at any other time?"

"No."

"Are you sure?"

She nodded.

"Norma, I have incontrovertible evidence that you called him on Thursday. His secretary told the police you called him on Thursday *and* Friday."

"I don't remember it."

"A lie."

"Really, Milt. That's the truth. I don't remember it."

"A lie."

She shrugged.

"Where did you call him from?"

"I don't know."

"A lie. You must know. Did you call from a pay phone?"

"I don't know."

"Another lie. How did you get his number?"

She closed her eyes for a moment, searching for an answer, but said nothing.

"Well, did you look his number up in the phone book?"

"I must have."

"Don't give me this 'must have' nonsense. Either you did or you didn't. It's real simple. How did you get his phone number?"

She thought for a moment, then looked back at me. "I just don't know. Why don't I remember that?"

"I don't know, Norma," I said, throwing my hands in the air as I paced back and forth. "Amnesia? Hypnosis?—"

"Oh," Beth interjected, "he was always doing that to us, too."

I stopped dead in my tracks. "Doing *what?*"

"Oh, hypnotizing us and stuff."

"Who?"

"Lovell."

"Lovell hypnotized you?"

"He tried to hypnotize both of us," Beth said.

"But he never hypnotized me," Norma added quickly.

"How do you know?"

"I just know." She giggled. "He didn't hypnotize me."

"But he did try?"

She nodded and giggled again.

"Is there something funny here?" I asked. Norma quickly became serious.

"Well, where did he try to do it?" I continued.

"At his house and at his office," Norma said.

"Who else was there?"

"It was Walt, Ellie, myself, and Beth."

"When did it happen?"

Neither Norma nor Beth could remember.

"Was it before or after your arrest?"

"It was after, I think," Norma said.

"Are you sure?"

"Well, I think so."

"Wait, mom, it had to be before," Beth said. "Remember, it was the week we spent at Walt and Ellie's, right after I told you about dad and me. I remember, because Frank was there, and he got upset with Walt for doing that stuff. It happened a couple of times. Once he tried it on both of us in his office, and then another time it was just you at the house, I think."

"Are you sure it was that week, Beth?" I asked.

"Positive. It was the week we spent at his house."

It was difficult not to make the connection: it was the same week Norma had called Anthony Pappas.

"Okay, Beth, tell me what happened in the office."

"Well, he told us to lie down on the floor."

"Then what?"

"This is ridiculous," Norma interjected. "I wasn't hypnotized."

I had once seen a stage presentation in which a man hypnotized thirty people. He had them taking off their shirts, acting like chickens, laughing, and crying. When the show was over, several of them insisted they had not been hypnotized.

"Norma, did Lovell have any training in hypnosis?"

"Well, he said he did."

"He was always telling us that," Beth added. "He said he had hypnotized Ellie so she could take her real-estate-license test. He said it was to make her relax. She was real uptight about the test —I guess she failed it once—and he hypnotized her to relax, and she passed it easily."

"Was this before you were hypnotized, Norma?"

"I'm telling you, I wasn't hypnotized."

"All right, Norma, if you're so smart and have all the answers, why don't you defend yourself?"

Norma said nothing.

"I want to look into this a little further. Did he tell you about any other people he had hypnotized?"

Norma shrugged. "He told me once he had hypnotized his former wife and that's how he got custody of their children."

"Did he say where he learned to do this?"

"He said he went to some school in San Bernardino," Beth said.

"Okay. Well, Norma, what happened at Lovell's house?"

"Just some silly parlor game. I don't see what's in this, Milt. I wasn't hypnotized."

"Well, let's try this. You are lying on the floor in his living room. Does that sound right?"

"Yes."

"Are you on your stomach or your back?"

"My back."

"Where's Lovell?"

"I don't know."

"Is he in the room?"

"Yes."

"Okay, does he speak to you, or do you speak to him?"

"He speaks to me. He tells me to imagine a tree. He says there is only a single leaf on the tree and that it is fluttering in the wind."

"What do you do?"

"I laugh," she said, laughing.

"Why?"

"Because I couldn't picture a tree with just one leaf on it."

"Did you try to picture it?"

"Yes, but I told him I couldn't."

"Then what?"

"Well, he told me to picture a wall that was all white and to imagine a single black spot on the white wall."

"Could you picture that?"

"Yeah." She shrugged.

"You did picture that, then."

"Yes."

"What happened next?"

"He said I was getting sleepy. That I was going to sleep."

"Did you?"

"I don't know," she laughed. "I had my eyes closed."

For the first time in the afternoon, I smiled. "Okay, then what?"

"He said that my arm was going to get real light and that I would raise it in the air."

"Did you raise it?"

"No."

"How do you know for sure? You said your eyes were closed."

"Well, I didn't feel it rise."

"Did it feel lighter?"

"I don't know. It might have, I guess."

"Then what?"

"He said there was a feather tickling the end of my nose."

"And what did you do then?"

"Well . . ." She paused for a moment. Then, as if by reflex, she raised her right hand to her face and with her index finger gently rubbed her nose.

CHAPTER 21

Norma Winters remembered
nothing of what had happened after she'd scratched the end of her
nose, and she insisted that nothing else had happened. She also had
trouble remembering exactly when she'd been in Lovell's house
and when she'd been in the office. Beth, however, had gone outside
for more than half an hour during one session at the house, and
when she had returned, Lovell had been with her mother in the
bedroom, talking to her in soothing tones, and Norma had been
talking in a little girl's voice. Beth remembered something else: on
a couple of other occasions when Lovell had hypnotized them, or
tried to hypnotize them, he had said, "Now, you won't remember
any of this," over and over again.

Tucker was shaking his head in amusement. "You know, Milt,
we've got incest and suicide and diet pills and computers named
Norm in this case already," he said. "Have we really got room for
black magic?"

I grinned. "No, not for black magic. But this is a possible explanation for all those memory blocks, and I think we should follow
it up."

I had only limited knowledge of hypnosis, but I did know that
it was a recognized method of treatment for some mental problems,
and that in itself removed it from the realm of witch doctors and
quack miracle healers. I also knew that someone could be hypno-

tized to perform a specific act and remember nothing about it afterwards. Was it possible that Norma's memory had been blocked through hypnosis? Was it possible that Lovell had tried to "erase" Norma's knowledge of his involvement in this crime? Was it possible that he had erased key parts of her own involvement from her mind? If he had, it raised one other chilling possibility: that Lovell had planted a hypnotic suggestion for Norma to commit the crime.

It seemed preposterous. It was common knowledge, I thought, that people could not be induced to do under hypnosis what they would consider morally wrong in a normal state of consciousness. Even if Lovell had hypnotized Norma, she would surely have resisted a suggestion to have her husband murdered. Still, I felt the issue needed further study. Once again I called Dr. Ellison, this time expecting to be laughed off the phone.

But Ellison was intrigued. Given her passive personality traits, he explained, influence from hypnosis was not as farfetched a notion as it might seem. He recommended a serious look into the possibility by a psychiatrist with a special interest in hypnosis. He suggested a couple of people for me to contact.

Over the weekend and on Monday, the twentieth, I gathered a few more names and settled eventually on six people to consult. Each of them led me to the same person, Dr. Barry Unger.

Dr. Unger, I was told, had worked with hypnotherapy since his psychiatric training in Baltimore in the early 1960s, most recently in connection with an experimental "pain center" in San Diego, in which he used hypnosis to help treat patients suffering severe pain. By both background and experience, he was a leading authority in the city on the psychiatric and medical uses of hypnosis. He was also a hard man to reach. After leaving messages for him all day Tuesday, I finally got him at his home at ten o'clock that evening.

Dr. Unger sounded skeptical when I explained why I wanted him to examine my client.

"Dr. Stanley Ellison suggested I pursue this," I said, hoping the authority of a colleague's name would diminish the doctor's doubts. Then I told him in detail about the case.

Dr. Unger was still reluctant to get involved. He had never testified in court before and said he knew nothing about criminal law. "My practice is limited to seeing patients and teaching at the University of California," he said.

"Well, I understand that, doctor. That's not a serious problem. I just need to know if my client could have been hypnotized to commit a crime, and if she was, would you be able to find out?"

Dr. Unger said nothing for a moment, but finally broke his own silence. "I don't know. Can she remember going to Pappas's office?"

"Vividly. She can remember exactly what she said to him, what he said, and how she left."

"How do you know her version is accurate?"

"Pappas told the police exactly the same thing."

After several more questions touching on what Norma could and could not remember, Unger asked, "Do you have any evidence that something occurred in these sessions with Lovell that your client could not recall?"

"Yes, I remember one thing. Beth told me that she had left to go outside during one session and that when she returned, Norma was lying on the floor talking about her childhood, about when she was a little girl. Norma told me she didn't remember talking about anything like that."

"Well, it seems highly improbable. I've been using hypnotherapy for twelve years, and I've never heard a story like that." He paused. "But some of what you say is consistent with the use of hypnosis. It certainly is worth further study."

"Then you can see her?"

He paused again. "I'd like to think about it. I'm not sure I want to testify in court. Do you think I'd be required to do that?"

"Doctor, if your analysis turns up any information that might be relevant to Norma's case, then, yes, I would want to call you as a witness."

"Well, give me a night to think about it."

I gave him my office phone number, and he promised to call me the next day. After I hung up, I glanced at my watch. It was nearly midnight. We had talked almost two hours.

The next day Unger called back. He would see Norma, he said, and he set up a three-hour appointment for her and Beth on Friday, the twenty-fourth.

Norma stopped by at the office after her visit with Dr. Unger, but had little information. She described him as a "nice man" and said that he had spent all afternoon with both her and Beth and that he wanted to see her again the next day.

"He said he needs to spend more time with me," she reported.

That was encouraging. At least he hadn't dismissed the notion outright after one visit.

In fact, on Monday he saw her for a third time, and when Norma stopped by to report on that visit, I called Dr. Unger myself.

"The examination so far is quite interesting, but it is still incomplete," he said. "But I have a couple of questions for you. Can you determine from Norma's mother whether she had a refrigerator on the back porch when Norma was three years old, and whether they moved from that house before Norma's fourth birthday?"

I called him back in an hour. The answer to both questions was yes.

Meanwhile, I sent Dr. Unger a thick folder of evidence in the case, ranging from transcripts of Norma's conversations with the police to her medical chart from Dr. Richard and the letter she had received the preceding May from Anthony Pappas.

After seeing Norma for a fourth visit on Tuesday, the twenty-eighth, Dr. Unger called me. His work with Norma was still incomplete, he said, but he hoped one last session with her would answer the question. And he wanted an outside observer to be present for it. I asked Tucker to attend.

Late the next afternoon Tucker walked into my office. He seemed shocked and bewildered. His face was ashen.

"What happened, Gene?"

He shook his head and sighed.

"Did Unger hypnotize her, or what?"

He looked at me. "Yeah. He sure did."

"Well, what happened?"

"You'd better have Dr. Unger tell you that."

I jumped for the phone. Yes, Dr. Unger said when he answered, he had indeed reached some conclusions about the case.

When Dr. Unger had first met Norma Winters the previous Friday, he had been skeptical. Somebody had been watching too much television, he figured. But within five minutes of their meeting, Norma had put some of his doubts to rest.

"Milt Silverman thinks I may have been hypnotized," she had said. "I think it's a lot of hooey. But he thinks seeing you might help the case, so here I am."

Later in their conversation she admitted that she had committed the crime, that she considered herself guilty, and even that she thought she deserved to be punished. That didn't sound like someone who was trying to get away with something.

Unger spent the entire first session—three hours—and most of the second one getting the story from Norma and Beth, including a description from each of them of Lovell's efforts to hypnotize them. Lovell had spoken soothingly to them, held their hands— important for establishing rapport—and had had them imagine a variety of images, all consistent with the practice of hypnosis. Beth had recalled three separate times when Lovell had hypnotized her mother in his office and his house on August 8 or 9. And she remembered his repeating over and over again, "You won't remember any of this."

Unger was surprised by that suggestion. You don't tell a person in a hypnotic trance not to remember something unless it's something terribly traumatic, he thought. In twelve years of using hypnosis in therapy, he himself had done that just twice.

At the end of the second meeting, on Saturday, January 25, Unger decided to hypnotize Norma on a trial run. Almost immediately she was in a light trance, obeying his simple suggestions. She was remarkably easy to hypnotize, he thought.

On Monday she was in his office again, and this time he put her in a deeper trance, in which she recalled some details of an earlier hypnotic experience. The hypnotist was Walt Lovell.

Since it was possible to lie under hypnosis, Unger "regressed" her in age back to her early childhood, and she described a scene on a porch with a refrigerator on it and her mother nearby. It was the scene that Norma's mother had confirmed as true, and it established for Unger that he had hypnotized Norma and that she seemed to be telling the truth.

During the fourth session, on Tuesday, he put her in still a deeper trance, and asked her to recall the specific events surrounding Lovell's three attempts to hypnotize her around August 8 or 9. She recalled her neck being rubbed and her lying on the floor, but she broke off that hypnosis and began to describe another session, one that had occurred on June 13, a day on which she and Ellie had also driven to Los Angeles to deliver some papers on Norma's escrow business to the California Department of Corporations. Unger tried to move back to August 8, but Norma would say nothing. She was blocked. When he brought Norma out of the trance, she could recall nothing special about June 13. But she had clearly resisted much elaboration on the events of August 8 or 9.

Now he had come to what he hoped would be the final day with Norma Winters. Not only did he have other patients to meet, but he was reaching a point where, though convinced she had been hypnotized the day before she walked into Pappas's office, he was not sure he would ever get the information he needed to make the connection. Hypnosis can be exhausting for the subject. Although often characterized as a stage of sleep, it is actually a heightened awareness of a very specific band of consciousness, and it can be an intense experience.

Both Tucker and Norma arrived right on time for the 9 A.M. appointment in a pleasant, moderate-sized room on the second floor of a large Victorian home that had been converted to doctors' offices in an established section of San Diego. It was a bright room, with large windows, and appointed with shelves lined with books, lush green plants and leather furniture, including a sofa, a chair, and a recliner, in which Norma took a seat.

Dr. Unger asked Tucker to be as unobtrusive and quiet as possible, motioning for him to sit on the sofa, just a few feet away from the recliner. And he asked Norma if Tucker's presence bothered her at all.

"No," she said with a half laugh. "I think Gene and Milt know all of my dark secrets already."

If there were any other secrets hiding somewhere in Norma's mind, two sessions that morning could not uncover them. Norma remained blocked. And she was tired. That afternoon Unger made what he decided would be the final attempt.

He asked Norma to count backwards to herself and to relax, and for several minutes he talked softly to her, before finally reaching for her left hand.

"Okay, Norma. Just relax. I'm going to move your arm back and forth, back and forth." He raised her arm up, as if she were flexing her biceps, then set it back down on the arm rest. He raised it again —"back and forth"—then lowered it.

"Norma, your arm is getting lighter and lighter, and I'm holding it lighter and lighter. Back and forth. Back and forth. Now your arm has a will of its own. It is moving on its own."

He let go of Norma's wrist, and her arm moved back and forth, back and forth, like a metronome, slowly, seemingly in time with her breathing.

"It's moving all on its own now, and almost nothing can stop it."

He reached for her wrist and pulled against it. Norma's arm resisted, pulling, straining to keep its rhythm as Unger applied more and more weight, until he was almost holding against the arm rest with both hands. Norma's body wrenched as she strained to keep her hand moving. Tucker sat on the edge of the sofa, transfixed. Unger let go, and Norma's hand moved back and forth, back and forth, resuming the original cadence.

The trance was well established and as deep as any she had been in during earlier sessions.

"Okay, Norma, let's go back several years to your childhood. Let's talk about a time when you were twelve."

As Unger asked her questions, Norma began to talk about living in Holtville with her mother and father and "making cookies with my mother."

She spoke not in her normal voice, but in that of a twelve-year-old.

Unger proceeded to move on in time, asking her about meeting Bruce. Her face brightened visibly, and she smiled as she relived the happy moments of their first meetings. "I was wearing a red sweater and pedal pushers," she said with a grin. But when he asked her to remember the latter years of their marriage, she cringed and withdrew in fright and meekly answered his questions.

Then he moved once again to August 8, and the hypnotic sessions with Lovell. Because of her earlier difficulty in recalling those sessions, Unger asked her to describe what she saw and heard as if she were there, observing it first hand.

"Where are you, Norma?"

"In the bedroom."

"What's happening, Norma?"

"Walt's rubbing my neck. He's asking me to imagine a nail in the wall. And he's telling me 'relax, just relax, everything will be okay.' He's telling me to imagine a single leaf on a tree."

"Are you doing that?"

"Yes." Her voice drifted off as if she were listening. She started to speak, and then frowned, as if offended.

"What is that you hear, Norma?"

She said nothing, but wrinkled her brow in apparent disgust.

"Is it offensive?"

"Yes."

"Is it obscene?"

"No."

"What is he saying, Norma?"

She shook her head. "He loves me, and . . ." She moved uncomfortably in the seat.

"Okay, Norma, what happens next?"

A puzzled expression crossed her face. "His mouth is moving, but I can't hear the words. It's blank. Numbers. One. He says one. It's blank. He's counting. Two. He's moving his lips, but I can't hear what he's saying. There's no sound."

She was describing the beginning of a hypnotic session, and Unger suspected, on the basis of what Beth had told him, that these blocked portions involved Lovell's instructions to Norma that she would not remember what had occurred. He had to get the information some way, he thought. He also had to be on guard against a phenomenon in hypnosis called "interviewer bias." He phrased his questions carefully, so he wouldn't suggest the answers to Norma and color the examination. Yet, he had come close to this point several times before with her, and she would go no further. He decided to go right to the point.

"Norma, go back exactly to the time Pappas's name popped into your mind."

Norma said nothing for a moment. Then she muttered, "In Walt's office."

"How did the name come up?"

"The letter," she said.

"Who is with you?"

"Walt and Ellie and me."

"Is anyone talking?"

"No, no." she said. It was not a negative answer, however. She was indicating a reluctance to talk. She became more agitated in the chair. Unger was cautious.

"Is someone talking?" he asked again.

Norma said nothing, but nodded slightly.

"Is that person talking to you?"

Again Norma nodded.

"Who is talking to you, Norma?" His voice was steady and soothing; he maintained the same quiet tone he had used from the beginning.

There was a long pause. Finally she said, "Ellie."

"What is being said?"

Tears formed in her eyes and spilled onto her cheeks. She seemed to be struggling with the memory. The steady cadence of her arm continued, but she rolled her head from side to side, moaning softly. "No, no, no . . ."

"It's all right, Norma," Unger murmured soothingly. "Do you feel that you would be betraying Ellie if you told me?"

"Yes."

"Can you just tell me generally what it's about?"

She paused for a moment. "Bruce," she sobbed.

"Is Lovell saying anything?"

"No."

"When you're in the room and Ellie is talking, how do you feel?"

Norma's eyes fluttered, and her breathing became heavy and labored.

"Do you feel angry?"

"No."

"Do you feel hurt?"

"Yes."

"How else do you feel?"

"Sad," she cried.

"Do you do anything, Norma?"

"Pick up the phone," she answered. Unger was uncertain whether she was describing an event or reporting a command.

"Is somebody telling you to pick up the phone?"

Norma recoiled as if she were ducking a punch. "No!" she said.

"Norma, is someone . . ."

"No! No! No!" Norma's body writhed in the chair. Her arm movement began to waver and move irregularly. She groaned, then cried out.

Unger moved quickly, taking her wrist. "It's all right, Norma. Back and forth, back and forth. Back and forth." She seemed to relax. "Do you go somewhere and pick up the phone?"

"No, I pick up the phone right there."

"Who do you call?"

"Pappas."

"Anthony Pappas?"

"Yes."

"Is it in your mind to call Mr. Pappas when you walk into Walt's office?"

"No."

"Does it come into your mind after you walk into the room?"

"Yes."

"When you walked into the room was there something on your mind that you were going to do?"

"No, nothing."

"Is it your idea to call Pappas?"

"No." she sobbed. She began to cry again. Unger didn't know how much longer she could take it. It was her third session of the day, and it was nearly 4 P.M. They had started seven hours ago. He had another chance to break through to her, and that would be it. He feared that she might go into an anxiety panic. He would not be able to hypnotize her again. It would be too painful, too traumatic. He would either get it now, or he would never get it.

He reached for her arm once again and moved it back and forth to maintain the trance. "Okay, Norma, you are at the telephone, right at the telephone. Is somebody talking to you?"

"Yes," she cried, twisting in the chair.

"Are they talking about Bruce?"

"Yes."

"Does it concern having Bruce killed?" Unger asked softly.

Norma let out an anguished cry. Her breathing made a loud, gasping sound. "Yes."

"What is said?"

"The phone. Pick up the phone."

"Do you want to do this, Norma?"

"No, no, no," she cried out, making a low moaning sound as if she were in pain. "Oh, God, no."

"Okay, Norma, we're only trying to get the truth. We're just trying to learn what happened. Now, who is telling you to do this?"

"No, no, no!"

"It's okay, Norma. Who is talking? Who is telling you to do this?"

She moaned. Her body heaved and lashed against the chair. Finally she answered. The word seemed to be pulled from her throat, in a loud, hoarse whisper.

"Ellllllieeeee."

Unger was stunned, unable to speak for about fifteen seconds. He was so certain Lovell had given the command that he was taken completely off guard. Norma continued to cry; her body writhed in the chair. At last Unger spoke to her.

"Do you make the call, Norma?"

"Yes," she said slowly. "I pick up the phone and call."

"Is Lovell in the room?"

Norma's arm wavered again. She was almost out of the trance. Unger reached for it again, moving it back and forth.

"Yes, he is," she said finally.

"What is he doing?"

Again her body heaved in the chair almost convulsively. "He is sitting in the corner, nodding," she cried. "He agrees."

Unger decided Norma had had as much as she could take. He had more questions, but to ask any more was to risk a breakdown.

"Okay, Norma, when I tap on the table the third time, you'll open your eyes and feel alert." He tapped slowly. Once. Twice. Three times.

Norma opened her eyes and sat up. Her arm stopped moving. She continued to cry. No one spoke for a few minutes.

"I didn't want Ellie to get involved in this," Norma said finally, slightly more composed. "I don't want to do anything to hurt her. She's my best friend. I can't hurt her."

"Norma, we're just looking for the truth now," Unger said again. "We're not trying to prove anything or get you out of anything. And we're not trying to get Ellie or anyone else in trouble. We're just looking for what really happened. You know, Ellie herself might have been hypnotized, too. Has Lovell ever hypnotized Ellie?"

"I don't think so, not that I know of," Norma replied. Then she remembered the episode about the real-estate exam.

"What did he say to her?"

"Oh, he just rubbed her neck and told her to relax and—"

Norma looked up at Unger startled. "That's the same thing he said to me."

CHAPTER 22

"**I**'m prepared to testify," Dr. Unger said as our telephone conversation continued, "that Norma Winters was hypnotized by Walter Lovell on several occasions, the first of which probably occurred last June 13. I'm prepared to testify that he subsequently hypnotized her on either August 8 or 9, just before she made a telephone call to Anthony Pappas to arrange the murder of her husband. I'm prepared to testify that the call was made from the office of Walter Lovell, in the presence of Mr. Lovell and Ellen Harris. I'm prepared to testify that when Norma Winters entered the office, she did not have in her mind the idea to call Pappas and that that suggestion was made to her by someone else in the room whom she loved and trusted."

"The suggestion came from Ellie?" I asked.

"Yes. The suggestion was made to her to call Pappas and to meet with him to arrange her husband's murder."

"Well, why wouldn't Lovell just tell Norma to do it himself? Why did he have to have Ellie tell Norma?"

"For Norma to accept a suggestion like that," Unger explained, "it would be much more effective if it came from someone she trusted. Ellie is her closest friend, and the sister of the proposed murder target. Lovell may have tried to make the suggestion, but it would be much more effective and likely to succeed coming through Ellie."

"I thought it was impossible to hypnotize someone to perform an act that in a normal state they would find morally wrong."

"Generally, that's true, at least in a direct sense. But exceptions are possible. You could accomplish the same thing by distorting someone's perception of circumstances." For example, he explained, it would be possible to "regress" a Vietnam veteran back to a day when he was in combat, give him a gun, and recreate a scene in which a Vietcong soldier was about to kill him. "Under those circumstances, it could well be morally acceptable for him to kill."

"How does that fit into the facts of this case?"

"Well, there's the circumstance of the incest. I don't know exactly how that might have altered Norma's perception of right and wrong, but it did provide her with a reason for wanting her husband dead. I'm sure she had murderous thoughts toward him. Lovell certainly knew about all that and could have capitalized on it. Also, there is the issue of distance. Norma did not accept a suggestion to kill her husband, but to ask someone else to kill him. By removing her from the act of pulling the trigger, Lovell made it even easier for her to consider the suggestion to commit the crime."

Before he made any other firm statements, Dr. Unger said, he wanted to talk to Dr. Ellison and consult with colleagues who were familiar with hypnosis, amphetamines, and thyroid. Harper had just told us that he had finally detected thyroid in one of the pills Norma had been taking.

While I awaited further word from Dr. Unger, I had some work to do myself. If Lovell was indeed a coconspirator, I wanted some evidence, in addition to Norma's and Beth's stories, to establish that he had actually driven her to Pappas's on August 9. That meant looking for witnesses at the Associates Office Tower, particularly at the shop where Lovell and Beth had had coffee while Norma had gone to the eleventh floor to meet Pappas. We would need photographs of the two of them to show to people who worked there. Norma provided a picture of Beth, but getting one of Lovell posed a problem. Eric Miller, my law clerk, was a good photographer; so I sent him to stake out Lovell's office from a distance and get him with a telephoto lens when he came out. The next day Miller handed me three glossy color photos of Lovell, showing him not outside his door, but sitting right at his desk, his left hand on his calculator and a big smile on his face.

"How did you get that?" I asked, laughing.

"Well, the light wasn't good for the telephoto, so I went in. I told him I was a photographer thinking of opening a studio and needed some information on setting up my books. We talked for a while, and I told him if I opened up a shop, I'd come and see him. Then I said I'd take a picture of him for his wife if he liked. He said he'd like that. So here you are."

As good as the idea was, it didn't pay off. Tucker and I showed the photographs to the manager of the coffee shop and to others at the Associates Office Tower, but no one could place the faces. After all, it was six months since Norma had called on Pappas.

I also wanted additional proof that Lovell actually knew enough to have been able to hypnotize Norma. Neither she nor Beth could remember where Lovell had said he'd taken hypnosis classes, and Lovell had kept Ellen away from Tucker when he'd tried to interview her. Since he had bragged to Norma about hypnotizing his first wife, we decided to track her down. That effort included telephone calls from San Diego to Philadelphia and finally to Kansas City, where she had last worked. When she'd left a company there, however, she had not left a forwarding address. We could go no further.

Both efforts to solidify our information on Lovell had reached dead ends. It was February 3, two weeks away from the scheduled trial date. After nearly six months of working on the case, I had yet to visit El Centro and the scene of the crime. When I was in law school, I used to visit courtrooms to watch lawyers at work, and I remembered vividly a shoplifting case in which a defense lawyer asked a witness questions that indicated that the lawyer had never been in the store. He was investigating his case in the courtroom, and it didn't surprise me that his client was convicted. After that I made sure always to visit the crime scene, no matter how nondescript it might be, before I stepped into a courtroom for trial. I told Tucker I wanted him to go with me to El Centro.

It is only about 120 miles along Interstate 8 from San Diego to

El Centro, but the two-hour drive joins two different worlds. San Diego, once a conservative city dominated by its navy base, is a Southern California boomtown. Its temperate climate and the aura of California culture have helped lure about 400,000 people to it in twenty years, bringing its population to more than a million. The established sections of the city include the internationally known zoo and Balboa Park, a vast, almost tropical garden in the middle of the city. Not surprisingly, however, the throngs of new residents have spurred a building rush. Mile after mile of stucco apartment complexes, concrete shopping malls, and plastic neon signs have popped up like dandelions along the freeways that cut across the city.

Within a thirty-minute drive east, as the highway starts to climb, the homes begin to thin out, although new gray foundations and wooden building frames hold the promise that before long the sprawl will cover the lush, tree-covered western ridge of the mountains that separate San Diego from the parched sand and blistering heat of the desert.

Midway on the trip to El Centro, near the crest of the mountains, is the town of Pine Valley. It has a hotel, a couple of gasoline stations, a restaurant, and a fast-food stand. People who are heading east, into the desert, often stop there to put water in their car radiators. On the way out of the desert, they stop to get a drink for themselves.

A few miles beyond Pine Valley, our car filled with dry heat. We had passed Crestwood Summit, at 4,181 feet, the highest point of the highway, and were heading down into Imperial Valley, among mountains and hills strewn with boulders and dry scrub brush instead of pine trees. Even at sixty-five miles an hour and with the windows open the car was hot.

We passed by a town called Plaster City, as dry as its name, and then a sign that read, "Elevation: Sea Level." And the road was still going down. El Centro, like the desert floor itself, lies below sea level. Now the air before us shimmered in the heat. Everything but the black asphalt of the highway was parched and baked for miles across the valley to the lavender and brown mountains that enclosed it on the other side.

Twelve miles from El Centro, however, the earth suddenly turns lush. There is no gradual blending of brown to green as in the mountains. The line between miles of sand and miles of green is marked precisely by the irrigation ditch that is the first section of a massive watering system converting thousands of acres of dusty earth into one of the most productive growing areas in the United States.

Just before nine o'clock a tall plastic sign loomed against the desert sky, partially obscured in the haze of heat, as if it were encased in a gel. Gradually, the orange letters came into focus: "Denny's," it read. We turned off the exit, drove slowly past the restaurant, and took a short drive through the business area before meeting Norma. It was a town where the pace seemed slow, conditioned perhaps to the relentless heat; even on a February morning the temperature was near ninety degrees. We saw men working in pickup trucks, women in cotton print dresses, all deeply tanned— not the golden, glamorous brown of the beach crowd, but one burnished into their skin, like a callus that had built up a protective layer that seemed to shield them from the sun.

"Let's pull in here, Gene," I said.

He wheeled the car into the parking lot and looked at me.

"What do you want to stop here for?"

I pointed to the Baskin-Robbins sign on a nearby store. "I want some ice cream."

"At nine o'clock in the morning?"

"Sure. You want some?"

He shook his head. "Are you playing with a full deck?"

Ten minutes later we arrived at the Reliable Escrow Company, a pleasant single-story concrete-block building that was especially appealing because it was air-conditioned. When we walked in, Beth was working at a typewriter. She greeted us with a smile, introduced us to another woman working in the office, and went to fix us some coffee.

Norma walked out from behind a partition just after we entered. She said hello with a broad smile and seemed cheerful and comfortable in the surroundings of her office. Just in her stride, she appeared to be confident, happy, and oblivious of her pending trial in San Diego.

We chatted briefly over coffee, and then Norma and I set out for

Denny's. We walked around the parking lot and then into the restaurant, and Norma pointed to the first pink-and-tangerine vinyl booth, in which she said she and Hanscom had talked that afternoon nearly six months before. I could hear the clatter of the dishes coming from the kitchen, sounding much as it had on the tape of their meeting. Then we walked around to the back of the restaurant to the hotel area, where a maid cleaning rooms allowed us to look into one while Norma described her second meeting with Hanscom. It was not a complicated crime scene, to be sure, but now I had a mental picture to refer to when I confronted Hanscom and Ryan on the witness stand.

"Okay, Norma, now I'd like to go to one other place, the old shack where Bruce shot himself. Will you show me?"

She shrugged and nodded. "Okay, sure."

It was an eight-mile ride on Highway 8, past acre after acre of farmland that yielded principally lettuce, cotton, and hay. The heat was dry, and cars and trucks on the two-lane highway kicked up dust that settled on the surroundings like a thin layer of chalk.

I slowed the car down and pulled off the highway in front of an old rounded metal house trailer that was at least twenty years old and that sat in the middle of a yard filled with clutter. She pointed to a shack across the highway. "That's it," she said softly.

It was a small, run-down building, barely large enough for four rooms. The outside walls were made of tar paper, wooden shingles on the roof were torn up, and paint around the windows and doorways, where it existed, was peeling. It looked as if no one had maintained the building since Norma and Bruce had lived there twenty years earlier.

As I got out, I looked over at Norma.

"Do you mind if I wait here?" she asked.

"No, not at all. I won't be long."

I stepped quickly across the road and walked past an old mattress and a barrel overflowing with beer bottles, to the back of the house and a door. I pushed it open and went in. The floor creaked under my weight as I walked from what looked like the kitchen into a small dining room containing a large wooden table, one of the few pieces of furniture inside. I walked into the front bedroom, where, according to police reports, Bruce had taken his life. There was a window that looked directly onto the highway and from which Bruce could have seen clearly anyone who approached.

Back outside, I took a second look at the mattress, which, judging by its appearance, hadn't been there very long. It was much cleaner than the bottles and other litter in the yard. I picked up a corner of the mattress and turned it over. There, in the middle, was a large, dry dark-red bloodstain. I started at it for a moment, then let the mattress fall back to the ground. Then I took one last look at the shack and remembered the first words of Bruce's suicide note: "This is where our lives together started and a fitting place for mine to end."

I got back in the car. Norma wiped tears from her eyes, and we headed back to El Centro.

The desert light had faded from the sky by the time Tucker and I left El Centro to return to San Diego. It had been an instructive, fruitful visit, giving me a chance not only to see the crime scene, but to spend time with Norma where she was most comfortable. Now, during the two-hour ride back, Tucker and I had a chance to think and talk through the whole case.

I had talked again with Dr. Unger the day before, and his consultations with his colleagues and Dr. Ellison had confirmed his opinion that Norma had solicited murder while under hypnotic influence and against her own will. She had called Pappas in the presence and under the direction of Lovell and Ellie. She had walked into his office like an automaton and blurted out her request, as if she had been complying strictly with a hypnotic command. And to assure success, Lovell had driven her to Pappas's office and remained downstairs. Unger felt that Lovell's staying close to Norma was significant, because it had provided the hypnotist greater control and influence over his subject.

But when Norma had talked to Hanscom, Lovell had been about 110 miles away. I wanted Unger to hypnotize Norma again to see what we could learn about the Hanscom meeting. But the doctor said another session might induce anxiety panic or even a psychotic episode in Norma. We checked Norma's telephone records at Unger's suggestion and found that she had called Lovell's number between her two meetings with Hanscom. Lovell could have maintained some control over the telephone, Unger said.

Although the findings of Dr. Unger were encouraging, I felt that we might also need to argue that Lovell had had a motive of his own for wanting Bruce Winters out of the way. I thought we could establish that Lovell had both a sexual and a financial interest in having Bruce dead and Norma under his control.

But we still had a problem. Nearly all of the evidence regarding Lovell's involvement and motives came from Norma and Beth. We needed something independent of them to corroborate their stories. Without it, I felt, the whole defense was vulnerable to rebuttal testimony from Lovell himself. The district attorney could call him to the stand, where he could deny, as he had to me earlier, that he had driven Norma to the Associates Office Tower. He could deny any knowledge of the incident with Pappas. He could deny any knowledge of hypnosis. And the DA could argue that Norma and Beth were making it all up. With such an unusual defense, that argument, I imagined, could be very persuasive.

"Gene," I said, as we neared San Diego in his car, "you've got to find something that I can use to impeach Lovell if he gets on the stand. We've got to have something."

Tucker shook his head. "I've tried. I've tried like hell, Milt. But Lovell won't talk. Ellie won't talk. And you know how we've tried to track down his ex-wife and those hypnosis classes. We just don't have enough of a lead."

As we continued talking, Tucker switched on the dome light, and I looked through the documents we'd collected in the case—the police reports, Tucker's witness-interview notes—hoping something would jump out at me, some idea we hadn't tried. But it seemed we'd tried everything.

As we drove from the mountains down into Mission Valley, the bright lights lit up the sky. We passed the Mission Valley Inn, where several months before Tucker and I had confronted Wayne Connors. Further up, on the hillside, was the Presidio, the city's oldest landmark, with its commanding view of the valley.

And then it hit me.

"I've got it." I slapped Tucker on the arm. "I've got it, Gene. Why didn't I think of it before?"

"What?"

"We'll ask him."

"Who?"

"Lovell."

"Awww, come on," Tucker said, his voice deflated. "I think the desert heat has fried your brain. You know Lovell's not about to talk to us."

"But, Gene, he's got to talk to us."

"What do you mean, got to?"

"He sued Norma, remember? We'll get him to talk, under oath. We'll take his deposition."

CHAPTER 23

If Walter Lovell hadn't sued Norma Winters, he would never have exposed himself to the witness chair prior to her trial. In a civil case, but not in a criminal one, a witness can be subpoenaed to testify under oath as part of discovery before a trial. Larry Hannaford, Norma's civil attorney, who was working under Don Rushmore, could subpoena Lovell and take his deposition.

I called Hannaford the next morning. Coincidence, which had seemed to plague us early in our investigation, now rallied in our favor. He had already scheduled the deposition for February 7 in his law firm's office. I would not be present for it, but I thought if we carefully buried the questions I needed answered among the dozens Hannaford would ask, Lovell and his attorney would not be suspicious. Hannaford would want an explicit and complete listing of what services Lovell performed for Norma, anyway, especially of those rendered during the week of August 6 to 11, since he had charged her thirty dollars for nearly every waking hour she'd been with him in National City. He'd already told her that driving her to San Diego to shop for office furniture was among the services he'd provided. I thought Hannaford could legitimately ask him whether he'd also charged her for a trip to Anthony Pappas's or for an afternoon of hypnotic sessions.

Hannaford and I spent the afternoon of February 6 planning the questions. The deposition itself began on the seventh, but Lovell cut it short, saying he had a long-standing appointment for that afternoon. The rest of the statement was taken on February 11. By the fourteenth I had a complete copy of what Walt Lovell had said under oath about his business relationship with Norma Winters. It was also a study in Lovell's character. Hannaford's first three questions set the tone for the entire 220-page document:

Q.—Will you state your full name for the record, Mr. Lovell?

A.—Walter Nelson Lovell, L-o-v-e-l-l.

Q.—Have you ever been known by any other name?

A.—I am known daily as Walt Lovell.

Q.—Any other name?

A.—Negative.

When Hannaford asked him when he had married Ellen, Lovell replied, "Two days before Bruce Winters met his demise."

"Ellen is the sister of the late Bruce Winters, is that correct?"

"Correct—qualified," Lovell answered. "As I am told."

"What do you mean by that? I don't understand the qualification."

"Well, I wasn't there. I'm just being nitpicky right now. They have both told me they are sister and brother. I just want to make sure it was understood that I do not know that of any other knowledge."

Under persistent questioning Lovell conceded that he had not credited to Norma's account the $3,000 check she had written to him on the weekend she had told him she was hiring an accounting firm. Then Hannaford asked him about his office practices.

Q.—Do you keep any books or records which would indicate the status of each person's or entity's interest in moneys in your trust account?

A.—Not really. I sit down and pull them off just like this, off my check stubs and deposit tickets when necessary.

Q.—If you make a check payable to the order of some third party, is there any notation on that check which indicates that it is with reference to a particular client of yours?

A.—At times I have and at times I have not.

Q.—You just rely on your memory when you don't make such a notation as to what the balance in the trust account would be for any particular client?

A.—I do. You say I rely on memory. I run an adding machine

to find out where I am.

Q.—But how do you know, if there is no notation on the check?

A.—I rely on memory.

He also testified that despite having released Norma and her company as a client on September 14, he had deposited an insurance check of $1003.47, payable to Norma, into his trust account on October 14.

Q.—How was the check negotiated?

A.—Put in my trust account.

Q.—Who endorsed the check?

A.—I did.

Q.—How did you endorse the check?

A.—Norma Winters.

Q.—Did you have a power of attorney from Norma?

A.—No, I believe I had done this before with some of Norma's checks.

Hannaford referred to Norma's letter of September 30, informing Lovell she had retained an accountant.

Q.—Did you take this letter to mean that Norma Winters did not want you handling her affairs. . . .

A.—That's exactly how I took it.

Q.—Yet you received the check at some point in time subsequent to your receipt of the letter, is that correct?

After conferring with his attorney, Lovell replied, "Yes."

Q.—And you nonetheless went ahead and endorsed that check and deposited it into your trust account?

A.—It was—yes.

Lovell said he had still been transacting business for Norma's personal expenses and could not say precisely when their business relationship had ended. It sounded to me, however, as if he'd misappropriated a check made out to Norma. He had deposited the check in his trust account, but a review of the transactions in that account indicated that many checks written on it were for Lovell's personal expenses and not for the business expenses of his clients. One check was for a car he'd bought for Ellie. And a review of the bill he'd prepared as part of the suit showed no entry crediting Norma's account for $1,003.47.

When the deposition continued on the eleventh, Hannaford

asked about how Norma and Lovell had arranged for his consulting fees.

Q.—Do you recall during that conversation ever telling Norma that there wouldn't be any charge for your services because you were sort of in the family?

A.—No, sir, I made no such statement.

Q.—Do you recall in substance making such a statement?

A.—No, sir, I made no such statement, or, as you put it, in substance, such statement. My comments—if you're using it, a particular application of thought—my comment was that "I am too close, involved, in order to give a reasonable price. For that reason, I suggest you see an accountant in Imperial Valley and get a price from him and . . . I'll do it exactly for that."

It had been much later, he said, when he had informed Norma that his fee would be $30 per hour, significantly more than the $250 retainer and $50 a month fee he had originally agreed to after Norma had consulted an accountant. Norma had insisted that Lovell had never mentioned a fee of $30 per hour.

Lovell confirmed that he had been denied a Small Business Administration loan and that he had used a computer in his office.

Q.—Have you named that computer?

A.—Will you ask your question again?

Q.—Do you have a nickname for your computer?

A.—I do not.

Q.—You never referred to your computer as "Norm," being named after "Norma?"

A.—No. Oh, there was another computer. I have a computer, yes. I answered you correctly. There was another computer that I kicked out of my office a long time ago.

Q.—Did you ever refer to that computer's name as "Norm?"

A.—Yeah, that was a derogatory name, but that's beside the point. It was not intended to be, and I didn't find that out till later, that Norm and Norma are the masculine- and feminine-type names.

Q.—Did you ever tell Norma that you named that computer after her?

A.—Absolutely not. If I had done that, that would have been rather stupid, because I was having tremendous trouble with that particular computer, and it was the dirtiest thing I could call it.

He insisted that he had never planned to use some of Norma's SBA money to set up practice in El Centro, but he acknowledged his plans for an El Centro office.

Then Hannaford asked about the bill that broke down the hours Lovell had listed for Norma.

Q.—Is it correct to say that you were charging Norma Winters for sixty-nine hours of your time at thirty dollars an hour for assistance you provided to hold funerals for Bruce Winters and for assistance that you provided in flying the body of Bruce Winters to Tennessee?

A.—No, sir.

Q.—How is this statement incorrect?

A.—I was asked to provide. Other than that, that statement is correct.

Q.—Are you charging Norma Winters for those sixty-nine hours?

A.—It would seem that I am charging Norma, because she's the one who so requested my services.

Q.—Bruce Winters was your brother-in-law, wasn't he?

A.—Yes, Bruce Winters was my brother-in-law.

Q.—How would you characterize your relations with Bruce Winters just prior to his death?

A.—That would be difficult to say, because I had no direct, eyeball-to-eyeball contact with Bruce Winters just prior to his death. I think it had been a month earlier since I had seen him last.

Q.—I'm trying to determine whether or not you would, if Norma Winters had not asked, or purportedly had not asked, you to arrange for Bruce Winters's funeral—whether you would have done it as his brother-in-law on his behalf.

A.—No.

Q.—You didn't provide the services on behalf of Ellen, who was Bruce Winters's sister and your wife, did you?

A.—I did not.

Q.—It was only on behalf of Norma Winters?

A.—Absolutely. My wife had an additional responsibility that was thrust on her that should not have been put on her, and that is to go down to Imperial Valley and represent the family and take the body back to Tennessee, where a dutiful wife would have been present instead of my wife having to carry the responsibility and, also, under the responsibility of keeping her mouth shut.

Lovell charged Norma for sixty-nine hours of services between the time of Bruce's death and his funerals in El Centro and Tennessee; this came to more than eleven billable hours per day, according to Hannaford's calculations. Lovell said those services included telephone calls to find a minister, to contact an airline to fly the body to Tennessee, and to arrange for a casket for burial and another for transporting the body.

"I believe you indicated previously," Hannaford continued, "that it was at Norma's request that you performed these services. . . . What was the substance of what she said to you?"

A.—To arrange for the funeral—funerals.

Q.—Did you understand her to be saying, "I will pay you at your rate of thirty dollars an hour to arrange for these services?"

A.—When they're asked of me in my office, I understand that, yes.

Lovell could not recall specifically what Norma had said.

Q.—There was no mention, for example, of the thirty-dollar-an-hour figure?

A.—No.

Q.—It was strictly a businesslike conversation, as far as you're concerned?

A.—Uh-huh. Absolutely.

When Hannaford asked Lovell to review his handling of Norma's insurance checks, Lovell admitted that he had refused to turn over to her three checks from Prudential and that he had finally mailed them back to the insurance company on the advice of his attorney. He also said he had received a telephone call from a woman at Prudential, informing him that they had received a call from me asking for a stop payment on the three checks.

Q.—What was your response?

A.—I told the young lady that I had, at the time, which I had, turned the checks over to my attorney for mailing back, or the proper disposition.

Q.—What else can you recall regarding that conversation?

A.—Prudential indicated that they thought the checks probably should go to Norma. The lady asked me who Milton Silverman was, attorney-at-law, and I said he is representing Norma in the criminal complaint here in California, which was involved in Norma attempting to have Bruce Winters murdered.

After a brief conversation between the attorneys, Hannaford moved to the questions I was most concerned about.

Q.—Have you ever hypnotized Norma?

A.—No.

Q.—Have you ever told anyone that you have hypnotized Norma?

A.—No. Those answers are in direct response to your communication to me. I'll wait till you ask one that I can answer.

Q.—I don't understand what you're saying.

A.—I'm waiting for you to finish your line of questioning. I'm saying—answering no to the ones that, no, I've never hypnotized Norma.

Q.—Explain to me your interpretation of my question.

"Just a minute," Lovell's lawyer interrupted.

Lovell and his lawyer conferred for a moment.

"There was an attempt," Lovell said. "Norma Winters asked me to hypnotize her, and there was a winded discussion about people not being subject to hypnosis, and also the fact that I am not a hypnotist, that hypnosis is something more suggestive and responsive between two people. And Norma and Beth both at the same time—and I have no qualification in this area, and I have never purported to have any qualification in this area—both lay down on the floor in the living room, with my wife present—and I don't know who else may have been there—may have been other people, that place was constantly crowded—and I attempted to talk her to sleep. She was having violent headaches and complaining of this, that, and the other thing. This was a matter of in-house, home, personal-type thing."

Q.—Did that occur—

A.—Among the many hours that she was in my residence, and I don't remember whether it was before or after her arrest, or Bruce's death, or anything else. I really don't recall. I'd forgotten about that, in fact. . . .

Q.—How could you talk her to sleep?

A.—I didn't say that. I said I tried.

Q.—How could you try? Did she go to sleep?

A.—No. This is, to come back to your original question, I have never hypnotized Norma. I have no qualification in that area. Maybe someone capable could have done it, but I am not.

Q.—You said you attempted to talk her to sleep?

A.—Yes, sir, that's right.

Q.—What did you say to her during your attempt to talk her to sleep?

A.—In the parlor games of attempting to talk her to sleep, I said, "You are going to sleep," and I kept repeating it in a monotone that would have put a class to sleep, had I been lecturing to a class.

Q.—Did you ever during that time, request her to envision a single dot on the ceiling or a single leaf on a tree fluttering in the wind?

A.—I may have. I don't recall.

Q.—Did you ever tell Norma as she was lying on the floor that her arm or arms were becoming lighter, or something to that effect?

A.—I probably did.

Q.—Did you ever tell her that her nose or some other portion of her body itched?

A.—I probably did.

Q.—Can you tell me what her response was to those suggestions?

A.—She laughed.

Q.—Do you have any educational training whatsoever in hypnosis?

A.—I believe that I have already so indicated.

Q.—You have no educational training in hypnosis?

A.—That's what I already said just a few minutes ago. I'm not qualified. I have never had any educational courses.

Q.—Have you ever had any informal courses which you have attended regarding hypnosis?

A.—Yes.

Q.—How many such courses?

A.—They were not a course. As you specified in your question, they were informal, by a man called Leo Cook, who is, or was at the time, a police officer . . . who also, at the time that I knew him, had already published one or two books on the subject of hypnosis. . . .

Lovell said he had attended about ten sessions around 1963, all but one in Mr. Cook's home.

Q.—What did Leo Cook attempt to do during these sessions?

A.—Perform hypnosis. . . .

Q.—Did he ever attempt to impart any knowledge as to how to hypnotize a person to you?

A.—In generality, not in specifics.

Q.—Have you ever hypnotized anyone?

A.—Yes.

Q.—Whom?

A.—An ex-wife.

Q.—What was her name?

A.—A Mrs. Lovell.

Q.—Her first name?

A.—Janet.

Q.—But you have never placed either Beth or Norma under hypnosis at any time?

A.—I don't believe I ever have. That's why I so answered. When somebody laughs at what you say, obviously, they're not placed under hypnosis.

Q.—You have never told Gene Tucker or Milt Silverman that you have ever—

A.—I don't ever make a mistake like that.

Q.—either Norma or Beth under hypnosis?

A.—I don't recall that I ever have, no.

The "I don't make a mistake" remark intrigued me. It seemed clear that he had already made several under Hannaford's questioning. He had filled in one of our biggest holes: he had indeed been instructed in hypnosis, and he had admitted to hypnotizing his ex-wife. That he had denied having succeeded with Norma made no difference after that. We had another witness who knew better.

Then Hannaford asked Lovell about charges that Norma may have incurred during the time she had spent at his house right after Beth had told her about the incest.

Q.—Was Norma Winters staying at your apartment in National City during the week of 8/4/74 to 8/10/74.

A.—Probably.

Q.—Did you charge her for that?

A.—No.

Q.—And you aren't charging her for that?

A.—I am not charging her for that time or the many other weekends and week days and nights that she spent at my apartment.

Q.—Did you provide transportation for Norma at any time during that whole week?

A.—Norma Winters most generally had her own transportation, and when she did not, . . . she was welcome to use my car.

Q.—Did she use your car during that week, would you say?

A.—I don't recall.

Q.—Did she use your car on several occasions in August of 1974?

A.—I don't know if she has ever driven my car personally. I think perhaps Beth has driven my car. I know my wife has chauffeured them around considerably, and I know that I have chauffeured them around considerably.

Q.—But you don't recall Norma, herself, driving your car?

A.—No, I don't.

Q.—Did you let Norma Winters use your business or residence telephone during that week?

A.—It was always available to her to use.

Q.—Both telephones?

A.—Wherever she was.

Q.—Was it during that week, that is, the week 8/4/74 to 8/10/74 that Norma went to Anthony Pappas's office?

A.—I believe it was.

Q.—Do you know how Norma got there?

A.—If it is the occasion that I am aware of, I drove her to the Associates Office Tower.

Q.—Which occasion are you aware of at this point in time?

A.—There was a time, a date—I don't remember the date—that I did drive her to the Associates Office Tower. She had a letter from Pappas, which I had read, that offered her a free meal and drinks.

Under further questioning, Lovell acknowledged that he had "no basic yardstick" for making the distinction between the business and nonbusiness aspects of his relationship with Norma, but that much of the chauffeuring he had done for her—driving her around to look for office space, to pick up business forms, to shop for carpeting and office equipment—was charged as a business expense, at thirty dollars an hour. I wondered as I read the deposition why Norma hadn't taken a taxi instead. I also wondered whether the trip to Pappas's had been business or personal.

Personal, Lovell explained, and on that basis, his lawyer thwarted Hannaford's persistent efforts to determine whether Lovell knew why Norma had paid Pappas a visit or whether he had discussed it with her beforehand. But that would have been frosting on the cake. The deposition had been successful beyond my most fervent hopes. Lovell had filled in the two critical holes by acknowledging his skills in hypnosis and by admitting that he had driven Norma to Pappas's. We now had more than enough evidence to deal with Lovell if the prosecution decided to call him to the stand.

The investigation of the evidence was complete. Now we faced our final problem: we needed a defense, a legal context in which to present this bizarre set of facts to the jury. This was not a case of did she do it or didn't she. Norma did it. She solicited the murder of her husband. Our investigation established that she did not *intend* to commit that crime. The cornerstone of Anglo-American law is the principle that guilt is personal and that a person cannot be convicted of a crime unless there is a concurrence of an evil act *(actus reus)* and an evil intent *(mens rea)*. It was one that I'd been exposed to in my first week of law school. The case books were filled with examples: the man who sits all day contemplating the murder of his neighbor, but who performs no act of murder, is not guilty of any crime; the sleepwalker who discharges a gun into the air and kills a bystander is likewise not guilty of a crime. I remembered no examples in the casebooks with evidence quite like that which we'd uncovered in the case of Norma Winters.

In order to find the legal context that we needed to argue that Norma had indeed lacked criminal intent, I reviewed my book of California Jury Instructions, Criminal, commonly known as CAL-JIC, a compendium of instructions that a judge gives to juries just before they begin deliberations.

The instruction that most closely fit Norma's case was the rarely used one on unconsciousness, which reads:

> When a person commits an act without being conscious thereof, such act is not criminal, even though if committed by a person who was conscious, it would be a crime. This rule of law applies only to cases of the unconsciousness of persons of sound mind, such as somnambulists or persons suffering from the delirium of fever, epilepsy, a blow on the head or the involuntary taking of drugs or intoxicating liquor, and other cases in which there is no functioning of the conscious mind.

Norma was definitely a person of "sound mind," according to Dr. Ellison. And, in a legal sense, she had taken the drugs involuntarily. The courts had held that anyone using drugs without knowing their contents or their effects on the body was taking them involuntarily. Furthermore, Norma had taken the pills by prescription, under the direction of a physician.

It was the last sentence that gave us problems. Dr. Unger had explained to me that a person under hypnosis has a definite "functioning of the conscious mind" and that he would so testify. The person is aware of his or her actions, but is powerless to stop them because the hypnotic suggestion capitalizes on a strong underlying emotion. The suggestion Dr. Unger said, impinges upon or compromises the will, not the functioning of the conscious mind. We would have to research the case law to see whether any precedents existed that coincided with the evidence.

Late one night shortly before the trial Eric Miller and I adjourned to my law library on the third floor of my office and began the search. Within an hour the room smelled of strong coffee and cigar smoke. Books had been pulled off shelves and were lying open in piles on the table. We pored intently over the volumes.

Finally, Eric broke the silence. "Unconsciousness includes not only a state of coma or immobility, but also a condition in which the subject acts without awareness," he said.

"What case is that?"

"*People* v. *Harrington,* 32 Cal. App. 3rd 10."

"It's not right on," I said. "We need to nail down volition, not awareness. Check out the key note on this one," I said, pointing to *People* v. *Sedeno,* "and see if you can track it down through the digest system."

The books in a law library are systematically and elaborately indexed and can direct those who know how to use them to precisely the points they need to cover. Those who don't know the indexing system can be driven nuts by it.

We continued to work quietly for a while, gulping coffee, making notes, and pulling still more books off the shelves.

"All right, Milt!" Eric exclaimed. "All right! Paydirt!" He walked toward me, holding a book in his hand and reading as he approached.

"*People* v. *Hardy, People* v. *Metherver,* and *People* v. *Rothrock* all contain language that this instruction, the unconsciousness instruction in CALJIC, 'contemplates only unconsciousness of persons of sound mind who suffer from some force that leaves their acts without volition.' That's our case!"

"You're damn right it is," I smiled. "Sheppardize it and see if it's still good law."

Eric checked the Sheppard's index and soon emerged with the verdict. "Clean as a whistle," he said. "That's the law. That is the law!"

Meanwhile, I found another case, that of Black Panther Huey Newton, in which the court indicated that a "hypnotic drug" would qualify a defendant for the unconsciousness defense.

It was a few more hours before we exhausted the trail of cases and satisfied ourselves that there was a consistent theme to them and that nothing was hidden in the volumes that the DA could use to sabotage our argument. We went back to the CALJIC instruction, penciled out the last line, and wrote in our own: "Unconsciousness also contemplates persons of sound mind who suffer from some force that leaves their acts without volition."

At the proper time I would argue from the cases we'd found and urge the judge to modify the instruction to accommodate that language. Whether that motion was won or lost could well determine the outcome of the trial and the fate of Norma Winters.

Finding the defense was the culmination of a month of incredible discoveries and good fortune: we'd learned of the hypnosis; we'd found Dr. Unger; we'd gotten Lovell's deposition. And now we'd found buried in a law book the phrase that was the key to our case. It was a heady time. Six weeks before, I'd had a bunch of unanswered questions and an otherwise straightforward case with a guilty client. Now not only had we turned up evidence of the most bizarre crime I'd ever encountered, we had put the evidence together into a coherent and logical defense, with the law to back us up.

The trial was imminent. It was the end of February, and we were trailing—waiting for one of the courtrooms, now all busy with trials, to open up. The wait was nerve-racking, and a time for second thoughts.

Late one afternoon, I asked one of my law partners to make himself comfortable in a big leather chair in our office, and I described the case to him. It took more than an hour to tell the story. I wanted to make sure that nothing critical was left out. He listened intently and with fascination, interrupting occasionally to ask a pertinent question. Finally, I explained that I felt the unconsciousness instruction would be changed and that because Norma had been hypnotized, the jury would find her innocent.

There was silence for a moment.

"Is that it?" he asked finally.

"Yes, that's it," I said. "What do you think?"

He nodded slightly, his index finger touching his lips. "Honest opinion?"

"Yeah, honest opinion."

"Milt, I think you're nuts."

I respected my partner and his assessment was sobering. I had no doubt Norma was innocent. Our investigation had uncovered the truth. Still, the trial was a gamble. From here on, the case was a chain of ifs—*if* we got a fair judge, *if* we got a decent jury panel, *if* we picked the right jurors, *if* we got Ellison's and Unger's testimonies in, *if*. . . . Were we going to get laughed out of the courtroom?

It went further than that. I thought our evidence on the first count—involving Pappas—was solid. Norma had blurted out her request. Lovell had been waiting for her outside. She had revealed the involvement of Lovell and Ellie in dramatic and convincing fashion during the hypnotic session with Unger. But the second count was more tenuous. Had Norma been trying to avoid getting caught with her concern over payments and her scheduled date with Wayne Connors, or had she truly been under the influence of a posthypnotic suggestion? It was a difficult question, and while I trusted and unequivocally believed Dr. Unger's opinion, it was an issue, it seemed, on which reasonable people might disagree. If only Unger could have hypnotized Norma one more time. What would she have revealed about her meetings with Hanscom?

Yet, what could we lose? The prosecution had offered no deal worth considering: plead to one count and dismiss the other. That was no deal. One count was the same as two. If we went to trial and lost both counts, the judge would surely sentence Norma to concurrent terms.

I explained all of this to Norma and asked her what she thought. She left the decision to me.

Alone in my beach house that night, I scanned the books I had aligned along the fireplace mantle, books about Darrow and Fallon and Rodgers and Streicher and Bailey and Erlich. They were the great criminal lawyers America had produced. I'd read and reread their cases. The men were quite different in style, in manner, in approach to their cases and the law. But they all shared at least one important quality—courage.

If Norma Winters were their client, I asked myself, would they take her case to trial? Absolutely.

So, I decided, would I.

PART III

The Trial

" 'A singular case,' remarked Holmes."

The Sign of the Four

CHAPTER 24

The San Diego County Courthouse is a modern, sprawling structure that occupies two city blocks in the downtown area. It was built with expansion in mind, and unlike courthouses with marble pillars and wisdom etched in granite, this one has a steel-beam-and-concrete facade, a strictly utilitarian design. Inside, a maze of corridors and stairways winds around and through the four to seven floors, depending on which section of the building you're in, and the unitiated need a map to avoid getting lost.

I had hoped to try only one of Norma's charges in this courthouse—the one involving Anthony Pappas. Two weeks earlier, before another judge, I had argued a motion challenging San Diego County's jurisdiction on the second count, concerning her approach to Al Hanscom. Except for Hanscom's telephone call from the San Diego police station, the entire episode had occurred in Imperial County, and that's where I thought that charge should be tried. If Hanscom had called from Nebraska, I argued, would that mean authorities in that state would have jurisdiction over the case? The prosecution had maintained that the governing action on both counts was Norma's visit to Pappas's office—in San Diego. The judge agreed, and ordered both counts be tried in San Diego.

Splitting the two charges would have worked to Norma's advantage, I figured. The Pappas count standing alone seemed weak, because Norma's inept approach to him made her intent arguable.

Trying the second and stronger count—where Norma had paid money and provided a description and other information that suggested a clearer intent—in Norma's backyard might cast her in the role of victim and evoke sympathy from the jury. After all, what was a big-city police department, especially the unit that investigated underworld assassinations, doing in El Centro, ganging up on this ordinary, unfortunate woman whose daughter had been sexually violated by her father?

I had one other reason for filing the motion. If the court erred in its ruling, and Norma was then convicted, the case might be reversed on appeal. In some circles, this is referred to in whispered conversations as "creating error." I think it's an important and legitimate way to protect a client.

But that was behind me now as Norma, Beth, David, and I rode up the escalator to the third floor and walked down the long hallway to department nine, the presiding department of the criminal calendar for the superior court. That courtroom was crowded with lawyers, clients, and witnesses, some of whom, like us, were trailing and waiting for an open trial department. I'd been walking the hallways for the past week, checking calendars and talking with lawyers and clerks to see what might be opening up. As we walked into the courthouse that morning, March 4, 1975, I knew of two departments where trials had been completed. And I knew we were near the top of the list.

Although the judicial system, ideally, should offer equal justice from courtroom to courtroom, every trial lawyer knows that the judge sitting on the bench can make a substantial difference in the kind of trial that plays out in front of the jury. The judge who sat in one of the two open courtrooms was widely respected as one of the fairest and most attentive judges in San Diego County—Judge Thomas Maine in department five. I'd had a run-in with the judge in the other courtroom, and I suspected I'd have a difficult time with him, especially with a defense as unusual as the one I was to present. (That judge is no longer sitting.)

"The People versus Norma Winters," the clerk in department nine announced.

"People ready," the prosecutor said.

"Ready for the defense," I said, approaching the bench.

The judge looked down at us. "Gentlemen, we have one department that hears short-cause matters on Friday and is available on
a four-day basis. Is that satisfactory?"

"That's satisfactory," the prosecutor said.

I rocked back on my heels. Did department five hear short-cause
motions on Fridays? "That's satisfactory to the defense."

"Very well," the judge nodded. "This matter is assigned to
department five, Judge Maine."

Edward Morrison, the deputy district attorney prosecuting the
case, and I headed for the customary pretrial meeting with the
judge. We stepped quickly through the courtroom, where the trial
would be held, to a back corridor that led to his chambers. His
clerk ushered us into a small, pleasant room with a couch and red
leather chairs. The judge greeted us by our first names and nodded
for us to sit down. He sat intently behind his desk while we briefed
him on the case. The trial would run seven to ten days, we es-
timated. Morrison outlined the prosecution's case. I told the judge
about Bruce Winters's suicide and suggested that if the jury knew
that my client's husband had killed himself three days after she had
sought to have him murdered, it could influence its view of the
case. If the issue came up in court, I said, I was prepared to call
witnesses to explain those events—that Bruce took his life out of
fear of the consequences of his relationship with his daughter, not
out of grief over his wife's action. Both Judge Maine and Morrison
agreed that the suicide was not germane to Norma's case and that
all witnesses should be directed not to mention it in their testimony. I also asked the judge to allow Dr. Nyquist to sit with me
at the counsel table during jury selection. With no objection from
Morrison, the judge granted the request. Within fifteen minutes our
business was concluded, and we returned to the courtroom to await
the beginning of the trial.

The courtroom was small, about the size of two school class-
rooms, just slightly longer than it was wide. It was informally
paneled with dark-brown walnut and a gold carpet, establishing a
comfortable, almost intimate setting for the trial. Books lined the
wall on the left as we entered. The jury box was on the right. There
were no ornate murals or shiny mahogany pillars to lend an air of

grandeur to the setting. A simple gold seal of the state of California hung behind the judge's bench, which was elevated about three feet and provided a clear view of the witness stand and the jury box to the judge's left and the counsel tables several feet in front of the bench.

By tradition the prosecution occupies the table closest to the jury box, the defense the far table. Norma took the seat to my right at the defense table, between Morrison and me, providing a small measure of privacy for my notes and whispered conversations. I told Beth and David to sit in the gallery directly behind, and slightly to our left, so that when the jurors looked at Norma, they would also see her children. Many of the other seats in the gallery were occupied by the thirty-one members of the jury panel from whom we would select twelve jurors and two alternates to hear Norma's case.

We rose in unison as the bailiff announced the judge's entrance. The judge stepped up to the bench, smiled, and took his seat.

"Good afternoon, ladies and gentlemen," he said.

"Good afternoon, Your Honor," I replied.

"This is the case of the People of California versus Norma Winters."

"Ready for the People. Edward Morrison on behalf of the People."

"Ready for the defendant. Milt Silverman on behalf of the defendant, Mrs. Winters."

"Would you swear the prospective jurors?" the judge said.

Maine spoke in a deep, resonant voice. He had wavy gray hair and a stern face. In appearance and demeanor he was the prototype of a judge.

With the prospective jurors sworn, the clerk called out twelve names, and one by one the vacant seats in the jury box were filled. "It shall be the duty of the trial court to examine the prospective jurors to select a fair and impartial jury," the judge announced.

The juror, in my view, is the most important person in a trial. It doesn't matter how good the case, how able the lawyers, how great the cross-examination, or how persuasive the summation. What matters is, what does the man or woman in the box think of it?

Jury selection, although a slow and sometimes tedious process, is thus one of the critical stages of a trial. Indeed, one mistake by either the prosecution or the defense in qualifying jurors means failure, for in a criminal case it takes twelve jurors to acquit and twelve to convict. Eleven out of twelve doesn't count.

Each juror brings to the box a certain set of attitudes based on such factors as educational background, age, sex, religious convictions, and marital and job status that come to bear in a variety of ways, depending on the nature of the case. A juror sitting at a trial of a husband accused of murdering his wife might react differently if it was, instead, the wife who was accused of murdering the husband. A high-school teacher who is Catholic may respond to the same case otherwise than a truckdriver who is Catholic. The key is to determine the critical themes in the evidence and then to figure out how each juror will respond to them emotionally.

Nyquist and I met for several hours to discuss the case and to determine the kind of juror we preferred to hear it. We outlined the themes with key words this way:

A *mother* learns that her *daughter* has been *assaulted* and *incestualized* by her *natural father*, who is a *federal officer*. The woman has been taking *diet pills* containing *amphetamines*. The mother and daughter agree on an *abortion* when the daughter thinks she is *pregnant*. The incest has occurred for several years, and the mother has just learned about it. A *bizarre* set of events then takes place. The mother is *hypnotized* by her *financial consultant* and *brother-in-law* to solicit the murder of her husband. The suggestion comes from the *sister* of the target. The woman can't remember certain things until placed under *hypnosis* by a *psychiatrist* who is a *professor*. The prosecution's case is *overwhelming*, but if you *wait* until you hear the defense, you'll see that she is *innocent*.

From that, and from Nyquist's study of the psychological and sociological literature and his own clinical experience, we also characterized an ideal juror: a married woman who had two children, aged seven to fourteen, who worked, who went to church (any faith), who joined the PTA, and who lived in a middle- to upper-middle-class neighborhood—a woman much like Norma Winters.

We also decided on an ideal male juror and on the potential

jurors, both male and female, whom we would automatically challenge.

As Judge Maine asked his preliminary questions of the prospective jurors, however, it was clear that we would have to rely on more than our "ideal juror" profile. Only eight of the thirty-one members of the panel were women, and the judge immediately excused three of them because they were nearing the end of their jury duty. But we also used a technique Nyquist had used in previous trials. We would not only listen to the jurors as they responded to questions from the judge, Morrison, and me. We would also watch them.

Nyquist is an expert in the science of kinesics, more commonly known as body language. Slight changes in gestures, shifts of the eyes, arms, or legs, and their timing can alter the meaning of what a juror is saying. Did a juror lean away from me as I spoke? As he spoke? Did another shift in her seat and cross her legs? Did another straighten his tie when the woman next to him spoke? I don't understand kinesics and don't know what to look for. But I knew that Nyquist did, and he had Hank Lansford, a graduate student, in court with us to help out. As the jurors responded to the questions over the next day and a half, I listened carefully. Nyquist and Lansford listened and watched.

The judge elicited the biographical information—age, marital status, home, prior jury experience—that was helpful in drawing our profiles. Nyquist scribbled the information on sheets in front of him and jotted down his impressions. He also kept an eye on Lansford, who was unobtrusively sending him signals from a seat in the gallery.

When the judge finished the questions, it was my turn to approach the jury. This part of the trial is known as the *voir dire,* and although it is designed only to select the jury, other forces are inevitably at work. For both attorneys it is the only opportunity to present themselves instead of the case to the jury—and thus to establish some rapport. It also gives the defense lawyer an opportunity to suggest the parameters of the case even before the presentation of the evidence begins. Indeed, I consider the selection of the jury the most important component of the trial, and it seemed especially significant in the case of Norma Winters.

"Ladies and gentlemen," I began, "my first question is my most important one. Since you have all served as jurors before, you know that someone has to go first in this case. That is going to be the prosecution. Before the close of the case, you are going to wonder what I'm doing here in the courtroom, because the prosecution's case is going to sound quite formidable. I want to know from each of you as my first, most important, question that you will wait and keep an open mind until you have heard the defendant's side of this case." I paused. "Do I have your personal assurance from each and all of you in that regard?"

The jurors nodded. I intended to remind them of that promise at the end of the trial.

Then I drew on the themes of the case for several more questions.

"There will be evidence in this case of repeated violent sexual assaults upon the daughter of Mrs. Winters. Has any member here had any experience at all that they feel would disqualify him from sitting as a juror in a case of this kind?"

The jurors shook their heads. A few seemed uncomfortable with the question, but I didn't make any guesses about the significance of their response; that was Nyquist's responsiblity.

"Does any juror have any experience in the area of diet pills?" I continued. "Does anyone here have an opinion as to what effect a rapid weight loss has on someone's mental condition? By rapid weight loss I am talking about a weight loss of sixty to eighty pounds within a period of four months."

No one indicated they had.

"Has anyone had any experience with amphetamine tablets?"

No one had.

Initially, there was little verbal response to my questions. After all, it's not easy to speak up in a crowded courtroom and tell a stranger your feelings about incest, abortion, and amphetamines. But after several general questions, addressed to the entire panel, I talked directly to each juror.

"Miss Maguire," I said, addressing juror number one, a twenty-eight-year-old woman who sat in the top left-hand corner of the box, "do you have any information as to the scientific value of hypnosis?"

"I have been to hypnosis shows," she said. "That is about my extent of knowledge. On a theatrical basis only."

"All right. You have no opinions as to the scientific validity of the discipline of hypnosis? Its power? Its scope?"

"I imagine that my opinion would be, if the person being hypnotized really believes in the person that was hypnotizing them, I'm sure it would have some effect on them."

"Why might you believe that? Is that from seeing these shows, or have you read anything?"

"No, I haven't read anything in particular on hypnosis, no."

"Thank you."

I looked to another juror, Mr. Edwards, asked him the ages of his daughters, and then raised the subject of hypnosis again. That brought my adversary to his feet.

"I'll object to the question," Morrison said. "I don't feel it goes to the cause as defined by the penal code."

"Yes," the judge answered. "The objection is sustained."

"Could I be heard at the bench, Your Honor?" I asked.

He nodded, and Morrison and I walked to the side bar where we could confer with the judge over legal points without the jury's hearing us.

"Your Honor," I said, "there will be testimony in this case from a psychiatrist who will testify relating to the defendant's state of mind at the time this offense was committed, and he will give an opinion relating to whether she was under hypnosis at the time that the offense was committed."

The judge considered the statement, and glanced toward Morrison.

"I think the question as phrased, Your Honor, asks the jurors to make a prejudgment of the evidence, or a prejudgment."

"Let me have the language of the question," the judge said.

The court reporter read the question: "Have you an opinion as to the scientific reliability of hypnosis?"

The judge leaned forward. "Well, I think for the purposes that you have indicated, that it probably is proper. I will reverse my decision and let you go into it."

"Thank you," I said.

As I returned to question the jurors, the judge looked at the panel. "I had sustained the objection," he said. "I feel my ruling was wrong, and at this time I will overrule the objection."

The question was read back to the juror.

"No, I don't," he answered.

"Mr. Edwards, would you have any strong feelings if evidence came in relating to the feasibility of an abortion—conversations between Beth Winters and Norma Winters?"

"I don't think so. I read pro and con on abortion. I think it all depends on the circumstances that are involved."

It is often important to appreciate the obvious. Can a juror hear? Is he or she able to comprehend technical, scientific evidence? And I'm particularly wary of jurors who show "dissonance"—the housewife dressed like a flashy college student, the businessman in a three-piece suit and dirty fingernails and scruffy shoes. Are these people trying to be people they aren't? Are they fooling themselves or you?

Although the final decision regarding a juror is mine, I have never accepted one whom Nyquist had rated a minus on his four-point scale of plus, plus over minus, minus over plus, and minus. I was impressed with one juror's answers to my questions. When I glanced down and saw that Nyquist had scored him as a minus, I tapped my finger on the sheet, indicating I wanted him to reconsider. Then I asked the juror more questions. Again, his answers seemed fine. But Nyquist drew another minus. When Morrison took over the questioning, I sat down and whispered, "I like seven." Nyquist shook his head. "He's lying through his teeth." Seven was my next peremptory challenge.

Jury selection continued through the first day and into the morning of the second. Morrison and I alternated frequently as jurors were challenged, opening up a spot for a new juror and more questions. I liked a middle-aged Mexican woman who had a cross dangling from her neck. Morrison challenged her. Although he was working alone, his questions and his challenges demonstrated his understanding of the few soft spots he foresaw in his case. The defendant, he said, was a pleasant, attractive woman. Would that be reason enough for a jury to acquit her? Would they be influenced by pity for her? Did they agree to follow the law and not vote out of sympathy or compassion for her?

He presented one line of questioning that seemed particularly effective. Would the mere fact that the case was going to trial cause the jury to doubt the prosecution's case? The inference invited sympathy for his position. Here he was, a prosecutor going about his job, discharging his public obligation, and the defense lawyer was telling the jury the case against his client was overwhelming. Was he supposed to be blamed for that? Were they going to hold him to a higher standard of proof just because the defense lawyer told them the case was formidable? He advanced the position well, making the point that while the guilty had a right to a fair trial, they didn't have a right to an acquittal.

Some questions were designed not so much to elicit negative answers, but to make the jurors think carefully about their responsibility in the case.

"If you were the defendant in this case," I asked Miss Maguire, who was still ensconced in the first chair in the box, "if you were sitting where Mrs. Winters is sitting, would you want yourself as a juror in this case?"

She paused a moment, as if imagining herself at the defense table. "Yes," she said, "I would."

I had no doubt I wanted her on the jury, and eleven others like her.

By noon on the second day, we'd selected a jury of ten men, including one black, two women, and two male alternates. Nyquist and I were satisfied with the *voir dire* and each of the jurors. I was convinced we had a fair jury, one that would at least be willing to hear and carefully consider the evidence we were to present. I suspected that, with questions about incest, drugs, and hypnosis running through their minds during the lunch recess, at least some of the jurors couldn't wait to hear it.

CHAPTER 25

T he trial opened that afternoon. Morrison had Al Hanscom with him at the prosecution table. I sat with Norma at the defense table. The children were behind us.

"Mr. Morrison," the judge asked, "are you ready to make your opening statement?"

"Yes, Your Honor."

Morrison assumed an air of formality as he strode to the lectern between our tables and the judge's bench and faced the jury.

"Ladies and gentlemen," he said, "what I am about to tell you is not evidence, just as nothing you have heard to this point in the trial is evidence, because the evidence in this case is going to come to you in the form of testimony from this witness stand." He gestured to the empty seat between the judge and the jury box.

Morrison apparently wanted to minimize the effect of the *voir dire.* Evidence or not, I thought the unusual series of questions had suggested to the jury that we intended to present some evidence worthy of their consideration.

"What is this evidence?" Morrison continued. "First of all, by virtue of a stipulation and agreement between Mr. Silverman and myself, we are going to establish that during the time in question, that is, between August eighth and August fifteenth of 1974, Norma Winters, the defendant in this case, was the beneficiary on a number of insurance policies. These policies were in the amounts of $21,926.51, two policies each in the amount of $5,210.32, and, finally, a fourth policy in the amount of $25,000. Now, these policies, we will agree . . . are policies which insured the life of the husband of Mrs. Winters, Bruce Winters, with Mrs. Winters being the beneficiary under those policies."

Then he previewed for the jury the basic elements in the case: Norma's two telephone calls to Pappas on August 8 and 9; the 4 P.M. meeting on August 9, in which "one of the first things out of her mouth" was her request for him to help kill her husband; the phone call from Al Hanscom; her two meetings with him at Denny's and the hotel room in which she paid him money and provided a photograph and other descriptive information, and her arrest by Sergeant Ryan.

"The evidence will show, ladies and gentlemen, that Mrs. Winters, on August the ninth, when she contacted Mr. Pappas, . . . solicited his aid in attempting to have her husband killed, and on the subsequent date, when she met Officer Hanscom at the Denny's Coffee Shop and at the Holiday Inn, did, in fact, solicit the crime of murder, and it will be based upon this evidence that at the conclusion of the case the people will ask you to return a verdict of guilty."

It was a brief statement that outlined an uncomplicated case. In terms of Norma's specific act—soliciting murder— it seemed quite simple. It was her state of mind that we thought was in question. Morrison didn't know that yet. His first statement of evidence to the jury concerned the insurance policies. I jotted the word "insurance" down on my legal pad. Did he really think this was an insurance case?

It was the defense's turn to make an opening statement, but I asked the judge to reserve that right until the conclusion of the prosecution's case. I exercise that option whenever possible. Some attorneys think it spots the People an advantage, because it leaves a major statement of their case unanswered in the jury's mind. But I had already suggested elements of the defense during the *voir dire,* and I prefer to present my opening statement when I know exactly what the evidence is against my client. If the DA tells the jury he will prove the defendant pulled the trigger of a murder weapon, it doesn't help your case to admit that in your opening statement, only to find out later that the prosecution can't prove it.

Morrison read into the record our stipulation about the insurance policies, subject to my request that the evidence include the dates the policies were issued. All of them had been in effect for several years; there was no recent increase in the amounts to suggest a motive for Norma's wanting her husband dead.

Morrison then called his first witness, Al Hanscom.

Hanscom walked smartly to the stand. He was wearing a brown sport jacket over a brown print Qiana shirt and tan pants. His long curly hair and full mustache gave his face a mischievous rather than a mean look, and he smiled broadly as he took the stand. He didn't look like a hit man.

Morrison's first order of business with Hanscom was the recorded telephone call the policeman had made to her on Monday, August 12, the day before he had gone to El Centro. Under the court's procedures, Morrison asked the bailiff to hand out copies of the transcript of the call to the jurors, so they could read along as the tape was played in the courtroom.

"Your Honor," Morrison said, turning to face the judge, "while these are being passed out, at this time I would make a motion to exclude witnesses."

"All witnesses?" the judge asked.

I rose slowly to my feet and turned to look first at the children and then at the judge. "Your Honor, may I be heard on that?" I sensed Morrison was working for a delay here, to give the jury time to read and fully digest the transcript. I wasn't happy about that, but the issue of the children was more important.

"The only two witnesses that I have in the courtroom are the daughter and son of Mrs. Winters," I said, "and I would request that they be allowed to remain." I looked over at them again. "Their mother is on trial here."

The judge called us to the bench for a conference out of earshot of the jury. Morrison said he didn't know why the children were going to be put on the witness stand, but they would hear testimony throughout the trial.

"It's going to solidify in their minds . . . certain facts, I think, and will not allow us the freedom of cross-examination to point out any inconsistencies in their testimony, if their testimony is allowed." He was particularly concerned about testimony regarding the incest issue.

"Well, I'm not willing to exclude any witnesses," I said. "The only two that happen to be present in the courtroom that I could conceivably anticipate calling are the son and daughter. . . . I can't see how anything that Al Hanscom would testify to would in any way influence [their] testimony."

"There is another problem, Your Honor," Morrison countered. "And I don't know if the court can see it now, but the daughter, Beth Winters, was crying. I think there is also a problem with potential emotional outbursts." Such incidents, he argued, tend to influence a case, even though they are not evidence.

"Your Honor, there has not been, in my view, a single impropriety on the part of the children. They have sat there quietly."

The judge paused for a moment, regarded Beth and David seated near their grandmother, then looked back down at us. "Well, this is somewhat of an unusual type case," he said. "It is not a question, for the most part, at least from the standpoint of this witness— perhaps other witnesses—of a factual difference, and I think under the circumstances that I will exercise my discretion and not exclude witnesses in this case." Morrison's motion was denied.

Norma turned around in her chair to look at Beth and David, then faced the front of the room again, and with her handkerchief wiped tears from her eyes. Morrison had given me an unexpected opportunity to introduce the children to the jury before they took the witness stand. They added an important psychological element in the courtroom, I thought. I wanted the jury to see Norma as a warm, clean-cut person and a caring mother. I knew that image would clash at least for a while with what was to come, especially with the first real evidence to be presented in the case—the recording of the phone call.

The tape was not played at a high volume, but it didn't have to be. Norma's voice was crystal clear, and the critical, damaging phrases filled an otherwise silent courtroom.

"I understand you have a problem," Hanscom said.

"On what?"

"Something you want to get rid of."

"Mmmm, yeah."

Then Norma: "I don't know if we're talking about the same thing, I don't know."

"I'm talking about something you want done."

"Yes. Okay."

Norma again: "I hope you're not setting me up, I swear to God I do."

And then Hanscom asks, "Are you interested or not?"

"I am," Norma replies. "Most definitely."

When the tape ended, Beth and David were pale. Norma seemed as if she had never heard the voice before. But her facial muscles appeared strained. For the first time since we had entered the courtroom, she looked frightened.

The transcripts were collected, and Hanscom resumed his testimony, confirming that he had met Norma at Denny's Coffee Shop the next afternoon. Since the tape of their conversation there was all but obliterated by the clatter of dishes and other background noise, Morrison was unable to have it played in the courtroom. Instead, using a transcript, he took Hanscom through the conversation, almost line by line. The evidence began to stack up against Norma.

Hanscom informed the jury that, from the beginning of their conversation, Norma had kept pressing him to see if he was "on the level," to see if he was a cop. And she had said she was "serious, dead serious."

He testified that Norma had told him she wanted her husband killed because she was scared of him and because of the sexual attacks on her daughter.

"Now, at that time, after she told you about the daughter," Morrison asked, "did you make inquiry of Mrs. Winters as to whether or not she was going to receive anything as a result of Mr. Winters's demise, or death?"

"Yes. I asked her how much she was going to get out of the insurance."

"And what, if anything, did Mrs. Winters say to you about that at that point in time?"

"She said that she hadn't even thought about it."

The prosecution's first witness, on the first mention of insurance, had undermined it as a motive. It seemed like an unusual strategy if Morrison wanted the jury to consider the insurance policies.

Hanscom testified about Norma's concern over explaining the $10,000 fee, and then about her request that he give her husband a message.

"She said she wanted you to give her husband a message?" Morrison asked, repeating the answer to make sure the jury heard it again.

"A message before I killed him."

"And did she indicate to you what this message was to be?"

"Yes. I was to tell him that 'this is from your wife for what you did to your daughter." . . . I indicated to her that she sounded like she really was serious and really wanted him—I think I used the word 'planted.' She replied, 'I hate his guts. I hate his goddamned guts.' "

When he had said he wanted to do the job by Friday, Hanscom testified, Norma had objected, saying, "You're going to screw up my weekend." He told the jury she hadn't wanted it done on Saturday night, because she didn't want to have an alibi for where she was going to be that night, so he had agreed to do it Sunday night as her husband went to work.

He testified about the arrangements for the second meeting, set up so Norma could pay him and give him the items he needed in order to find her husband. "She told me she already had the stuff I needed, that she didn't bring it the first time because she didn't know whether or not to trust me," he said.

The judge adjourned the trial for the day, and the next morning, March 6, Hanscom took the stand again. He told the jury that when Norma had walked through the hotel room door, she had immediately reached into her pocketbook and handed him one hundred dollars in cash and the other items in her purse. Then Morrison introduced the physical evidence—the money and the map, the picture of Bruce and the photocopy of the picture she had given to Hanscom, and the list of license-plate numbers of the family cars.

Just before she had left, Hanscom testified, "I told her to tell me the *real* reason she wanted him killed."

"And what, if anything, did she say to you about that?" Morrison asked.

"She said, 'That's exactly the reason. I hate the son of a bitch.' I said, 'That's all?' And she related to me that he had been mean to her. She said that she was scared of him and that she wanted to divorce him but she was scared of him, scared to death of him. I asked her, had he ever threatened her, and she said, 'Hell, yes, he has threatened me.'"

I stood up at the defense table to make an objection. I thought Hanscom was simply reading from the transcript rather than using it to refresh his memory. We had a brief conference with the judge, and Morrison asked Hanscom another question.

"Your Honor," I interjected, "I'm not sure the last question was answered. I interrupted."

"Oh, I'm sorry," Morrison said. "Let's go back to that previous question." He turned to the witness. "I'm sorry, you asked her if her husband, I guess, had ever threatened her. Can you tell the ladies and gentlemen of the jury, Officer Hanscom, what, if any response Mrs. Winters made to that statement?"

"She said, 'Hell, yes, he has threatened me. He has never left bruise marks on me. He hit me where you can't see them.' She said he is big, and he grabs ahold of her hair and bangs her head up against the wall."

Morrison's response to my request served to impress the jury with another part of the psychological evidence in the case—the violence in Norma's marriage.

"Now, would you tell the ladies and gentlemen of the jury, then," Morrison continued, "if after that statement by Mrs. Winters, you brought up another statement."

"I did."

"And what was that subject?"

"Insurance money." He smiled.

"Okay. Can you tell us, please, what it was that you said concerning insurance money at that point in time?"

"I told her I was going to be a little pissed off if I found out she was getting a couple of hundred thousand. She replied, 'I'm getting some insurance money.' I asked her if she was scoring big, and she said, 'No.'"

Then, he said, she had said that her husband had a $10,000 policy and a $24,000 policy with a $3,000 loan on it and that she didn't know how much he had at work.

"And how much longer did you talk with Mrs. Winters at that point in time?"

"Oh, just a few seconds, and that was it."

It wasn't quite it, according to my version of the transcript, but I was about to clarify that point. Morrison quickly completed his examination, and the judge nodded to me.

"You may cross-examine."

Norma's defense had little to do with what Hanscom had testified to, or with what we anticipated Ryan would tell the jury. Their testimony was solid: Norma had indeed committed the act of solicitation to murder. I saw no gain in avoiding the issue or in attempting to evoke any doubt in the jury's mind about those facts. Outside of the context of our defense, Norma was dead guilty. Nevertheless, it was possible to place some of that evidence in a context more consistent with our position and I approached my cross-examination of Hanscom with that in mind.

I stood up behind the defense table, so that Hanscom would have difficulty looking at both me and the jury at the same time and would appear to the jury to be talking out of the side of his mouth. I spoke in a clear but low-key tone.

"You testified that when you inquired of Mrs. Winters as to why she wanted her husband killed, she had responded that Mr. Winters had molested her daughter, is that correct?"

Hanscom agreed that she had, and he also acknowledged that he had replied, "That's cold," and "That son of a bitch belongs in the ground. He is rotten."

I continued, "You indicated you asked her how much money she was going to get out of the insurance, and she said that she hadn't even thought about it?"

"That's correct."

I reminded Hanscom that he had agreed to kill Mr. Winters on Sunday night, on the way to work.

"Did you ever check to see if Mr. Winters was, in fact, working on Sunday evening?"

"I didn't."

"Do you know if anyone did?"

"I don't know."

He said Norma had told him she could pay him only one hundred dollars and couldn't get four hundred more until two days later.

"Did you make the statement that Mrs. Winters was pushing you for Sunday night?" I continued.

"Yes, I did."

"You had suggested other times, hadn't you?"

"I had."

"The route that is drawn on the map that you have there, do you know of your own personal knowledge whether that is the route that Mr. Winters, in fact, took to his work?"

"I don't."

Morrison had left harmful inferences about some issues by asking "half questions" that had elicited only half responses from Hanscom, especially on the insurance question, and I wanted to clarify some of those matters for the jury.

"When you testified earlier, you stated in response to the prosecution's question that she had told you that she had a $24,000 policy, a $10,000 policy, and she didn't know what he had at work. There was a $3,000 loan on the $24,000 policy, and then you stopped. Now, I'm wondering if your notes reflect whether she said anything after that."

"Yes, there was another sentence that she said, 'It's not the insurance.' "

"It's not the insurance?"

"Yes, sir."

"Now, referring your attention to the first transcript, did you ask Mrs. Winters the question, 'So he's been balling her since she was twelve years old?' "

Hanscom flipped the pages on his transcript, paused a moment, then looked up. "Yes, I did."

"Okay. Now, can you recall, after looking at those notes, what her response was?"

"Yes. She answered, 'Well, not really. He was playing with her, fooling around and playing with her. I don't know how to put it in nice words.' "

"Did Mrs. Winters ever tell you that, in fact, what had happened, is that her husband had been playing with her daughter's private parts and that he had climaxed twice between her legs?"

"I believe that was in the interview at the police station."

"And you were present when that occurred?"

"Yes."

I thought the jury might see a substantial difference between "fooling around, playing with her" and his climaxing between her legs.

I had established all the points I thought I could with Hanscom, and after a few more questions from both Morrison and me, his testimony was completed. Morrison called Mike Ryan to the stand.

Ryan wore a brown suit and a gold shirt as he stepped to the witness stand. He had a serious expression on his face, but he always seemed on the verge of cracking a smile.

After answering preliminary questions about the investigative support unit, Ryan told the jury that on the night of her arrest Norma had continually denied knowing about any threats against her husband until Hanscom had walked into the interview room at the Imperial County Sheriff's Office and shown her his badge.

"Did Mrs. Winters say anything at that point in time?"

"Yes."

"What, if anything, did Mrs. Winters say?"

"She said, 'I knew you were a cop.'"

Morrison paused, letting the jury ponder the statement.

Ryan reviewed about forty minutes of the interview with Norma, in which she admitted to the crime, and in which she first denied knowing anyone named Manny and said she had just been testing Hanscom when she mentioned that name on the telephone.

After a break for lunch Ryan testified that Norma had told them a man named Emanuel had cashed the check for Hanscom's down payment.

"At that time," Ryan continued, "Hanscom said to her, 'Emanuel, that is the proper name for Manny, isn't it?' and Mrs. Winters replied, 'Yes.' Then Hanscom followed up by saying, 'So that is Manny, isn't it?' and she said it was." She had also said that Manny had nothing to do with the case, Ryan added.

The rest of the conversation was on tape and although not as clear as the telephone call, it was clear enough to be played in the courtroom. As Morrison set up the tape recorder again, he asked the judge whether the bailiff could pass copies of the transcript to the jury.

"Your Honor," I said, "I would prefer not until the tape is ready."

"Let's wait until the tape is ready to go," he agreed, "and then we will pass out the transcript."

Morrison and Ryan fumbled with the tape and the recorder for several minutes. Without the objection the jury would have had time to read most of the transcript.

When they were ready, Ryan pushed the "play" button, and once again Norma's voice filled the courtroom. This time she wasn't committing a crime; she was confessing to it.

The jury listened as Norma admitted to Ryan that she had hired Hanscom to kill her husband, that insurance was not her motive, that she just wanted to be left alone. The taped confession related the details of Norma's marriage as she told Ryan she had taken the blame for sexual problems in their relationship because of her affair, only to find out that he'd been molesting Beth long before she'd met the other man.

Ryan: "Have you made an agreement with anybody else to kill your husband besides Al, here?"

Norma: "No, no, no. I told you that before. No."

Ryan: "Have you talked to anybody else about having your husband killed?"

Norma: "No."

Ryan: "Can you see what our concern would be—that maybe someone else who's talked to you might go ahead and harm your husband?"

Norma: "Yes. But frankly, I wouldn't care if they did."

Later on the tape Hanscom, who participated in the interview, says, "you mentioned some insurance policies to me—"

"Yes," Norma interrupts, "I mentioned some insurance policies to you, but that has nothing to do with it whatsoever."

Hanscom: "Would you go over the amounts on a number of insurance policies?"

Norma: "We have a $24,000 policy, which we have a $3,000 loan on, and we've got a $10,000 life insurance policy on him, that's a family plan."

Hanscom: "Does he have insurance where he works?"

Norma: "I don't know, I think so, yeah. I'm sure he does."

Hanscom: "Are you familiar with any of the policies—do they pay double indemnity or triple indemnity or anything?"

Norma: "No, I don't believe so. The only thing I was concerned about the insurance was getting enough to pay you. I don't care anything about that damn money. All I want is peace and quiet in my life."

As I followed the transcript—the same one the jury had—I was surprised to see that it read, "The only thing I was concerned about the insurance was getting enough to pay *me.*" I distinctly heard it in the courtroom as "enough to pay *you.*"

The tape ended, and I asked Judge Maine for a conference and explained the discrepancy.

The judge sent the jury out of the courtroom, and that portion of the tape was played back twice.

"I think it was *you,*" the judge agreed. "That really makes sense under the understanding of the evidence as I have heard it."

The jury was called back, and the judge carefully went over the change with them. It was an innocent but fortunate error in the trial, which served to reinforce in the jury's mind that there was no connection between the insurance and the crime. As the judge read the corrected version, I noticed that several jurors nodded.

Morrison then asked Ryan about his second conversation with Norma and elicited details of Norma's second confession.

Morrison soon concluded his questioning, and I began cross-examination. My strategy with him was the same as with Hanscom: to flesh out the conversation where the information would help place Norma in a more sympathetic light and establish the foundation for the defense.

Before we adjourned until Monday the tenth, Ryan told the jury about Norma's concern that Hanscom would "plant her in the desert" if she failed to go through with the plan. Then, when he resumed the stand Monday morning, I asked about his personal contact with Norma when he arrested her, bringing out Norma's apparent surprise at the threat to Bruce's life and the fact that she barely recalled talking to Hanscom.

Ryan's testimony concluded the presentation of the prosecution's case on the second count of Norma's indictment. Morrison moved to count one, Norma's meeting with Anthony Pappas.

One witness, Pappas's personal secretary, was ill. I agreed to stipulate that she would testify that she knew of Norma's attempts to reach Pappas on Thursday, August 8, had herself attempted to reach Norma on the ninth, and, at about 4 P.M. on that day, had seen Norma enter Pappas's office and leave shortly afterward.

A bookkeeper testified that she had received a telephone call from a woman identifying herself as Norma Winters on the afternoon of August 8. I had no questions for that witness.

Then Sharon Elliot testified that she had been sitting at a reception desk outside Pappas's office at about 4 P.M. on August 9, when Norma Winters had stepped off the elevator, approached her, and asked to see Pappas. She said she had directed Norma to his office.

"Now, after you did that, did you ever see Norma Winters again that afternoon?" Morrison asked.

"Yes."

"About how long was it after you had initially given her directions to Mr. Pappas's office?"

"It was a very short time, not even five minutes."

"Not even five minutes?"

"Not to my recall."

"What was Mrs. Winters doing the next time you saw her?"

"She came back to the front and pushed the elevator and stood facing the elevator until it came."

The witness pointed to Norma in the courtroom and identified her as resembling the woman she had seen at the elevator.

It was my turn to cross-examine. I had one question.

"Was Mrs. Winters alone?"

The witness looked at me, puzzled. "Yes, sir."

"Thank you."

The jury seemed puzzled as well, but it would know before long that she hadn't been alone that afternoon when she'd walked into the lobby of the Associates Office Tower.

Then Morrison called Anthony Pappas. That morning, in the judge's chambers, Pappas's lawyer had met with Morrison and me for a conference about Pappas's testimony. His lawyer, a flashy, expensively dressed man, told Judge Maine that he was afraid I would try to impeach Pappas's credibility with the felony conviction for offering a federal official a "gratuity" to treat his father well. Morrison expressed concern as well. Under a decision in *People* v. *Beagle,* the lawyer argued, his client was protected from such tactics. He also pointed out that Pappas's conviction was on appeal.

I was surprised by their concern. I had no reason to impeach Pappas. I had no doubt he would tell the truth. And I certainly didn't want the jury to know that Norma had approached a convicted felon to find someone to murder her husband. I wanted the jurors to consider him a reputable businessman.

"Well," I said to the judge, "I think *Beagle* applies to testifying defendants; I'm not so sure it applies in this case to a testifying witness. But frankly, Your Honor, I have no intention of asking Mr. Pappas about any prior felony convictions."

"Okay," the judge replied. "Then we'll proceed on that basis."

But I did have a score to settle with Pappas's lawyer. At the beginning of the case, he'd turned down my request to talk to his client as part of the investigation of Norma's case. He was under no obligation to help me, but I didn't see any reason why he couldn't.

"Your Honor, there's one more thing," I added before we left the chambers. "Mr. Pappas's attorney here is a very impressive lawyer, and he looks like a very impressive lawyer, and I think Mr. Pappas should not have his lawyer in the courtroom when he testifies. It might give the jury some unwarranted impression of who Mr. Pappas is, or the importance of his testimony, and I just think it's better if his counsel is not present during the course of his questioning. I move that he be excluded."

The judge agreed.

Pappas's attorney looked at me with a smile and shrugged. I smiled back. We were even. When we returned to the courtroom, he patted his client on the shoulder.

"Give me a call if they put you in jail," he said with a grin.

Pappas just smiled.

Pappas's testimony was straightforward and contained no surprises. He said he had met Norma when she had closed an escrow involving the exchange of his home for a motel in Calexico, and that he had sent her flowers and a letter inviting her and a guest to dinner at the hotel. He had not seen her again until she had come to his office at 4 P.M. on August 9, 1974.

"Can you tell us what happened when she arrived?" Morrison asked.

"She walked in the door to my office, which my desk faces. She shut the door and sat down in front of my desk."

"Did you say anything to her before she walked in and shut the door and sat down?"

"Nothing more than hello."

"When she sat down, did she say anything to you, or did you say anything to her?"

"She immediately said, 'I have a problem.' And I said, 'Oh, what is that?' And she said, 'I want you to help me kill my husband.' "

"I want you to help me kill my husband?"

"Yes."

"And was she laughing, or did she appear to be joking in any way?"

"No."

Pappas testified that he had asked her to leave and had then called his attorney, who had agreed that he should call the police.

During cross-examination I introduced the letter Norma had received from Pappas, and he confirmed that it was the one he had written.

He also confirmed that he knew both the chief and the deputy chief of the San Diego Police Department personally. Then I had just one other question.

"It would be fair to say, would it not, that your only relationship with Mrs. Winters was in a business capacity with the closing of a hotel in Calexico?"

"That is correct."

"Thank you."

After Pappas stepped down, Morrison stood to face the judge.

"The People rest, Your Honor," he said.

CHAPTER 26

At each recess and daily adjournment, when the jurors leave the courtroom, the judge instructs them not to talk about the case or to form any opinion about the case until all the evidence is heard. It was not difficult, I suspected, for the jurors to refrain from discussing the case, but now that the prosecution had completed its presentation, I wondered how each juror could avoid thinking that it was indeed a formidable case against Norma Winters. The phone call, two meetings with Hanscom, two confessions, and the meeting with Pappas —six times the jurors heard uncontested evidence that Norma had solicited the crime of murder. Would they be willing to listen to the evidence I was about to outline for them in my opening statement?

Morrison asked the court to rule out any testimony that would establish whether Bruce Winters had in fact molested Beth. He argued, and I agreed in principle, that such information was not relevant to Norma's innocence or defense.

I had two witnesses, David and Madeline Peters, to whom Bruce had admitted having had relations with Beth, but I intended to call them for that purpose only if the prosecution attempted to discredit any of my witnesses by questioning the truth of the incest itself.

The jury filed back into the courtroom, and I stepped up to the lectern about five feet from the jury box, placed my notes in front of me, and began my opening statement.

"Ladies and gentlemen of the jury, the purpose of an opening statement is to give you an outline for what is to follow. Sometimes in cases the evidence may get complex . . . and my only purpose in making an opening statement is to provide you with a map so that as the evidence is coming in, you will have some idea of how it connects with the other facts that may follow."

I stepped away from the lectern and began pacing slowly along the jury box, taking care to look at each juror individually. It was important, I thought, to establish some sense of rhythm, both physically and verbally, as I delivered this statement, but it was also important that it be very low-key. This was not a case for courtroom histrionics, for table pounding and sarcastic gibes. The prosecution's case was too strong, and the defense was, well, too bizarre. Anything but a deliberate, serious approach could shatter my credibility, and that of the defense as well.

"In order to understand the sequence in this case, we have to move from the month of August back to the month of February," I continued. "The evidence in this case will show that on February 28, 1974, Mrs. Norma Winters weighed almost 190 pounds, and that she visited the offices of a Dr. Alfred Richard in El Centro.

"Prior to that time Mrs. Winters had been employed in an agency capacity, always working for someone, either as a typist in a steno pool, as a secretary for an aircraft company, and between the months of February and August, her life dramatically changed."

I told the jury that Dr. Richard's medical records were in code, but that witnesses would be called who would identify the drugs Norma had taken during those five months—drugs that came in packages with no clear identifying labels and that included dextroamphetamine, a dangerous drug, and thyroid.

"The evidence will show that Mrs. Winters did not know what the pills contained and that she was never told. The evidence will show that from February 28, 1974, through the month of August, Mrs. Winters's personality changed. When she would wake in the morning, she would stumble, and she could not be very active until she took these pills. The evidence will show that for the four- or five-month period preceding August the sixth, 1974, Mrs. Winters suffered a tremendous weight loss of some sixty pounds.

"The evidence will show from a psychiatrist called by the defense that Mrs. Winters is inherently a passive-dependent personality; that a passive-dependent personality is one characterized by complete passivity, nonviolent behavior, and nonaggressive behavior, and that by virtue of this medication, Mrs. Winters's passive-dependent personality changed and that the pills made her susceptible to the events which followed."

I paused for a moment, stepping back to the lectern to check my notes. The jury was attentive.

I noted that Beth Winters had spent part of the summer in Europe, a graduation present from her parents, and that she had missed her period while there.

"When she returned, she spoke to her grandmother, the evidence will show, and on the evening of August the sixth, she imparted the following to her mother: she told her mother that since the age of twelve . . . she had been the victim of repeated violent sexual assaults by her natural father, Bruce Winters.

"The evidence will show that she thought she was pregnant by her father. The evidence will show that she denied that Mr. Winters ever actually sexually penetrated her, but that he came so close in climaxing between her legs on two occasions that she believed she was pregnant, having missed her period."

I described briefly for the jury how Beth's father had jimmied her door and had threatened her with scandal if she ever told anyone what he was doing.

"The evidence will show that on that evening when Mrs. Winters heard this, she cried. The evidence will show that, in Beth Winters's opinion, she had never seen her mother more upset than she was on that evening."

The next day, I said, Norma and Beth had gone to San Diego to see Ellen Harris and Walt Lovell, who took Norma to a lawyer and Beth to a doctor, where she found she wasn't pregnant.

"Then, the evidence will show this: that either on Wednesday or Thursday of that week—we are moving to August 7 and 8—Beth Winters and Norma Winters were made to lie down on the floor of Mr. Lovell's office. The evidence will show that . . . Mr. Lovell had them imagine a single dot on the wall, and further had them imagine a single leaf fluttering in the wind. The evidence will show that Mr. Lovell attempted to hypnotize Norma Winters and Beth Winters."

I kept walking slowly in front of the jury box. The jurors' eyes were riveted on me. Norma didn't think she was hypnotized, I said, but "the evidence will show that either on Wednesday or Thursday she was placed under hypnosis on three separate occasions. . . . The evidence will show that Mrs. Winters does not remember these events. In fact, the evidence will show that Mrs. Winters remembers nothing other than the initial hypnotic sessions where she was told she would become more sleepy."

I explained that Dr. Stanley Ellison had encountered continual unexplained blocks in her memory when he had examined her and concluded that it was possible she had been hypnotized. And I told the jury that Dr. Barry Unger, another psychiatrist, had placed Norma under hypnosis and concluded that she had indeed been hypnotized by Mr. Lovell.

I described the two phone calls to Anthony Pappas, including one that Norma didn't remember—the one from Walt Lovell's office. "The evidence will show that a suggestion was made to Mrs. Winters that she call Anthony Pappas to have her husband killed. The evidence will show that that idea did not begin or emanate from the mind of Mrs. Winters. The evidence will show that that suggestion came from Ellen Harris, the sister of Bruce Winters."

I paused. The air in the courtroom was tense. No one moved or made a sound.

"The evidence will show that on the next day Mrs. Winters was physically driven in an automobile to the Associates Office Tower by Walter Lovell," I continued, adding that she had gone to the top floor of the building alone.

"The evidence will show that Mr. Lovell knew why Mrs. Winters was going to Anthony Pappas and that he had suggested that she do that.

"The evidence will show that when Mrs. Winters came downstairs, she said, 'He kicked me out of his office,' and Mr. Lovell responded, 'Hmm, maybe he thought you were trying to set him up.'

"The evidence will show that Mrs. Winters cannot remember

anything about driving back to the office or home of Walter Lovell. The evidence will show that according to the testimony of Dr. Barry Unger . . . Mrs. Winters had been told not to remember those facts while under hypnosis."

Then I began to wrap up my statement.

"The evidence will show from Dr. Stanley Ellison . . . that Mrs. Winters's personality changed dramatically between the months of February and August, and the evidence will show that his findings are consistent with those of Dr. Unger, which are that Mrs. Winters had been placed under hypnosis by another person; that she visited the office of Anthony Pappas as a result of that hypnotic session; that the idea to call and visit the offices of Anthony Pappas did not originate with her, but from someone else; that Mrs. Winters had no capacity or very limited capacity to resist that suggestion; that when she did visit those offices, her conduct on the following morning was completely consistent with the existence of a hypnotic suggestion that she have her husband killed.

"The evidence will show that despite the hypnotic suggestion there are at least three pieces of evidence which show a certain amount of uncertainty in her own mind as to what she wanted done.

"The evidence will show on the Sunday that her husband was to be killed while going to work, Mrs. Winters was aware that he was not working that Sunday evening.

"The evidence will show that on the day she told Al Hanscom she couldn't get the $500 together, because she didn't have that much money in her account, that she had approximately $1,400 in the very account which she wrote the check out on to Manny Lopez.

"The evidence will show that the route to work which was drawn on the map may have been a route that her husband took, but whenever she went to the border station with him, she characteristically took the highway route, and she felt that would be the more likely avenue he would take."

The jurors were on the edge of their chairs. The air seemed electric. I had never felt such intensity coming from a jury box before.

"The evidence will show that Mrs. Winters, on the date that she visited the offices of Anthony Pappas, did not have the specific intent to solicit the crime of murder, and that as a consequence of that, on the following days, in her conversations with the police officer, the evidence will show that Mrs. Winters did not have the specific intent to solicit the crime of murder.

"Thank you."

One of the jurors said, "Whew." The others seemed to sigh collectively and settle back slowly in their seats, emotionally drained.

"Ladies and gentlemen," Judge Maine said, "we are about to take our noon recess."

The timing was perfect. Ending right at the lunch hour would give the jury a lot more than food to digest before it returned to the courtroom. And when it did return, I was convinced, it would be ready to hear my case.

Before its return Morrison and I still had a legal issue to resolve with the judge—his request that his psychiatrist be permitted to examine Norma. Morrison assumed that we were basing our defense on either insanity or diminished capacity, each of which, by statute and case law, concedes to the prosecution the right to have the defendant examined by a psychiatrist.

I argued against Morrison's request, however, because our defense was not insanity or diminished capacity, but the lack on Norma's part of the specific intent to commit the crime. It was the People's burden to prove she did have that intent.

I told the judge that the language in the case law on the issue referred to instances when defendants were, for whatever reason, unable to form the specific intent to commit a crime, while Norma's seemed to turn the question around: Dr. Ellison would testify that it was precisely because of these pills that Norma had been able to form the intent, and that in the absence of those pills, she would have been incapable of forming such an intent, that it would have been inconsistent and incompatible with her essential nature.

Morrison argued, however, that we were introducing Norma's emotional or mental state as evidence in this case and that his request therefore did not violate her Fifth Amendment rights.

"Well, this is a most unusual defense," the judge said, his voice suggesting his interest. "There is no question about it. But it does involve the emotions of the defendant, and . . . since the defendant herself will be calling experts to testify as to that emotional state . . . I think the People should have the right to an examination of the defendant."

Judge Maine urged Morrison to arrange for the examination as soon as possible, so that the trial would not be delayed.

I called our first witness, Beth Winters.

Beth had changed significantly in the six months since she had first walked into my law office. She was no longer a child, but a woman, and that caused me some concern, since I wanted the jury to see her as she had been at the time of the incident, as Norma's daughter, as a girl who had been the victim of incest. By now she had lost her adolescent fat, she had become more independent, and she had recently celebrated her nineteenth birthday. At Dr. Nyquist's suggestion we made sure Beth dressed attractively, but conservatively.

"Beth, where do you live?"

"In Holtville, with my mother."

I asked her first to tell the jury what she had told her mother on the evening of August 6, 1974.

"Well, I told her that my father had been trying to mess around with me since I was about twelve years old," she said. She spoke softly and haltingly. "And that I thought I was pregnant by him, and she wanted me, she asked me, she was crying, and she asked me if it couldn't have been anyone else, somebody in Europe. And I told her that I wished, you know, that I could say that, but I couldn't."

Tears began to well in her eyes. Norma was crying, too, as she sat at the defense table. She was more concerned about her daughter's testimony than her own because Beth had to tell a courtroom full of strangers what her father had done to her. Norma had hoped Beth would not have to testify at all.

Beth then related to the jury the essential parts of the conversation in the car with Norma—that her father had once cracked a rib chasing her, that he had jimmied the lock on her door, that she hadn't been able to tell her mother about his advances, because he had threatened her with scandal and hit her in the head, and that he had never actually penetrated her.

Beth occasionally looked over to her mother, who was crying softly at the defense table, seeming to relive the conversation of six months ago. I stood motionless at the end of the jury box and said nothing for several seconds, letting Beth regain her composure. It was painful for me to hear her tell her story, and I had heard it so many times that I was partly conditioned to it. The jury seemed particularly anguished by her ordeal.

"What else did you tell your mother that evening?" I continued.

"Well, she just—she wanted to know why I hadn't told her, and we kept on going over the same points, and I think we talked about it after my dad left for work that night, with my grandma, and everybody was all upset. I have never seen my mom more upset—"

"Did she seem surprised when you told her this?"

"Objection," Morrison interrupted. "It calls for a conclusion on behalf of the witness."

"Overruled," the judge said.

Beth was taken aback slightly by Morrison's interruption. "Yes. My mom did," she said softly. "She seemed surprised very much, and—"

She couldn't complete the answer. There was a pause.

"Just relax and take a deep breath for a moment," the judge said. "Tell us when you are ready to go again."

When she could speak again, she described her trip to San Diego the following day, her visit with the doctor, and the finding that she wasn't pregnant.

"Do you recall anything else occurring on Wednesday?"

"Either Wednesday or Thursday my uncle tried to hypnotize my mom and myself."

The courtroom was silent as Beth, by now more composed, described how Lovell had told her and her mother about his taking lessons in hypnosis, how he had helped Ellen calm down before a real-estate exam, and how he had then said, "Let's see if we can hypnotize you."

"Would you describe what, if anything, Walter N. Lovell did with relationship to your mother."

"He held her hand, and he told her to relax and picture a hole or a black spot on a white wall, and just concentrate on that. First he told her to picture just a single leaf on a tree, blowing in the breeze, and she laughed at him, because she couldn't imagine anything like that; so he told her to picture a spot on the wall; so she did. Then he told her that she was getting sleepier and sleepier and sleepier."

"Were her eyes closed?"

"Uh-huh."

"Okay."

"And he told her that she wouldn't remember anything that happened, and when she was fully asleep, he told her that her arms were getting light, and they didn't."

"They didn't rise?"

"No. And he just told her that everything was going to be okay, and that she wouldn't remember anything that happened."

She also described a second session in which she was talking to Lovell about when she had been a little girl.

"He asked her name. She said, 'Norma Holden.' She was just talking about what she was doing at school. It was weird."

Finally, I asked Beth why her mother had gone to the doctor in February and March of 1974.

"Because she was fat and wanted to lose some weight."

"How much did she weigh, approximately?"

"About 190."

"Do you know what her approximate weight was on August the sixth, 1974?"

"About 135."

"During those months in question, between March and August, did you note any change in your mother?"

"Yes. She got irritated really easy, and she would stay at work and work longer, and when she'd come home, she would go to her room, and she'd bring work home and any little thing would get on her nerves. If I didn't have the house cleaned up to her expectations, she'd get mad at me, and she just flew off the handle real easy."

"And was this unlike your mother?"

"Yes, it was."

"How long have you lived with your mother?"

"All my life."

"And how old are you now?"

"Nineteen."

"You just had a birthday?"

"Uh-huh."

"On August the sixth, 1974, you had lived with your mother for approximately eighteen years?"

"Yes."

"And in your opinion, did your mother change between the months of March and August?"

"In my opinion, she did."

We had laid part of our foundation for three key parts to the defense—the incest, the hypnosis, and Norma's personality change. It was Morrison's turn to cross-examine.

He stood near the end of the counsel table and looked at her coldly. It was apparent from the first few questions, that he was not showing sympathy toward her, did not share what I thought certain was the compassion that the jury had for her. He asked her about telling her mother the details of her father's advances.

"As you were driving to Mr. Peterson's house, you told your mother about this?"

"Yes."

"And she became upset, is that right?"

"Yes."

"And she started crying?"

"Yes."

"And you were crying?"

"Yes."

"Did you stop the car anywhere? I mean, did you become so overwrought, perhaps, that you couldn't drive?"

"No."

His tone was similarly strident when he asked Beth about the hypnosis episode.

"Now, it was on a Wednesday or Thursday that your uncle tried to hypnotize your mother, is that correct?"

"Yes."

"And you said she laughed when he told her about the leaf on the tree?"

"Uh-huh."

"Were you there to watch this entire episode?"

"Yes."

He looked at her out of the corner of his eye. "And when your mother was told to raise her arm, her arm was getting light, her arms didn't fly up or anything?" He fluttered his arms as he asked the question, mockingly emphasizing the words "fly up."

"No," Beth answered quietly.

"Was she told to do anything else?"

"Something about her nose itching."

"Did she scratch her nose?"

"Yes."

"Do you remember that?"

She nodded.

He asked if Lovell had hypnotized her. I objected, thinking the question irrelevant, but the judge overruled me.

"Were you hypnotized?" Morrison asked.

"I don't know."

"You don't know?" he repeated, with a tone of disbelief. "Is that your answer? You don't recall if you were?"

"Yes."

Then he tried to question her about the impact of the pills on her mother.

"These pills, they seemed to make her a little more nervous. Is that what you're telling us?"

"More irritable and nervous, yeah."

"She never appeared to lose contact with reality, did she?"

"I'm going to object," I said, standing at my table. "That is irrelevant. We are not contending that she did."

"Overruled."

Beth looked at Morrison. "What do you mean by 'reality'?"

Morrison stammered a moment, unsure of what to say. The effect of his question was gone. "Well, did she ever seem to see things that weren't there?"

"Well, I don't know. Not that I know of, because, like I said, she would stay to herself more and wouldn't hardly talk to us unless she was mad."

"But when you did talk to her, did she appear to have any

trouble understanding you?"

"No."

"And after you told her about this, did she appear to you to have any trouble understanding you that evening, when you were talking with her about what had gone on?"

"She understood, but she didn't, she didn't want to believe it, because—"

"Did she appear angry?"

"She was upset. She was crying."

"Did she appear angry, though?"

"Didn't seem like anger to me."

He asked whether her mother ever called her father names.

"She probably called him a son of a bitch a couple of times."

"Did that indicate to you that she might be mad at him or angry with him?"

"Well, I did too. I was mad at him and angry at him."

"I have no further questions."

I asked just a few more questions of Beth, in which she testified that her mother had been able to compose herself when she'd had to and that she'd kept her personal problems to herself. I wanted to make certain the jury didn't misread her emotional state, as a result of Morrison's questions. I didn't understand his tactics. He had tried to break Beth, to expose her as a liar. She wasn't lying; she was a victim. You get little sympathy from a jury when you try to hack up a victim.

I called the next witness, David Winters.

I wanted David on the stand for one reason: to tell the jury about his telephone conversation with his mother when, shortly after her arrest, she had told him to tell his father that she loved him. But when I asked David to relate the substance of that phone call, Morrison objected. The answer was hearsay, he said. The judge agreed and sustained the objection. We approached the bench.

"I don't think it can come in with this witness," he said, suggesting that perhaps Norma could testify to it herself in direct examination.

"She doesn't remember it," I said.

The judge held his ground. Since I had no other questions of

David, he was excused. As he stepped down from the witness stand, he frowned at Morrison, clearly disappointed that he didn't get to give his testimony.

The judge called an afternoon recess. I checked my evidence-code book, and I found the exception I was looking for: section 1250, which I thought allowed for his testimony: a hearsay statement that would explain a defendant's then-existing state of mind was admissible, it said.

With the jury already back in the courtroom, Morrison and I met the judge in chambers. I read the rule in question and explained that the conversation was important, because it related to the state of Norma's emotion and because it was essential for my expert witnesses to form a basis for their opinion regarding her feelings during the week she had met Hanscom. And I noted that through Hanscom the people had introduced her statement, "I hate his guts, I hate his goddamn guts."

Morrison argued that Norma's statement could not be trusted as evidence because of the circumstances involved, particularly since she couldn't remember it.

When the judge was still in doubt about the question, I told him explicitly what the significance of the statement was.

"This is not going to be a Cartesian either/or analysis: 'I love him or I hate him.' It is possible for both of these emotions to be riding at the same time."

I told the judge that I thought Norma could have both loved and hated her husband on the same day, and that Dr. Ellison and Dr. Unger would testify that someone could do that.

"All we have right now is a picture of a woman who is demonic in the sense she is telling the police officers, 'I hate his guts, I hate his goddamn guts,'" I said.

"All right," Judge Maine said. He looked at Morrison. "What about 1250?"

"I have nothing further to say, Your Honor," the prosecutor said.

The judge looked back at me. "I think that probably you are correct. I think that under the circumstances, that probably it should come in."

It was an important victory. It was a small but critical piece of evidence, and now it was coming in. In addition, the jury would now get information it knew Morrison had not wanted it to hear. And twelve-year-old David would get his day on the stand.

"David, I'm going to ask you about one statement that was made on the telephone when you spoke with your mother, and I only want the statement that your mother said to you, okay?"

He nodded.

"On the evening of her arrest, did you talk to your mother on the telephone?"

"Yes, I did."

"Okay. Will you tell the jury what she said to you?"

"She told me that she loved me, and to tell my dad she loved him too."

Morrison had a couple questions of his own.

"How many times would you say you have been with your mother to see Mr. Silverman?"

"Just about five, I think."

"And you have talked with Mr. Silverman about your testimony here today, isn't that correct?"

"Yes."

"And you have talked with Mr. Silverman while your mother was present about your testimony here today?"

"Yes, but not all the time."

"In other words, she wasn't there some of the time, or what?"

"She wasn't there some of the time."

"No questions."

Morrison was out to make David a liar, too.

"David," I said, "on the time that we discussed that telephone call, we were alone, weren't we?"

"Yes."

"And did I tell you to tell the truth?"

"Yes."

David stepped down from the stand and looked at Morrison with a proud grin on his face. Then he smiled at his mother. Norma, tears in her eyes, smiled back. I waited for him to return to his seat, then looked at the judge.

"Your Honor, the defense calls Norma Winters."

CHAPTER 27

The courtroom was tense as Norma Winters rose from her seat at the defense table and walked past the judge's bench to take her place on the witness stand and be sworn by the clerk. Rarely during a trial is there more drama or more at stake than when a defendant takes the stand. The credibility of no other witness is considered as rigorously by the jury. A defendant who is honest, sincere, and believable on the stand can walk out the door at the end of the trial, no matter how awesome the evidence for conviction. The defendant who is not believed can go to jail, no matter how flimsy the evidence. And on the stand, the defendant, having waived Fifth Amendment rights against self-incrimination, is exposed to and must answer the big question: did you commit this crime?

At the same time the prosecution feels the pressure, for it has no better chance to destroy the defense and win its case than through cross-examination of the person accused of the crime.

I didn't need to put Norma on the stand to present her case to the jury. Other witnesses could provide all the pertinent evidence. But in order to win, I thought Norma had to testify and to endure cross-examination. The defense was too unusual, the evidence too bizarre, to permit the jury to leave the courtroom to consider the evidence without its seeing and hearing Norma on the stand.

We had one advantage in such a strategy: Norma was a "good"

defendant. She had a quiet demeanor as she sat at the stand in a blue dress, her hair cut short and neat. She was fidgety, not out of concern over what she would be asked, but just because this was a new experience for her. Here was a woman whose only other encounters with the law were a couple of speeding tickets. She was a mother, a small-business woman, not a criminal. She seemed no different from the two women sitting near her in the jury box, or perhaps from the wives of the men who would also judge her.

I thought she would bear up under Morrison's questioning as long as she was open and honest, not evasive. It served no purpose to challenge the physical evidence of what she'd done. We didn't want the jury to think we were hiding anything.

Under my questioning Norma told the jury about her visits with Dr. Richard; she identified thirty-two plastic sacks of pills that his nurse had given her; and she described her regimen of at least twelve pills a day. And she said she had almost no idea what drugs she had been taking or how they had affected her.

"Do you know what effect, if any," I asked, "dextroamphetamine has on the human nervous system?"

"I don't even know what it is," Norma replied.

Sometimes, she said, she hadn't even gone to the doctor's office to get her pills; a friend had picked them up for her.

Then she told the jury about her conversation in the car with Beth. And just as Beth had, Norma broke down frequently on the stand as she described the evening on which she had learned that her husband had been molesting her daughter. The jury was quiet and seemed to respond sympathetically to the story Norma had to tell.

It was Manny Lopez, she said, who had driven her and Beth to Lovell's house the next morning, and I asked what she had told him during the ride to San Diego.

"I told him that I was going to—something had to be done about Bruce, and that I was going to get a divorce from him. . . ."

"Okay. There was no discussion at this point about killing Bruce?"

"No."

Then I moved to the hypnosis, and Norma described for the jury Lovell's directions that she imagine a tree with a leaf on it, a wall with a spot on it, and a feather tickling her nose. Her nose had itched, she said to the jury, instinctively raising her hand to rub her nose as she described it, just as she had done in my office the day we had discovered the hypnosis.

"Can you recall making a phone call to the offices of Anthony Pappas on Thursday?" I asked.

"Yes," she replied.

"Could you recall making a phone call to his office on Friday?"

"No, I don't remember that. I don't remember but making one phone call to him."

"Mrs. Winters, since your arrest, have you been placed under hypnosis?"

"Yes."

"By whom?"

"Dr. Unger."

"All right. As a result of those sessions, can you recall matters that you could not recall at the time of your arrest?"

"Yes."

"Will you describe to the jury the circumstances of the phone call to the office of Anthony Pappas?"

"I'll object to the question, Your Honor," Morrison interjected, "and ask that we approach the bench."

Morrison argued that the reliability of hypnosis in extracting evidence a witness would otherwise not recall had never been established and thus such evidence should not be admitted in court. But I maintained that I could use anything to refresh Norma's recollection.

"And as far as the hypnosis is concerned," the judge asked, "that is the thing that did refresh her recollection, is that it?"

"As I understand it, yes." I told the judge the Los Angeles Police Department had recently hypnotized a woman whose child had been kidnapped, and she had been able to recall considerable detail that she had not been able to remember otherwise.

Morrison maintained his objection. "It is so new, Your Honor, that there are so few cases on it." He demanded evidence of scientific reliability and the right to rebut any evidence on that basis.

"Well," the judge said, "if it brought things to light and later made her remember things that she didn't remember before, I think it is proper to have it come in. If you have something from the scientific standpoint that would indicate it is unreliable, you have a right to attack it from that standpoint."

"Your Honor," Morrison responded, "the problem is, I am at a disadvantage in that I didn't know until counsel made his opening statement this morning as to what he was going to be doing."

"I understand."

"I would ask for a recess of several days, perhaps, so I can do that. I am stuck."

The judge said he would give Morrison whatever time he needed to rebut the testimony. "But I will permit it to come in for the limited purpose of refreshing her recollection."

We had won the first critical round on the hypnosis battle. It did not yet suggest that the judge would consider hypnosis as a legal basis for Norma's defense, but it was, I thought, an important first step.

Norma said she had been in Walt Lovell's office with him and Ellie when she had called Pappas and talked to him and set up an appointment for 4 P.M. on Friday.

"All right," I said. "Now, when you walked into that room, was it in your mind to call Anthony Pappas?"

"No."

"All right. Was a letter being discussed?"

"I don't even remember. I just remember . . . I got the letter out and got his telephone number off it, and I dialed his number. And the best I remember is I got ahold of him."

She conceded that the testimony of Pappas's office workers indicated she had not reached him that day.

I showed Norma the copy of Pappas's letter that we had already introduced into evidence. Norma said she had discussed the letter with both Lovell and Ellie shortly after she had received it in May, 1974, in order to clarify for Bruce whether Pappas had invited just Norma or both of them for dinner.

"So Walt Lovell and Ellie both were aware of that letter during the month of August?"

"Yes."

"Did you arrange to meet Anthony Pappas on Friday?"

"At four."

"All right," I said deliberately. "How did you get there, Norma?"

"Walt Lovell drove me."

"In his automobile?"

"Yes."

"Did he know why you were going to see Anthony Pappas?"

"Objection, calls for a conclusion, Your Honor."

"I think it is a conclusion she can rationally draw," I said.

"Overruled."

"Yes," Norma said. "He knew why."

I paused. The words seemed to hang in the air.

"And the reason—the understanding he had—was that you were going there for the specific purpose of soliciting a murder?"

"That's right."

She testified that Beth had gone with them to Pappas's although no one had told her why they were going. And she said Lovell and Beth had stayed downstairs in the lobby of the Associates Office Tower while she had gone to the top floor to see Pappas.

"When you came downstairs, and you met with Walt Lovell, what, if anything was said?"

"I think I told him that I was kicked out of his office."

"What did Lovell say?"

"Objection, hearsay," Morrison said.

"Sustained."

I wanted the jury to hear Lovell's remark, "Maybe he thought you were trying to set him up," but I said nothing then. I decided to take the matter up later.

"Do you know, on August the seventh or eighth," I asked Norma, "who specifically suggested that you call Anthony Pappas?"

"I do now."

"Who?"

Morrison objected to the question, but was overruled.

"Ellen," Norma said.

"Ellen Harris?"

"Lovell, yes."

"This is Bruce's—"

"Sister."

I paused a moment, then moved to her meeting with Hanscom.

"When you received the phone call from Al Hanscom, you knew what he was calling about, didn't you?"

"Yes."

"On Tuesday, when you met him, would you describe where you met him and what transpired?"

"I met him in Denny's Coffee Shop, and we talked, and it was —I was real scared of him, and he told me that if I tried to double-cross him, he would plant me in the desert, and he also told me that if I'd just say so, he would kill my mother if I wanted her killed."

"Did you believe him?"

"I don't know whether I believed him or not. I was scared of him."

"All right. Now, what items, if any, did you have in your purse when you met him?"

"I had Bruce's picture and a map. . . . And also the license-plate numbers of the cars."

"All right. When you went back to the office, did you think about what Al Hanscom had told you?"

"Yes."

"What did you think about, Norma, when you returned to the office?"

"That if anyone was going to be killed, I would rather it be Bruce than me, because I hadn't done anything, and he had."

Norma testified that she had met Hanscom again that afternoon and that he had agreed to kill Bruce at 11:30 Sunday night.

"Now Bruce usually worked on Sunday night, didn't he?"

"Yes, but they changed shifts on Sunday."

"It was your understanding that Bruce wasn't going to be working Sunday night?"

"No, he would be working Sunday. He was taking Friday and Saturday off, and he went to work at eight Sunday morning and got off at four in the afternoon."

Norma testified that although she had told Hanscom she had only enough money to give him $100 that day, she had actually had $1,400 in her checking account. And she said she had given him a map of the back way to Bruce's job, though every time she had taken him to work, they had traveled another route.

She also told the jury that after her meeting with Hanscom, she had called Lovell's house and talked to Ellie. When I asked her to relate the conversation, Morrison raised the objection that this was hearsay, and the judge sustained it. We had another bench conference, in which I explained that the telephone call was important because it was consistent with the posthypnotic suggestion that she make contact with Lovell again. Unger would testify, I said, that she had been ambivalent about her second meeting with Hanscom and that the phone call had reinforced her.

Morrison maintained, however, that while we had claimed that hypnosis had been involved in the Pappas meeting, there was no such contention regarding the Hanscom meeting.

I told the judge that Dr. Unger would offer such testimony. But Morrison disputed whether he would legally be permitted to render such an opinion in the presence of the jury.

"Your Honor," I said, "Dr. Unger has to base his opinion on something, and the opinion has to be based on the facts, and these conversations are probative of those facts."

The judge thought for a moment, then replied, "Well, it's going to be . . . defense counsel's responsibility to tie it up with the experts, and if he is not able to do it at the end, of course, all of it goes out."

On that condition he allowed the testimony. I had won another skirmish on the hypnosis question.

Norma told the jury that she had informed Ellie she needed five hundred dollars to give to Hanscom. "I told her I didn't have the money and didn't know where I was going to get it," she said. "And she told me not to worry about it, that she could get five hundred dollars more for me."

"All right," I said. "Do you know if you wanted your husband dead, Norma?"

"No."

"You don't know?"

"No."

The court recessed for the evening. Norma was bearing up well on the stand, I thought, but the real test would be during Morrison's cross-examination.

As they did on most evenings during the trial, Norma and her children drove to the home of a friend about thirty miles east of

San Diego, where they had dinner with Norma's relatives and, in general rested up for the next day. On a couple of the nights, Norma met friends for dinner elsewhere, but usually the stress of her own testimony and of seeing her children on the witness stand, or just the daily strain of sitting in a courtroom wondering how the judge and a dozen men and women in the jury box were viewing the case, was exhausting. A quiet evening and a good night's sleep were the best preparation for another day of the trial.

I spent as many evenings as possible the same way, relaxing at my beach house. Occasionally, I checked with Tucker on a question of evidence or made notes for the following day's examination. But I find a trial an intense, emotionally draining experience and generally work better in the courtroom when I'm rested rather than tired after a night of rethinking a full day of testimony.

When court resumed the next morning, I renewed my effort to get Lovell's remark to Norma at the bottom of the elevator before the jury. It was circumstantial evidence of his involvement in the case, I told the judge, and would be used by our expert witnesses to show not only that Lovell was an active participant in this crime, but that he orchestrated it.

The judge said, however, that this statement would not be subject to a cross-examination of Lovell. So, he ruled against me.

When Norma was back on the witness stand, I spent close to an hour marking and introducing thirty-two packages of pills that she had saved as evidence, so that later witnesses could refer to them in describing their effect on her physical condition and her personality. She identified all of them as similar to those she had taken between March and August of 1974.

Then I asked her about the evening Sergeant Ryan had met her at her office and told her that Bruce's life was in danger.

"He indicated in his direct examination that you seemed surprised by that. . . . Were you, in fact, surprised?"

"Yes."

"Did you associate, in any way, what Officer Ryan was telling you with what you had just done a few moments earlier with Al Hanscom?"

"No. . . . I had forgotten all about that."

"All right, so . . . would you describe what was going through your mind when they informed you that there had been threats on Bruce's life?"

"It scared me. I thought they were telling me the truth."

I noted that she had told the officers that she was afraid of Bruce, and I asked her to tell the jury why.

"He threatened me so many times. He held me at gunpoint one weekend, me and my mother."

I introduced Norma's marriage certificate, which she testified came from the Bible she had had when she had been married, and Norma testified that it had been ripped out of that Bible.

"By whom?"

"My husband. He ripped my Bible up."

"And what did he do with that item that you have there, if anything?"

"Objection, Your Honor. It is irrelevant."

The judge sustained the objection, and we approached the bench. I told the judge that I wanted to establish Norma's state of mind regarding the fear of her husband. "He ripped the piece of paper out of the Bible, and he used it as toilet paper, and he threw it at her," I explained. "And during this same sequence of events, he had an automatic weapon and said he was going to kill her and the grandmother together. And I think it is important to impart to the jury that . . . he was the type of person that one would normally be afraid of and that he had a past pattern of being brutal."

But Morrison argued that the evidence was no more than an attempt at character assassination and that its prejudicial effect on the jury would outweigh any value it had as evidence. "The use of the gun may characterize fear," he conceded, "but the reference to the Bible and this page of the Bible is purely extremist material which, I submit, has no probative value."

The judge agreed with him. The gun and threats on her life were sufficient, he said, and he kept the Bible incident out.

I asked Norma a few more questions and then stepped back. It was Morrison's turn.

Morrison's cross-examination quickly took on a sarcastic tone, as if in addition to each question he were also asking, "Come on, now, Mrs. Winters, do you really expect us to believe that?" Referring to the thirty-two packages of pills she had identified, he said, "I take it you got these pills sometime in September, is that correct?"

"Part of them," Norma replied.

"Oh. *Part* of them you got in September, is *that* correct?"

"Yes."

He pursued the issue with a long series of questions in which Norma could not say for sure which of those she had taken during what months prior to her arrest. Morrison seemed to suggest in his questions that Norma may not have taken any of them.

Then he changed direction abruptly. "Let me ask you this, Mrs. Winters: How long had you been thinking about having your husband killed?"

"I hadn't been thinking about it," she said quietly.

"You had never thought about it before, is that correct?"

"No."

"Do you recall telling Officer Hanscom of the San Diego Police Department that you had been thinking about it on and off for the past ten years?"

"That is what I heard."

"You don't remember saying that to him?"

"No."

"Is that correct?"

"That's right."

"Do you remember telling—well, is it your testimony that you had never thought of having him killed prior to August sixth of 1974?"

"That's right. Yes, sir."

"And I take it that prior to that date you never discussed that possibility with anybody, is that correct?"

"That's right."

After Norma testified that she remembered some parts of her conversations with Manny and with Sergeant Ryan but could not remember others, Morrison asked, "Would it be fair to state, Mrs. Winters, that you just don't remember certain parts of what went on during this five- or six-day period of time?"

"Yes, sir, there are some things I remember vividly and some things I don't remember at all."

She did remember her telephone conversation with Hanscom and getting a map from her office and a photograph of Bruce from her wallet, she said. And she recalled writing down the registrations of the three family cars on a slip of paper.

"And at that time, were you doing that, Mrs. Winters, so that you could furnish these license numbers to a person that you were going to hire to kill your husband?"

"I didn't know what I was going to do at that moment."

"Well, what was going on in your mind at that particular point in time?"

"I had gotten myself into something that I didn't know how to get out of."

"Mrs. Winters," Morrison said firmly, "would it be fair to state that at that time you wrote down those license numbers, you did so knowing that you were going to provide them to an individual that you were going to hire to kill your husband?"

Norma paused a moment. "I don't know."

"Mrs. Winters, can you tell the ladies and gentlemen of the jury, please, then, why you wrote down those license numbers?"

By now Norma was crying. She also seemed evasive. I wished she would just answer his questions. When she regained her composure, she said she hadn't known who Hanscom was when she had written the numbers down.

"Well, did you think Mr. Hanscom was a person you were going to hire to kill your husband?"

"I didn't know."

Morrison, though unsympathetic in tone, was patient and persistent. Norma conceded that she had written the numbers down in response to the phone call, but she maintained, "I don't know whether I intended to have my husband killed or not."

"Well, you just told us, ma'am, I believe, that you had gotten yourself into something that you couldn't get out of, is that correct?"

"I didn't know what to do."

He repeated the question.

"I didn't know what to do," Norma said again.

"Ma'am, did you just tell us a few minutes ago—do you remember just making the statement a few minutes ago?" There was anger in his voice now.

"Yes, I did," Norma said finally.

"Now, Mrs. Winters, what was it that you thought you had gotten yourself into?"

"I thought that I didn't know who Al was, and I just didn't know. I didn't know what I had gotten myself into."

"Did you think it was a dangerous situation at that point in time, this is as you were taking the license numbers down?"

"Yes."

"And did you think it was a dangerous situation because there was the possibility that someone was going to kill your husband?"

"Yes."

Morrison sighed. "Now, I want to ask you this question, if I may: At the time you filled out those license numbers, did you do so with the intention of giving them to the person who identified himself as 'Al'?"

"Yes."

"And did you do that with the intention, ma'am, of having those license numbers available to that person, because he said he needed them so that he could kill your husband?"

"Yes."

"So would it be fair then to say that you put those license numbers on a piece of paper to aid the person that you were going to be contacting the next day at the Denny's Coffee Shop to kill your husband?"

"Yes," Norma said.

Morrison looked at the judge. "Would this be a convenient time to break?"

"Yes," the judge replied. "We'll take our noon recess at this time."

It certainly was convenient for Morrison. After Norma had appeared to evade his questions, she finally gave in. It was effective and damaging cross-examination, I thought, and it left the jury with the impression that Norma was cracking under the questioning.

During the recess I told Norma she was being too protective of herself. "Look, you were meeting Hanscom to arrange your husband's murder, right?"

Norma shrugged. "Yes."

"Well, then, say so. The answer is yes. Just answer his questions."

After lunch, when Morrison used the same line of questioning on the photograph and the map, Norma quickly conceded that she had put them in her purse with the intention of giving them to a man in order to have her husband killed.

She told the jury that she had not been concerned about what might happen to her if she were caught committing the crime, but that she had been aware of that danger.

"And you knew that that danger stemmed from the fact that you were about to embark upon something that was wrong, isn't that correct?" Morrison asked. "Or illegal if you want to—"

"It was illegal," Norma said.

"And you knew it was illegal?"

"Yes. I didn't think that it was wrong."

"You felt in your own mind that you were justified in doing this, isn't that correct?"

"Yes."

"Hmmm?"

"Yes."

"And you knew it was illegal?"

"Yes."

"But despite this knowledge that it was illegal, you proceeded on with your contacts with Officer Hanscom in an effort to have your husband killed, is that correct?"

"Yes."

Norma also conceded that she had considered aborting the plan and that she had carefully weighed the pros and cons of carrying it out the night before her meeting with Hanscom.

"Now, do you remember what you were thinking during that period of time?"

"I remember I was undecided." She began to cry again. "I couldn't make up my mind. I was very torn up about what I had heard about my daughter."

Norma admitted that she asked Manny to find someone to kill Bruce, but she said that she had never contacted anyone or thought about contacting anyone before August 6.

"Had you ever thought about having your husband killed prior to August the sixth, 1974?"

"I was wishing he was dead." Norma spoke softly, with tears in her eyes.

"I'm sorry?"

"I wished he was dead sometimes."

Morrison paused for a moment. "For approximately how long a period of time did you wish your husband dead?"

"I didn't wish him dead all the time."

"Well, how often would you wish your husband dead?"

Norma seemed puzzled and choked up. She couldn't answer.

"I mean, I know that it is difficult to characterize, but did you wish him dead once a week?"

"Oh, no."

"Once a month?"

All Norma could do was shake her head.

"Just on two or three occasions?"

Norma wept, unable to reply.

"Just relax for a minute," the judge said. "We'll start again when you think you are ready."

When she nodded, Morrison continued, "How many times prior to August the sixth had you wished your husband dead?"

"I don't know how many times."

One of those times, I knew, was after Bruce had wiped himself with their marriage certificate. Morrison had blundered. He had reopened that issue, I thought. I decided to try again on redirect examination to get the Bible scene before the jury.

"Would it be fair to say that every time you had an argument with your husband of any substance, you wished he was dead?"

"No. No, that wouldn't be fair to say that."

"Okay, how about the time that you told us about when Mr. Silverman was questioning you about this incident with the gun. Did you wish he was dead during that episode?"

"Yes. I'm sure I did."

During a recess Norma had more time to compose herself. Morrison's questions had been good ones, I thought, but his manner seemed unduly harsh, and I wasn't the only one who felt that way. Out in the corridor I overheard another assistant DA telling Morrison, "You know, she's really crying a lot. She's really in tears." He seemed to suggest that Norma was suffering too much. But Morrison replied, "Yeah, she's crying, but she's admitting to everything."

He maintained that approach when he addressed the hypnosis issue.

"Were you under some form of hypnosis when you committed these acts?" he asked.

"I don't know," Norma answered.

He tried to pinpoint times when she thought she had been under hypnosis, and she said each time that she didn't know.

"If I were to have walked up to you during the five days in question," he asked, "August 8, 9, 10, 11, 12, and 13 and asked you, 'Mrs. Winters, are you under some form of hypnosis?'—as I understand it, your answer would be, 'I don't know.' "

"You could have asked me the day I was supposed—when I was hypnotized, and I would have told you, 'No.' "

"You would have told me, 'No'?" Morrison said with surprise. Norma nodded.

"Would it be fair to state that, insofar as you know, at this point in time, that you were not under some form of hypnosis during that period of time?"

"I honestly don't know."

After posing several similar questions, Morrison continued, "Other than the fact that you have been told by a physician that you may have been under hypnosis during the period in question, August 8 through 13, other than what Dr. Unger has told you, do you have any other reason to believe that you were under hypnosis during that period of time?"

"Walt Lovell tried to hypnotize me, or whatever it was."

Finally, Morrison switched to the insurance motive and attempted to establish that with a $10,000 loan, a $15,000 interim-financing loan, and a pending application for $30,329 from the Small Business Administration, Norma had faced the prospect of a $55,329 debt during the early part of August, 1974. At the same time Bruce Winters's insurance policies had amounted to $57,-347.15. Morrison was clearly suggesting to the jury a correlation between the figures, but Norma testified that she hadn't known the exact total of the insurance policies and that she'd planned to pay off the interim loan when the SBA application was approved.

Norma also admitted she had written the $100 check out to Manny so it would cover up the transaction and she admitted having urged Hanscom not to kill Bruce on Friday or Saturday, because it would have "messed up" her weekend.

Morrison was about to bring Norma's affair with Wayne Connors before the jury, and I hoped to prevent that. We had a brief hearing with the judge. I argued that Connors had contacted Norma purely by coincidence that week and that it was absolutely certain that he had not been involved in the plans to kill Bruce Winters.

Morrison noted, however, that she had agreed to meet Connors at the bar, and that she had used the date to ask Hanscom for some other night. Judge Maine ruled that the arrangements with Connors were relevant evidence.

Norma testified that by "screwing up her weekend" she had meant that her husband had planned to have the weekend off.

"You, in fact, did not plan to be home yourself that weekend, had you?" Morrison asked.

"I had to come to San Diego."

"And you were coming to San Diego for what purpose, ma'am?"

"I was coming to San Diego to be with—to see my financial manager."

"To see your financial manager?" Morrison said in a tone that suggested disbelief.

"Yes, Walt Lovell."

"And that was the only reason you had to come to San Diego, I take it?"

"It was one of the reasons, yes," Norma said.

Morrison paused just for a moment and then asked, "Mrs. Winters, wasn't the primary reason that you had planned to come to San Diego on that weekend was to meet a person by the name of Wayne Connors?"

Norma sighed and looked down. "Yes," she said quietly.

"Would you tell the ladies and gentlemen of the jury, please, who is Wayne Connors?"

"He is a man that I had an affair with five years ago."

The jury was visibly startled by her answer. Some jurors shifted uncomfortably in their seats. They all seemed suddenly to see Norma differently. I had no doubt our defense had been set back.

Morrision deliberately allowed Norma to testify that Connors had called her and that she had not been with him for four years. But she also had to say that her conversation with Connors had taken place on the day of the phone call from Hanscom.

"And you were to meet Wayne Connors where, ma'am?"

Norma didn't answer.

"It was at one of the hotels in Mission Valley, wasn't it?"

"Mission Valley, yes. I have forgotten the name of it—Mission Valley Inn."

"Mission Valley Inn?"

"Yes."

"And that is what you meant when you told Officer Hanscom that if he killed your husband before the weekend that he was going to screw up your weekend, isn't that what you meant?"

"No."

"Oh," he said sarcastically. "You were still concerned about your husband's two days off, is that correct?"

"Yes."

"Then Officer Hanscom, after the discussion about whether he should kill your husband before the weekend, he said, 'Well, I could do it Saturday'?"

"Yes."

"And you—didn't you tell him, 'No, don't do it Saturday, because I'm going to be some place Saturday that I don't want people to know about, . . . isn't that correct?"

Norma said nothing.

"In other words, you didn't want to have to use Wayne Connors as your alibi for your whereabouts on the night that your husband was going to be killed, because you would be meeting Wayne Connors for whatever reason in San Diego that night, isn't that correct?"

"Yes," Norma said finally.

Norma testified that she had seen Connors on only three weekends, in April, May, and August of 1970, during a time when each of them had worked in different offices for the same company.

He asked whether the offices had had toll-free lines between them. Norma said they hadn't.

"Well, I take it that you and Mr. Connors made some efforts to arrange these meetings, is that correct?"

"Yes."

"In secret?"

"Yes."

"Just as the meeting on the night that Officer Hanscom suggested as the night he was to perform the killing you were hiring him for was also to be secret, is that correct?"

"Yes."

"No further questions."

"I think at this time," the judge said, "we'll take our evening recess."

Morrison's timing was perfect. He left the jury thinking overnight about perhaps the most serious threat to the credibility of our case. Although I knew that the whole incident with Connors could be explained, we would have to deal not only with the facts of that incident, but with the jury's emotional response to it. Indeed, I thought Morrison had raised the issue primarily to leave the jury with the impression that another man was involved in the case. I had only two ways to address the problem: to call Wayne Connors himself to the stand and to confront it head on with Norma.

When Norma was back on the stand in the morning, that's exactly what I did.

Norma clarified for the jury that Connors had called her and that it had been so long since she had heard from him that at first she hadn't recognized his voice. It had been Connors who had suggested they meet at the Mission Valley Inn.

"What were you going to do at the Mission Valley Inn?" I asked.

"We were going to have dinner."

"Did you arrange to stay with him at the Mission Valley Inn or anything like that?"

"No."

"Was there any conversation at all about that?"

"No."

"Did you tell Wayne Connors anything at all about what you had learned had happened to Beth?"

"No."

"To your knowledge, did Wayne Connors know anything about it?"

"No."

Then Norma testified that during the months when she had seen Connors on those three weekends, she had been separated from her husband. She hadn't seen him again, she said, after she and Bruce had gone back together.

"So when you went back with Bruce and were living with Bruce, you again were completely faithful to Bruce?"

"Yes."

She admitted that she had called Connors back collect, at his request, but said that at the time, she hadn't even thought of Hanscom's call earlier that day.

"Why did you want to see Wayne Connors?" I asked.

"Just to talk to him."

"Were you planning on telling him that you were going to have your husband killed?"

"No."

"All right." I paused and then asked Norma very distinctly, "Was the fact of Wayne Connors calling you on Monday, August 12, 1974, a matter of complete and total coincidence?"

"Absolutely," Norma said.

Norma also told the jury how she had hidden in the bathroom that night in Palm Springs when Bruce had nearly killed Connors. Dr. Ellison had characterized those actions as typical of Norma's passive-dependent personality; they would stand in contrast to her efforts to have Bruce murdered.

Next, I asked Norma about her business and her relationship with Lovell.

Norma testified that she had begun to set up her escrow business in the spring and summer before August 6, and that after her first SBA application had been turned down, she had filed a second.

I asked her who had submitted the loan applications.

"Walt Lovell."

"Who filled them out?"

"Walt Lovell."

"Who suggested the amount that you requested in the Small

Business Administration application?"

"Walt Lovell."

"On both occasions?"

"Yes."

"Who had the books, all of your books and records prior to August the sixth, 1974?"

"Walt Lovell."

"Who had your insurance policies prior to August the sixth, 1974?"

"Walt Lovell."

"Who made the suggestion that you initially request $40,000 from the Small Business Administration?"

"Walt Lovell."

"Who was to receive a fee for submitting these loan applications?"

"Walt Lovell."

"Who negotiated the lease on the building in El Centro regarding Reliable Escrow?"

"Walt Lovell."

"Who was to control and manage the financial affairs of Reliable Escrow?"

"Walt Lovell."

There could be little doubt in the jury's mind about who had had control over Norma's financial matters.

"I'm going to ask you, prior to the month of August of 1974, whether Mr. Lovell expressed any romantic interest in you?"

"Yes."

Norma told the jury about the times Lovell had told her he loved her and how he had considered her business their child.

"How did you respond to these various advances?"

"I didn't like it."

"Did you tell him?"

"Yes, and I asked him, 'What about Ellie?' "

Earlier that morning I had attempted once again to have Norma testify about the marriage certificate. Morrison had objected on grounds that Bruce's holding a gun on her and his tearing up the Bible had occurred on the same weekend. But after Norma testified in the absence of the jury that the incidents had happened on separate weekends during the summer of 1970, the judge agreed that Morrison had "opened the door" for my question.

With the jury back in the box, Norma described one other time when she had wished her husband dead.

"We were arguing, and he tore the page, our marriage certificate, out of my Bible and wiped himself on it. He took his pants down and wiped himself with it, and said, 'That's what I think about our marriage,' and he threw it at me."

I asked Norma how she had felt about her husband when that had happened.

"I wished that he was dead at that time," she said.

"All right. Now, when you testify, do you make a distinction in your mind about having thought about actually soliciting his murder and wishing him dead?"

"Yes. I just wished that he was dead."

"Okay. But on those occasions, had you intended to go out and solicit someone to kill him?"

"No."

Norma was nearing the end of her second full day on the witness stand, and, inevitably, she was going over much of the same ground. We clarified once again any suggestion that she had had an insurance motive, and she told the jury that her $10,000 loan was actually a bond that had been necessary for the escrow business, that she had only paid interest on, and that she had intended to pay back the $15,000 interim loan with part of her SBA money. We made it clear that her actual debt would not approach the $57,000 value of her husband's insurance policies. And we continued to suggest Norma's ambivalence—the ambivalence consistent with our hypnosis defense—in her dealings with Hanscom and the peculiarly inadequate information she had supplied him with when she had hired him to kill her husband—the photograph, the plate numbers, and the route to work.

In his re-cross-examination Morrison, too, went over the material again, attempting to establish that it hadn't been ambivalence, but a deliberate effort to cover up any evidence that could have led to her capture. And he worked to undermine our contention that she had been hypnotized, by getting Norma to admit, once more, that she had no positive recollection that she had at any time been in a hypnotic trance.

"Mrs. Winters, have you seen any dramatic presentations or read any books wherein the defense of hypnosis in a criminal case might have been suggested to you, or a defense similar to this?"

"No."

"Have you ever seen a movie, *The Anatomy of a Murder?*"

"No."

"Never read the book?"

"No."

"Other than what may have been told to you by a physician, you have no personal feeling of being hypnotized at all during August eighth through the thirteenth, is that correct?"

"I said, I don't know."

When Norma stepped down from the witness stand, she was emotionally drained but relieved. Morrison had given her a tough time. He had constantly tried to imply that she was a liar. And he had been mean, she thought. His questions had pounded into her, and she was especially upset about his accusations that she had "selective recall." She thought she was honestly trying to answer the questions. He didn't have to beat the answers out of her.

I hoped the jury felt the same way. Norma had confessed over and over again from the stand to soliciting the murder of her husband. She had at times evaded Morrison's questions, less because of an attempt to cover up, I thought, than because of her instinct for self-preservation, aroused especially by his hammering. I had expected the prosecutor to make some points anyway: that was the trade-off I had to make so the jury could hear Norma talk, see her cry, and feel her respond to the evidence against her. While he had elicited some damaging testimony, it had often been offset, I felt, by the sympathy he had evoked for her from the jury. And I felt we had established without question a strong foundation for Dr. Ellison and Dr. Unger to refer to as they informed the jury of their opinions.

I was eager to get on with that, but I had some other witnesses to put on the stand first. The next one was Wayne Connors.

CHAPTER 28

Morrison seemed surprised that Wayne Connors was even in town, not to mention that I was calling him as a witness. As Connors walked into the courtroom, Morrison said to me, "I'll stipulate that he called her."

"No," I said, "the jury's going to hear him."

Morrison shrugged and then frowned as he turned back to the counsel table. He sensed, I thought, that Connors's testimony would hurt him.

Connors looked just as he had looked the night Tucker and I had met him at the Mission Valley Inn. He was a pleasant, plainly dressed man who presented a low-key, honest appearance. He was far from the flashy playboy who would turn a jury off. Indeed, if a "boyfriend" had to be involved in this trial, we couldn't ask for an image more favorable to Norma's case.

Connors confirmed that he had called Norma on the morning of August 12, 1974, first at her former business, where he had been given her new number. He said he had immediately called Reliable Escrow and been told that Norma wasn't in. He had called back and talked to her about 10 A.M.

"Why did you call Norma Winters on August 12, 1974?" I asked.

"Well, I separated from my wife in June of '74," he said. "She had entered my mind off and on for a period of a couple of months.

Three weeks prior to that, I had just completed a vacation in the area around Morro Bay, where I first met her. I had fond memories of that occasion, and it just seemed to me that morning that I wanted to talk to her and see how she was doing."

He said it had been during a second call that evening when they had arranged to meet for dinner at the Mission Valley Inn the following Saturday. He had made no reservations to spend the night with her, he added.

"Was it your intention to do that?"

"I don't really know."

Then I introduced his phone records, which confirmed his version of the sequence of calls, including Norma's collect call to him that evening, which, he noted, had come at his request.

"Mr. Connors, Mrs. Winters is on trial here for the solicitation of the murder of her husband. On that date that you made that phone call, did you have any knowledge whatsoever about any of Mrs. Winters's involvement in any of these matters?"

"None at all."

I paused a moment, and asked, "Is it a matter of pure coincidence that you called the very morning that Al Hanscom, a detective in the San Diego Police Department, called in the afternoon?"

"Yes, it was an embarrassing coincidence."

"It was a coincidence?"

"And that's all."

"Thank you, I have no further questions."

Morrison stood up to cross-examine.

"You stated that the reason you called Mrs. Winters was because you had fond memories of a time you had been with her in Morro Bay, California, is that correct?"

"That is correct." He said they had not spent a weekend together then.

"And it was subsequent to that meeting that you spent several weekends with her?"

"That's right."

"Three?"

"Three."

"And I believe it was your testimony, in response to Mr. Silverman's questions, that you didn't know whether or not you were going to spend the Saturday night with her or not."

"That's right," he replied. "Yes."

Morrison paused, arched his back slightly, and smiled at Connors. "Were you hopeful?"

Connors paused for a moment, looking back at Morrison, then nodded. "Yes," he said.

In the jury box one of the women nodded slightly, as well. It was a completely honest answer. Morrison had just established Connors's credibility as a witness more effectively than I could have hoped. I felt at that moment that the boyfriend issue in the case was resolved.

Morrison asked a few more questions, and Connors stepped down from the stand.

It was near the end of the day, and I called one minor witness, the chief supervisor at the Calexico border station, who testified that Bruce Winters had not been scheduled to work the evening of August 18, 1974, the Sunday that Norma had suggested as the day Hanscom should kill him.

Morrison and I then stipulated that the insurance policies in effect on Bruce's life at the time of the crime had been purchased in 1966 and 1968. And we stipulated that on the day Norma had told Hanscom she could not afford to pay him $500, she had had $1,465.75 in her checking account.

When I walked up the corridor on the morning of March 13, the seventh day of the trial, a small balding man, wearing a bright plaid sport jacket, was standing just outside the courtroom, chatting with Morrison. As I approached, Morrison walked away.

"Dr. Richard?" I asked.

"Yes."

"Hello, doctor, I'm Milt Silverman and I—"

"Let me ask you something," he said, squinting at me. "Are you saying that the pills I give my patients aren't of the highest quality?"

"No," I said, surprised by his charge. "I don't think I've said that."

"Well, let me tell you something, sonny, I've been around a long time, and I only give Cadillac pills to my patients—Cadillac pills, you hear—and you better not try to say otherwise."

I had no intention of embarrassing Dr. Richard on the witness stand. I had called him for one purpose, to explain the codes on Norma's medical records and to identify the drugs that she had taken. Assuming he would confirm that he had prescribed amphetamines and thyroid pills, my experts were prepared to explain their impact on Norma and their relevance to the case. Given his apparent hostility toward me, I didn't want him on the stand as part of my case for very long.

Once he was sworn, I introduced his chart of Norma into evidence, and, one by one, asked him to identify the medications Norma had taken.

"Directing your attention to the date on the first page there, I believe, doctor, you've got a 3/6/74, and there appears 'at breakfast,' the number 2660. Could you tell us what that represents?"

"Yes. That is an appetite depressant that carries its ability to depress appetite for about three to four hours," he said with a touch of arrogance in his voice.

"Does it have a name?"

"It is made by the Ardel people, and if it has a name, I don't recall the name. I usually don't use the name." He paused, then continued. "Again, the name is, some of these names are quite lengthy, and we use only the serial number the laboratory produces both on the container and, at times, on the tablet or the capsule itself."

"Now, with reference to lunch, it has the number 1650."

"1656."

"1656. What, if anything does that represent?"

"Well, that is a very similar product made by the same laboratory, and, again, the same thing holds true; that is, the serial number the laboratory gives that particular product."

The testimony continued in similar fashion, as I went over every number on two pages of Norma's chart. He identified some of the symbols as representing Bacarate, ammonium chloride, potassium chloride, and thyroid.

I moved to the month of April.

"Fourteen-ninety-nine. What, if anything, does that represent?"

"That is amphetamine, five milligrams."

"All right. Now, is that dextroamphetamine, do you know?"

"Yes."

I asked what "PB" meant.

"That is phenobarbital and belladonna preparation, and it is primarily given at bedtime to help the patient relax," he said.

"Actually, all I need to know is what they are, doctor."

It was a slow process, and several times I had to cut the doctor off. I wanted him only to identify the drug. I didn't need any more of his testimony, and I didn't want to open up a cross-examination that would allow Morrison to suggest, for example, that the pills were distributed under proper medical procedures and could therefore not have caused Norma harm.

The doctor's testimony did establish what David Harper had already determined: that Norma had taken fifteen milligrams of amphetamine and two to four grains of thyroid daily for more than four months prior to the crime.

We ran through the rest of the chart, which extended into February, and I completed my questioning.

Morrison rose to cross-examine.

"Doctor, I take it you were, during the summer months and the spring months of 1974, Mrs. Winters's physician, is that correct?"

"Relative to this problem."

"And what was the problem, as Mrs. Winters expressed it to you?"

"I'm going to object to that, Your Honor. The sole scope of my direct examination was to qualify the medical records and to establish what those numbers consisted of, and no other purpose, and my direct examination was specifically limited to that."

"I think this would go outside the scope of direct examination," the judge agreed.

Moments later Morrison tried again, and I objected again. The judge called us to the bench for a conference. If Morrison wanted to go into other areas with the doctor, I argued, he could call him as a rebuttal witness after I had presented my case.

Morrison noted that Richard maintained a part-time practice in El Centro and another one elsewhere and suggested that forcing him to wait could mean a delay in the trial, as well as an inconvenience to the doctor.

"If there is any harm that has been visited on anybody by the distance, it is my client's," I said. "The people didn't want to prosecute this case in El Centro; they wanted to do it here, and I have to pull all of my witnesses from El Centro, and I've got my people scheduled, and I called this doctor specifically for one purpose. And I am sure what Mr. Morrison wants to do is call him as a rebuttal witness in the middle of my case."

The judge suggested that since my experts were going to testify in part on the basis of Richard's testimony, Morrison needed an opportunity to get more information from the doctor in order to fully prepare to cross-examine my experts.

"Judge, I agree," I said, "but he can get the information by questioning, talking to him. I don't know if he has to get the information by cross-examination. I conduct my case by investigating it first."

My argument was to no avail. The judge let Morrison have his questions.

Dr. Richard testified that he had found nothing wrong with Norma during his first physical examination, except that her blood pressure was slightly elevated, that her weight was 187-1/4, and that "her measurements were commensurate with her weight." A urinalysis, a hemoglobin count, and an electrocardiogram had all been within normal limits, he said. And Norma had told him that she was taking two grains of thyroid a day.

"Can you tell us, doctor, does the human body produce thyroid in a, say, a normal, healthy individual?" Morrison's tone was congenial, in sharp contrast to his harsh manner when Norma and Beth had been on the stand.

"Yes, sir."

"In approximately what amounts, doctor?"

Richard didn't answer immediately.

"Is it about three grains per day?"

"Well, yes. It varies with the person, of course, and their build. I started to say physiognomy, but their build, and the normal thyroid produces within a certain range."

"And did you find that Mrs. Winters in any way, shape, or form to be overproducing thyroid in her system?"

"I'm going to object to that," I said. "There is no foundation for that."

"Overruled," the judge replied.

"The patient's thyroid function," Richard answered, "can be determined by, usually, blood pressure, pulse, the moisture of their palms, the contour of their body or whether the thyroid gland is palpable or not; whether the eyes, whether they were bulging or not, and such things. Also, we did a PBI, which is a thyroid function study, in the laboratory, and it was found to be within the normal range, 7.95, eight being the top of the normal range."

"And can you tell us, doctor, why you prescribed the thyroid medication for Mrs. Winters?"

I objected and again was overruled.

"The purpose of giving thyroid is to step up body metabolism to help burn off weight—excessive adipose tissue on the body."

"Doctor, . . . would you characterize two grains of thyroid twice a day as a near toxic dose?"

"By no means."

"Can you tell the ladies and gentlemen of the jury why?"

"Well, the PBI would suggest that it is within normal range, and the doctor who put her on the thyroid doubtless checked thereafter, and then, too, the fact she presented no toxicity symptoms."

I wondered what the jury felt about a doctor who just assumed another doctor would check such information without discussing it with either the patient or the other doctor.

Richard testified that toxic symptoms included feeling warm in a chilly room, high blood pressure, a fast pulse, hyperactivity, and nervousness. He had found no evidence of thyroid toxicity in Norma while she had been his patient, he said. She had complained to him on one occasion of feeling nervous, but the doctor stated that he had found nothing suggesting that the medication he had given her had been causing the nervousness.

Then he testified that in recent months, long after the crime, Norma's weight, which had been as low as 124 pounds in November, had increased slightly, and that he had increased the amphetamine dosage from fifteen milligrams a day to twenty-five.

"Now, doctor, had you been informed by Mrs. Winters that she had not taken any of the amphetamines which you have previously described, excuse me, prescribed for her, would you have increased the dosage?"

I stood up at the table. "Irrelevant and speculative."

"It is their expert, Your Honor," Morrison said.

"Overruled."

"Wait a minute," I said. "I would like to clear this one point up."
We approached the bench.

"He just made a statement that he is my expert," I told the judge.
"I had not called him as an expert, and I would like that made clear
on that point, Your Honor. I called him to qualify those records,
but I don't want the jury to think he is my expert witness."

The judge nodded and then instructed the jury that the doctor
was not our expert witness and that he had been called only to
substantiate the medical records. Morrison then asked the doctor
about his credentials. Dr. Richard was now the prosecution's expert. After several more questions it was my turn to take the doctor
on in cross-examination. Harper was at the defense table to advise
me.

"Doctor," I asked, "Are you familiar with the treatise entitled
The Pharmacological Basis of Therapeutics?"

"I'm sorry, I didn't hear."

He did hear; he was buying time. I repeated the question.

"Well, yes, but I think—" He fell silent.

"Well, are you familiar with it?"

"Well," he said finally, "that is like asking me if I am familiar
with the Bible. There are several books in the—I mean, the treatise
of pharmacology, is that produced by the FDA, which—what are
you talking about?—and in medical nomenclature we don't use
that term, so you'll have to bring it to my mind, so I know what
you are talking about. Are you talking about a textbook on pharmacology, or are you talking about some product that is the outcome of the FDA occasionally, or—"

"Am I to understand that you don't understand?"

"By that term, I do not, no."

"And which term are we referring to?"

"Well, you say, a 'treatise.' To me, a treatise—" He looked at
me with a frown. "Are you talking about a monthly publication of
the FDA?"

I said nothing, letting him struggle with the question. The book
was as basic to his field as *Gray's Anatomy* was to a surgeon's. He
said he received ten to fifteen monthly journals, each with an article

on some pharmacological problem or new product.

"What would the answer to my question be as to whether you are aware of anything other than a book entitled *The Pharmacological Basis of Therapeutics?*"

"Well, now, if you are asking me to tell you the name of some of the journals I receive relative to pharmacology, I could probably list you some, because each of them usually have an article, but I'm not a pharmacist nor pharmacologist, and I don't receive—and I don't think most doctors receive—specifically a book on pharmacology. Now, there are books that once a year, there is the product called *Current Therapy,* and that usually consists of—"

"Well, doctor, I think you have answered my question."

"And the *PDR,* we receive that once a year—the *Physicians' Desk Reference*—which has the pharmacological background of the drugs that are listed therein."

As soon as he mentioned *PDR,* I remembered Harper's vain scrutiny of that book for some of the drugs that Richard had prescribed for Norma. I knew right then that after the lunch recess Richard would spend some time on the witness stand, looking up his drugs in the *PDR* in front of the jury.

First I had a few other questions. Did *The Pharmacological Basis of Therapeutics,* I asked, contain information on the effects of phendimetrazine?

"I don't recognize the generic term," he said. "If you could just give me one of the trade names for that generic term, then I can probably respond to the question."

"All right. Would it also be safe to say that you aren't familiar with the term 'phendimetrazine'?"

"Well, phendimetrazine is, I recall, is one of the commonly used bases for various laboratory-produced products for appetite depressant, and these came out relatively recent. There was six or eight kinds that came out, and this particular one has a relatively easy generic name, but some of them are very difficult and have just had, haven't made a study of remembering generic nomenclature."

He compared what he thought the drug was to another one and said, "Now this, by the way, is why each physician has a *Physicians' Desk Reference* on his desk, because there is a few thousand products out, and each of us have our pet, and, characteristically, a patient comes in and has a product given to them by another doctor, and we all have the experience of looking it up to see what it resembles that we use in our armamentarium."

When we broke for lunch, Harper could not contain his astonishment at the doctor's demeanor and his inability to answer what should have been simple questions for someone in his field.

"He's prescribing phendimetrazine for Norma, and he doesn't even know what it is," Harper said, shaking his head.

That was only one of the points we intended to make with the jury as we reviewed Norma's chart and the 1974 edition of the *PDR* before returning to the courtroom.

You indicated on your direct examination that you weren't particularly familiar with, specifically, phendimetrazine."

"Well, with a qualified no."

"And you talked about the *Physicians' Desk Reference*, the *PDR*."

"Yes, sir."

Dr. Richard gave a discursive definition of the *PDR* that went on for several minutes.

"The *PDR*, I take it, contains information relating to the brand name of a drug, its manufacturer, the generic name, and its therapeutic effects?" I asked.

"Yes, sir."

"In layman's terms, is it somewhat an encyclopedia of drugs?"

"Yes. That probably would describe it to some degree."

I gave the doctor a copy of the *PDR*.

"Would you look in the *Physicians' Desk Reference* under the word 'Bacarate'?"

He located the word.

"What is the technical name for 'Bacarate'?"

Richard looked at me disdainfully. "Phendimetrazine tartrate."

"Phendimetrazine tartrate?"

"Yes."

"Now, you were prescribing Bacarate?"

"Yes, sir."

I could have asked him how he could prescribe a drug without even knowing its generic name, but I thought the jury would be asking that question, anyway.

"May I qualify my answer?"

The judge interrupted. "Can you answer the question without qualification, or do you feel that you cannot?"

"Well, I feel an illustrative answer may clarify the matter. Just primarily an analogy that may clarify your point."

"All right," I said.

"I drive a hydramatic transmission in my car."

"Uh-huh."

"But I cannot tell you the inner workings thereof."

"I see."

"It is named 'hydramatic.' "

"But you are not a car mechanic, are you."

"No, but I—"

"Thank you. . . . You mentioned that you were giving an amphetamine, dextroamphetamine," I continued.

The doctor nodded.

"Do you know what manufacturer you were using?"

"Ardel."

I walked over to the defense table and picked up a package of pills. The packages were marked B-1 through B-32 to identify them as defense exhibits. I picked one marked B-7, walked over to the witness, and handed it to him. Morrison approached the stand, as well, looking at the package with the doctor.

"Does that appear to be a five-milligram dextroamphetamine from Ardel?" I asked, walking away from the stand.

"That is the one known as fourteen-ninety-nine."

"And now would you please look up dextroamphetamine-Ardel in the *Physicians' Desk Reference,* 1974 edition?"

Morrison remained at the stand, looking over Dr. Richard's shoulder. The doctor paused and flipped through the pages of the book. He licked his finger and flipped through some more, back and forth. Suddenly, a look of recognition appeared on Morrison's face. He stepped quietly but quickly away from the stand toward his table.

Dr. Richard looked up slowly and in a soft voice said, "Well, I don't see it listed."

"It's not there, is it?"

"No," he said. His arrogant demeanor seemed to drain out of him.

"All right. Now, let's talk about the potassium, excuse me, ammonium chloride that you prescribed. What manufacturer do you use?"

"Well, ammonium chloride falls somewhat into the classification of about like an aspirin. There is probably fifty-five companies in the country that make ammonium chloride, and we purchase ammonium chloride—"

"Your Honor, I don't think the witness is answering my question."

The question was read back, and the doctor mentioned several companies from which he purchased the drug. "Just sort of depends, upon, I guess, how the weather is blowing," he said. "I don't know."

"How the weather is blowing?"

The doctor shrugged.

"I see."

"It's like aspirin. Many, many companies produce an aspirin."

"That's all I need to know right now."

I handed Dr. Richard package B-4 and asked him to identify the pill inside.

"It appears to be a grain two thyroid." He named the manufacturer.

"Now, would you look up please, in the *Physicians' Desk Reference,* that medication there?"

He stared at me and said nothing. I waited.

"It is probably not listed."

"It is probably not listed?"

He shook his head. "Huh-huh." He put the package down in front of him.

I handed him B-6, which he identified as menthol cellulose, a vitamin supplement he had prescribed for Norma, to make certain she would not be deficient in vitamins during her diet.

"Who makes that drug?" I asked.

"Ardel."

"Would you look that up, please, in the *Physicians' Desk Reference?*"

"It is probably not in here," he said again, this time without hesitation. "But there is many products that these companies make that is not in here. . . . they have many products that wouldn't fit in this thing. If they had all their products in, this book could be this thick," he added, stretching his hands out wide.

"I see. Did you find it?"

"I didn't take time to look for it. It is probably not there."

I stood by patiently and silently. Finally, he halfheartedly turned a few pages and stared back at me again.

"I don't see it."

"All right. Thank you." I gave him two other packages—potassium chloride and phenobarbital. Neither was in the *PDR,* he was forced to admit.

I handed him the package marked B-10. He identified it as a two-grain thyroid made by yet another company.

"Do you think they are in the book?" I asked.

"They may be."

"Do you want to look it up?"

He nodded, turned a few pages, pointed to an entry, and looked at me. "They are in the book," he said.

"Good. Finally got one."

I referred to his testimony that the top of the normal thyroid range was eight. "When you determined that Mrs. Winters's was at 7.9, did you continue to prescribe the same dosage of thyroid or did you increase it?"

"Stepped it up."

"Stepped it up?"

"Yes. . . ."

"How much did you step it up by?"

"Well, when she came to me, she was taking two grains, and we gave her three more."

"Uh-huh. Now, what is the effect of that much thyroid plus the amphetamines?"

"Well, a combination of the administration of the thyroid and amphetamine creates tachycardia."

"What is tachycardia?"

"Fast heart," he said softly. "Fast heart."

I proceeded to hand the doctor another package of pills.

"That one is not in the book, is that right?"

"Yes."

"The blue ones, these are the, oh, these two are thyroid?" I asked.

"Yes."

"Are either of those in the book?"

"No, sir."

"Now, these, here, these red ones," I said, giving him another package. "Are they in the book?"

"No, sir."

"The yellow ones, here, are they in the book?"

"No, sir."

"And these mustard colored ones, are they in the book?"

"No, sir."

"The white ones, what are these?"

"Meprobamate."

"And is it in the book?"

"Meprobamate is, but not that particular company."

"This meprobamate isn't in the book?"

"No, sir."

"And here, again, we have the mustard-colored ones. Now, you have indicated the injection that you gave—the parmain?"

"Parmon."

"That is not in the book either, is it?"

"No, sir. That book is like the social register."

I moved to other issues. Dr. Richard testified that he had never checked with the doctor who had prescribed the thyroid Norma had been taking when she had came to see him, that he had made no attempt to determine why she had been taking it, that it was possible Norma had been taking a chance with her body.

"What precautions, if any, did you take to make sure that wasn't happening?"

"Well, after a few thousand patients and twenty-three years of practice, my precaution is the veracity and truthfulness of the patient. If the patient can't tell me the truth about their own findings and feelings, and medication, they are putting themselves in jeopardy."

He testified that his "girls" had taken Norma's blood pressure when she had come to his office. Reading from her chart, he noted that she had reported nervousness, itchy skin, and tiredness.

I asked what those conditions meant to him.

"I look this over, and then I decide what medication—I have never seen anybody die from tiredness, but if a patient looks that tired, I doubt if they will be able to talk to me, that I'd be so impressed to be, as it were, impressed with tiredness. Some people may be born tired, but I'm not impressed with somebody saying, 'I'm tired.' Now, if they say 'I'm tired all the time, I get up in the morning, I am as tired as when I went to bed,' I think possibly in terms of clinical or subclinical-type of emotional or psychological depression."

"So you don't attach too much significance to someone writing down that they are tired?"

"I think most people are tired to a degree."

We took an afternoon recess, and I then asked him a few more questions, before concluding my cross-examination. I walked over to my defense table, where Harper was still sitting, picked up the remaining packages of pills, and walked slowly to the witness, barely able to carry them all.

"Now, I hand you—I won't take much more time—B-31, B-17, B-22, B-9, B-24, B-18, B-14, B-30, B-16, B-32, B-25, B-12, B-21, B-26, B-20, B-28, B-15, B-13, B-2, B-29, B-23, and B-27. I believe many of those pills are merely duplications of the first twelve that we have already talked about."

"That's right," the doctor said.

"Do you see any in there that we haven't already talked about that might be in the *PDR?*"

"No, I think they are just about like those."

"You don't think you could find any of those in the *PDR,* either?"

"I can find you a few ton that wouldn't be in the *PDR,* if we want to start hunting for non-*PDR* drugs. The local drugstore probably has 40,000 of them."

"My specific question is, if we went through each of those drugs that I have just put in front of you, do you think we can find any of those in the *PDR?*"

"No, as answered before, some of them are not."

"In fact, most of them are not."

"I said, some of them are not."

"Well, which ones are?"

"Well, the Ardel Company is listed. You were insinuating—"

"Ardel amphetamine?"

"Well, the reason why they don't list the Ardel amphetamine is they don't list the Ardel aspirin. It is as common as dirt, and that is why they don't list it."

I asked him again which ones were listed in the *PDR*. The doctor paused and sighed. Then he said softly, "I suppose none of them are."

"Thank you, I have no further questions."

Morrison asked just a few more questions, but did not try to rehabilitate his witness, and Dr. Richard stepped down from the stand. Then, just to make sure there was no confusion in the jury's mind about which side of the case Dr. Richard represented, I asked the judge to clarify it one more time. After Richard was excused, and after a brief recess, Judge Maine said, "Ladies and Gentlemen, relative to this last witness, Dr. Richard, he was called initially as a defense witness for the purpose of establishing the types of drugs that were administered to the defendant and solely for that purpose. Since Dr. Richard was here, I permitted the prosecution to use Dr. Richard as a prosecution witness for all other purposes. Ordinarily, he would be called in to testify at a later point, but for convenience, I permitted him to testify, so you can, in your mind, you can conclude that that testimony is the testimony of the prosecution."

The judge's statement was strong and helpful. Dr. Richard was hardly a credit to the quality of the prosecution's case.

I called Dr. Stanley Ellison.

CHAPTER 29

It was late in the afternoon on Thursday, March 13, when Dr. Ellison took the stand. He sat motionless in the witness chair as he answered questions in an almost muffled tone.

He listed his qualifications to the jury, including his experience as an expert witness on both the prosecution and defense sides of criminal cases, and he said his examination of Norma Winters included five hours of interviews and record evaluations and twelve hours of psychological testing.

"Do you have an opinion as to the basic personality structure of the defendant, Norma Winters?" I asked.

"Yes, it was my psychiatric impression that she had what was referred to as a personality disorder, a passive-dependent personality."

People with such a disorder, he explained, were neither insane nor severely neurotic. "They tend to be quite dependent upon other individuals. They are usually submissive, retiring. They fail to assert themselves. They don't ordinarily show much in the way of aggression. They have their feelings easily hurt. They are quite sensitive in that regard, but still are able to function in society and normally don't come in for treatment."

In general, he said, and in Norma's case, the disorder was nearly lifelong and usually recognizable during adolescence.

"Doctor, beginning from the months between February to August, and through August of 1974, do you have an opinion as to whether Mrs. Winters's personality remained the same or changed?"

"It is my opinion," he replied, "that her personality underwent a change during that time."

"Would you describe for us the nature of that change?"

"Her personality underwent changes in the form of becoming much more hyperactive. She was busy in many areas. She became verbose, that is, quite talkative. She had a flight of ideas—many things running through her mind—often intruding upon each other, so she had difficulty in completing tasks before racing on to some other thought or activity. She became quite irritable, was labile in her emotions, tended to have crying spells quite frequently, and then, other times, would be more euphoric. She was impatient. She tended to be somewhat confused in her thinking, didn't think things out clearly, and had difficulty getting along with other people in her surroundings."

"Is it your opinion that this personality change was the result of the combined influence of amphetamines, thyroid, and weight loss?"

"Yes, that would be my conclusion."

He also testified that her condition had rendered Norma more susceptible to suggestion, in the form of hypnosis or any other form.

"Do you have an opinion as to whether Mrs. Winters would have become engaged in conduct concerning Anthony Pappas and Al Hanscom in the absence of this personality change and in the absence of this combined influence of amphetamine, thyroid, and weight loss?"

"In my opinion, she would not have become so involved, because this behavior was certainly ego alien, that is, something entirely uncharacteristic for her normal personality."

I stated the basic facts of the case and asked, "Is it your conclusion that Mrs. Winters's basic personality structure is inconsistent with the conduct that we see described between the dates of August the sixth and August the fourteenth of 1974?"

"Yes, that would be true."

"I have no further questions."

Under Morrison's cross-examination, Dr. Ellison conceded that despite her passive-dependent personality, Norma could have committed the crime and been capable of forming the specific intent to do it.

"I take it you didn't perform any hypnotic tests with Mrs. Winters?" Morrison asked.

"No, I did not."

"Do you yourself use hypnosis as a form of therapy or treatment?"

"On occasion, yes."

"You then, I take it, did not arrive at any opinion as to whether or not Mrs. Winters was laboring under some form of hypnosis at the time, is that correct? Or did you? I don't know."

"Well," Ellison said, expressing emotion in his voice for the first time since he had taken the stand, "after reviewing Dr. Unger's findings, that certainly appeared to be a distinct possibility, yes."

Morrison paused a moment, seemingly surprised by the answer. The jurors shifted slightly in the box.

"Would you say," he continued, "that while you say it is a distinct possibility, would you state it was not probable in view of the conduct of Mrs. Winters on the day in question?"

"I don't think her conduct would tend to rule it out—or in, for that matter. I think she could well have acted in the manner she did with or without hypnosis."

Holding a copy of the CALJIC instructions, opened to the unconsciousness instruction, Morrison asked, "Doctor, would it be fair to state that during the period of time that Mrs. Winters was talking with Officer Hanscom and during the period of time between August the sixth and fourteenth, I take it there was a functioning of Mrs. Winters's conscious mind?"

"Yes."

"And as a matter of fact, doctor, would it be fair to state that these acts which were committed by Mrs. Winters on those occasions were a product of her conscious mind?"

"That is true."

"And it would not be fair to state that there was no functioning of her conscious mind, is that correct?"

"No, that wouldn't be true."

Morrison alluded to Norma's meetings with Pappas and Hanscom and asked, "Would it be fair to state that, in your opinion, at the time that she solicited in both of these cases, that she did this with the specific intent to have her husband killed?"

"Object to that, Your Honor. It calls for a legal conclusion on the part of the witness."

"I think that that is the ultimate conclusion to be drawn," the judge agreed. He sustained my objection. Morrison pressed his point at the bench, but I had to make little argument. The judge spoke to the issue.

"You've got the testimony already that she was capable of developing the specific intent at all times of these contacts," he said, "but to ask the ultimate question would be improper in this case. The jury is going to make an ultimate decision, and I think that is going to be really the sole issue in this case—whether there was the specific intent to commit the crime, and you are going to be able to argue both sides."

The judge added, "This is really akin to asking the psychiatrist, 'Do you think this gal is guilty or not guilty?' "

"Well, no, that is, not quite," Morrison said. "Almost."

"Well, I think it comes so close that we would be abdicating the responsibility of the jury."

Morrison pursued other matters, eliciting from Dr. Ellison the opinion that Norma had been able to consider the consequences of her actions, including the question whether she would be caught. And then he concluded, "Doctor, would it be fair to state that even though Mrs. Winters was suffering from the personality disorder and the syndrome you have described—that her capacity to form the intent to commit these crimes was in no way impaired?"

"That is correct," the doctor said.

"And would it be fair to state that despite this disorder and despite whatever else might have gone on—that there was during the period of August the sixth through fourteenth, the functioning of Mrs. Winters's conscious mind?"

"Yes."

"And would it be fair to state, doctor, from the reading of the transcript of the conversations with Mrs. Winters and Officer Al

Hanscom, that during those conversations, that Mrs. Winters has or did have the use of her conscious mind at that time?"

"That is correct."

"I have no further questions."

The court day was just about over. The judge excused the jury for a long weekend, and then we had a brief hearing before the judge concerning Morrison's request for access to the interviews Dr. Ellison had had with Norma. Morrison wanted his expert witness to study them in order to prepare a rebuttal to the defense. The judge leaned heavily toward Morrison's position, but agreed to read the transcripts of the interviews overnight before making a final decision.

As we were packing up, Morrison stood near the court reporter, holding his copy of CALJIC and reading the unconsciousness instruction. "This rule of law applies only to cases," he read, "in which there is *no functioning of the conscious mind!*"

"What are you doing, Ed?" I asked with a grin. "Summing up?"

He turned to look at me. "I just don't understand," he said. "I don't understand what you're up to."

Over the long weekend break Norma returned to El Centro, in part to spend some time away from the scene of the trial, but mostly to work. She had established her business quite well during our investigation of the case, and she wanted to maintain as much momentum as she could during the trial, even though she was away four days a week. Real-estate brokers and other customers and friends stopped by on Friday and Saturday to see how she was doing. And she kept taking business, without a thought to what would happen if she was convicted. She left the trial on the other side of the mountains.

During that weekend I couldn't afford to relax. I had to think seriously about Morrison's cross-examination of Dr. Ellison. It had been short but effective in undermining three basic defenses—insanity, diminished capacity, and unconsciousness. He had carefully left the impression in the jury's mind that despite the pills and her personality change, Norma had still been able to form the intent to commit the crime, and that her conscious mind had been working when she had formed it.

I prepared a long memo for Dr. Ellison and Dr. Unger, outlining our defense. While I wanted them to read it for background on which to base further testimony, writing it out in twelve pages helped me to understand it better, to think it through, and to prepare for my argument before Judge Maine when I would ask him to change the wording of the unconsciousness instruction.

Indeed, while Morrison's questions had seemed effective, they had addressed only the test of the instruction itself, not the case law we intended to use to change its wording, so that it would accommodate the circumstances of Norma's case. We were not contending that Norma's conscious mind had been dormant when she had committed the crime. We were not contending that the amphetamines, thyroid, and weight loss had impaired her judgment or lessened her ability to commit the crime; we thought they had *enhanced* it. And we were questioning not whether she had had the capacity to form the "specific intent" to solicit the murder of her husband, but whether she *had* formed the intent—whether the intent had been the product of her own will.

Morrison had worked over the weekend, too. Judge Maine had allowed him to see some of Dr. Ellison's records in the case. When the trial resumed Tuesday morning, he called the doctor back to the stand.

He referred Ellison to a section of the records of his conversations with Norma and asked him when she had first intended to arrange for Bruce's death.

"She said she went to bed thinking about it," Ellison said.

"Excuse me, doctor, was she speaking now of the evening that her daughter had informed her of these alleged molestations, the evening which we now know as August the sixth?"

"Yes, I believe so."

"And can you tell us, what did Mrs. Winters tell you at that time?"

"Well, that she—the thought then occurred to her about arranging for his death, and that she went to bed thinking about it. And then, I mentioned, 'That is, the night you found out, you decided you'd try to arrange for his death?' and she said yes at that point."

"In other words, you asked her at that point in time if she had decided to try to arrange for her husband's death on that date and her response was yes. Is that correct?"

"That is true."

"I have no further questions of this witness, Your Honor."

"Anything further?" the judge asked, nodding to me.

Indeed, I did have questions. All prior testimony had indicated that Norma had not been hypnotized at least until the day after that and probably two days after. But Ellison was scheduled to testify in another trial.

"I'd like to defer redirect examination of him until after my next witness," I said.

"The motion will be granted," the judge replied. "You may step down."

As Dr. Ellison rose at the stand, I changed my mind.

"Your Honor, could I ask Dr. Ellison to answer one question for me before he leaves?"

"Yes."

I remembered that Dr. Unger had determined that Lovell had hypnotized Norma on other occasions prior to August 6. And I remembered one other fact.

"Dr. Ellison, on the evening of the sixth, when she was lying in bed, this would have been after the phone call was placed to Walter Lovell's residence, isn't that right?"

"Yes."

"Thank you. I have no further questions. The defense calls Dr. Barry Unger."

CHAPTER 30

That Dr. Unger had never tes-
tified as an expert witness before was one of his most convincing
credentials. Although I thought we couldn't win the case without
Norma's appearance on the stand, Unger's testimony would be the
most important and most explosive. If the jury got the impression
that he was a professional witness who specialized in creative
defenses, we wouldn't have a chance. Nevertheless, I didn't want
him completely unprepared for cross-examination. A "virgin" expert witness can be easy prey for a veteran prosecutor. Before the
trial began, Eric Miller and I had grilled him in a mock cross-
examination, exposing him to the traps that could be set by a
careful prosecutor. Unger quickly learned to listen carefully to
each question, to force the definition of any term he didn't understand, and to avoid debate with the examiner. My purpose was not
to "coach" him—to concoct or distort his testimony—but to make
sure he expressed his opinions clearly and accurately to the jury.
It is important for expert witnesses on both sides of a case to
prepare for their testimony; the case is more likely to be decided
on the facts rather than by the clever legal machinations of either
counsel. The prosecution recognizes that principle: policemen and
other law-enforcement officials regularly get instruction in giving
testimony as part of their training.

Dr. Unger had other credentials, as well, and after he was sworn, he listed them carefully for the jury: graduate of the University of Michigan Medical School; resident in psychiatry at Johns Hopkins Hospital, Baltimore; fellow in psychiatry at the Johns Hopkins University School of Medicine, where he learned the use of hypnosis; assistant professor at the same school and staff member of the hospital from 1966 to 1970; member of the Department of Psychiatry at the University of California School of Medicine in San Diego, 1970–72; a founder and the first director of the Psychosomatic-Psychiatric Liaison Service, where he oversaw all uses of psychiatry with other departments in the hospital. In 1972, he went into private practice. He was currently associate clinical professor at UCSD. He was a member of more than ten professional organizations and health advisory boards, held staff appointments at six hospitals, consulted in psychiatry with the Veterans' Administration and the Scripps Clinic Research Foundation, and had written twenty-five papers on various aspects of psychiatry and psychosomatic medicine. In his work, he told the jury, he had used hypnosis with more than a hundred patients as part of his practice.

After Dr. Unger testified that he had examined Norma several times in connection with the case and that he had reviewed police reports, psychiatric evaluations, court testimony, and Lovell's deposition, I moved to one of the critical issues of the defense.

"Doctor, in medical terminology, what is meant by the term 'unconscious'?"

"Objection, Your Honor," Morrison said. We approached the bench.

Morrison argued that the medical definition of the word was irrelevant, since only the legal meaning—that there is no functioning of the conscious mind—was pertinent.

I noted several cases involving unconsciousness that contemplated "persons of sound mind who suffer from some force that leaves their acts without volition." Others, I said, "speak in terms of lack of awareness and indicate that to constitute what the law deems a crime, there must occur both an evil act and evil intent; therefore, the intent with which the unlawful act was done must be proved."

The judge heard our arguments, paused for a moment of reflection, and then overruled the objection. "I think, of necessity," he said, "we are going to have to go into certain areas that may not necessarily be applicable when it comes down to the final question, that is, the magic questions at the end, and it might be that we are going to have to have some sessions outside the presence of the jury during that time."

It was the first of several objections Morrison raised while Dr. Unger was on the stand, and as the questioning continued, Morrison persistently tried to keep the evidence regarding hypnosis away from the jury. But Judge Maine permitted it with the condition that I make legal sense of it later in the trial.

Dr. Unger described two kinds of unconsciousness, one involving a person who is knocked out, and the other involving feelings and urges that are essentially out of a person's awareness, such as unconscious fears.

Then he described hypnosis as an "altered state of consciousness," as opposed to "unconsciousness," in which "a person is in a state really of heightened awareness rather than decreased awareness. Their focus is on a very narrow band of thought, and on that band of thought they have a hyperawareness, and there is an extreme amount of suggestibility under hypnosis."

"Is it possible under hypnosis," I asked, "for a person to suffer from some force which would leave their acts—their subsequent acts—without volition?"

After another objection was overruled, Dr. Unger said, "I don't know if I would say that their acts would always be without volition after hypnosis. I think that would depend entirely on the situation. Depending upon how it mixed with the person's basic underlying personality type, and the conditions at the time, it might at various times compromise volition."

"Okay, under certain circumstances, though, it is possible for a person to suffer from that force which leaves their acts without volition?"

"It could happen."

He also said, "I think it is important for the jury to understand that hypnosis is not really black magic; that a person who is hypnotized talks just about the same as a person who isn't hypnotized and may act about the same as a person who isn't hypnotized, except possibly that they may talk in more of a monotone."

He told the jury that physical contact between a hypnotist and subject is important for establishing a rapport between the two. He said a person could learn to hypnotize someone in an hour or two. And he said he had found Norma Winters an easy subject to hypnotize.

"In your earlier sessions with her, prior to the hypnotic induction, was it a matter of concern to you that Mrs. Winters could not remember certain details about events leading up to her arrest?" I asked.

"Yes, I discussed that with her actually when she first came in. I asked her about the idea of hypnosis and her memory. She herself was somewhat puzzled. She did not believe she had been placed under hypnosis."

"I'm sorry," Morrison interrupted. "Could we have the last statement read back?" Unger repeated his answer.

"Is that surprising?" I asked.

"Not at all."

He told the jury of Norma's difficulty in recalling specific blocks of time, especially the evening after she had visited Pappas's office, and of her telling him that the idea to call Pappas just "popped into my mind." She had used the same phrase to describe her initial thought of having her husband killed on the night of August 6, after she had talked to Beth.

And he conceded that traumatic events, such as a mother's seeing her daughter killed, might induce amnesia, but he concluded that such a factor was not involved in Norma's memory blocks. If Norma had suffered some psychological trauma, he said, she would probably have forgotten the terrible humiliation of walking into Pappas's office, blurting out her request, and being ushered out, which she remembered vividly.

Then he told the jury of Norma's accounts of Lovell's attempts to hypnotize her—accounts aided by Beth's recollection.

"Did you form an opinion," I asked, "as to whether or not Mrs. Winters had been hypnotized on those occasions?"

"Yes, I believe she was hypnotized on those occasions."

I asked whether he was able to retrieve while Norma was under hypnosis any of the information that she could not recall while in a conscious state.

"Partially."

"You were not entirely successful?"

"No."

He said that he had tried several times to have Norma reenact the scenes of the three hypnotic sessions in August, but that she had remembered only a few details of the beginnings of the sessions.

"Toward the end, she described Mr. Lovell as counting, 'one,' and then there are words she can't hear; 'two,' and there are words she can't hear. And that was significant, because earlier her daughter had told me that Mr. Lovell had done the same thing in the living room and that in between his counting . . . he repeated the words, 'You won't remember this,' and would say the next number, and then, 'You won't remember this,' and the next number.

"When she reported them back under hypnosis, she reported the numbers and not being able to hear that something was being said," he continued. "So essentially, it was all blanked out."

Then I asked him to describe the details of the last hypnotic session with Norma, when she had revealed the circumstances surrounding her visit to Pappas's office.

"Two things kept bothering me," he said, after describing the frustration of running into the blocks. "They both tended to do with the words 'popped up.' As I mentioned, this was about the fifth session and the seventh hour, and those words had only been used in the first interview, so at the end I asked her essentially to go back in time to exactly the time that it popped into her mind, and she said, 'In Walt's office.' "

"This would be Walt Lovell?"

"Correct, as she later identified him, but she said, 'In Walt's office,' and I asked her what—how it had come up. And she answered simply, 'The letter.' "

"The letter?"

"Yes."

The courtroom was silent. The jurors sat motionless in the box, captivated by the testimony.

"Now, from what you know about the case, would this appear to be a reference to the letter that Anthony Pappas had written to her some time in May?"

"I thought it might be, but her answer was simply 'the letter.' That is all that she said."

"All right."

"And I said something to the effect of, could she describe what was being said, and she was listening, and she started saying, 'No! No!,' and looking very agitated, very uncomfortable. And I asked her again what was being said, and the same thing repeated, so rather than ask her again what was being said, I asked her who was talking during this period. And she paused for a long time and then said, 'Ellie.' And I asked her again, could she tell me what was being said, and she began having tears in her eyes. She looked very much like she was struggling with it, and I was beginning to get a bit concerned because she looked increasingly agitated. There was a lot of tremor in her face. . . .

"And then I asked, . . . did she feel that she would be betraying Ellie if she said any of this, and she said, 'Yes.' And I asked at that point, did this conversation about Mr. Pappas, Ellie's talking, 'concern killing your husband?' And she paused, and she could say yes to that. And I said, 'Is Walt talking?' And she said, 'No.' On asking her what he did, she said he was silent and nodding."

Dr. Unger said he had had to stop at that point, because she had begun sobbing. "I was kind of frightened that I might lose her in the hypnotic state. There is a danger that people can go into anxiety panics during these states, and she displayed more emotion over this naming of a person or retelling of something than she had displayed about anything, including her own fate, her daughter's fate, her husband's fate, or any other examples."

He described for the jury Norma's disclosure that she had made the telephone call to Pappas immediately, from Lovell's office.

"Did you ask her whether it was in her mind when she entered that office to make that phone call?"

"Yes. . . . I asked her specifically whether it was in her mind, and she said, 'No.' And I said, 'When did it come into your mind?' 'In the office.' And I said, 'Oh, you went into the office to see them?" And she said, 'No, we all went into the office together, and then it popped into my mind.' . . .

"When she came into the room, she was not thinking of either calling on Mr. Pappas or anything. Her mind was essentially on the events of the day, which was her daughter's visit to an obstetrician, a visit to the lawyer, and it was a rather harried day."

"All right," I said. "In this case, there has been evidence that Walter Lovell drove Mrs. Winters to the Associates Office Tower and waited downstairs while she went upstairs. There has been evidence from Mr. Pappas that Mrs. Winters walked into his office and sat down and said, 'I want you to help me kill my husband,' and he promptly asked her to leave. As a result of your five or six hypnotic sessions with Mrs. Winters, do you have an opinion as to whether Mrs. Winters visited the offices of Anthony Pappas while under hypnosis?"

"Objection, Your Honor," Morrison said. "It is irrelevant."

"As far as the jury is concerned," Judge Maine said, "we'll take a short recess." He paused. "As a matter of fact," he added, glancing at the clock, "I think we will take our noon recess as far as the jury is concerned at this time."

The jury filed out. The crucial legal argument over whether our defense could actually be considered by the jury was about to begin.

Judge Maine looked at Morrison. "Will you state your objection and the grounds for it?"

"Yes, Your Honor. It is my contention that the opinion which is sought by counsel at this time concerning whether or not Mrs. Winters was under hypnosis at the time is irrelevant in light of the doctor's description of, his medical description of unconsciousness in that it fails to comport with or comply with the legal requirements of unconsciousness as a defense as set forth by CALJIC." He mentioned two court cases to back his assertion.

The judge looked toward me.

"Your Honor, of course, the cases control what the law is, not the CALJIC instruction," I said. I listed a number of the cases that Miller and I had researched a few weeks before in my law library. They held, I said, that "an act done in the absence of the will is not any more the behavior of the actor than is an act done contrary to his will."

I noted another case which said that someone not conscious of acting could not have the will to perform that act—the precise circumstances, I explained, that Dr. Unger would testify we had in this case.

Then I said that the unconsciousness instruction, where it stated there should be "no functioning of the conscious mind," did not directly relate to the cases we had found. "I think what these cases relate to is a question of control over one's will and over volition . . . and the person's ability to control their specific acts. . . . I submit that if the testimony were to show that Mrs. Winters— Norma Winters—was hypnotized and was directed to go to that office, not to pull a trigger, but to utter certain words, and if the doctor's testimony is that, as I think it will be, that those acts were outside her volition, and the predicate to those acts was not a function of her conscious mind, then I think we've gotten to the substance of what the defense of unconsciousness is all about."

Even without an instruction on unconsciousness, I added, the hypnosis issue went directly to the question of whether Norma had been able form the specific intent necessary to solicit the crime of murder.

"If I am in a hypnotic state and I am directed that my arm will rise, I may be conscious that my arm is rising—my motor activity is functioning—but I may be powerless to control it, and I would think it would be a sad day in our literature if a person were to commit an act under those circumstances and could, nevertheless, be found guilty of a crime requiring an evil intent, which has been supplied to them by someone else. And that is all I have to say on this."

The judge paused a moment. "Well," he said, "is this witness going to testify that her acts in soliciting Mr. Pappas were totally involitional?"

With the judge's permission, I conferred with Dr. Unger.

"The language that the doctor would prefer to use," I said, "is that her volition was severely compromised and that she was seeking to resist the suggestion, particularly with relationship to the manner in which she approached Anthony Pappas and the manner in which she conducted her interviews with Al Hanscom. There was a reservoir of the functioning of the conscious mind which was resisting the hypnotic suggestion that she continue to solicit her husband's murder. So if volition was exercised, it was exercised in the effort to put the brakes on the hypnotic suggestion."

The judge nodded slowly. "In other words, Mr. Lovell put the defendant under hypnosis, and somebody, whether it was him or

whether it was Ellie, made the suggestion that she contact Pappas
for the purpose of soliciting the murder of her husband, is that the
idea?"

"Yes."

"I gather," the judge replied, "that it will be his testimony that
she did not have the capacity or the will to ward off this suggestion?"

"Essentially."

"Suppose we do this," he said. "I want to look at some of these
cases. Also, I think we are going to have to have further testimony
of the doctor outside the presence of the jury before we finally
decide what path to take."

The judge made notes on the case references, and we took a noon
recess. As we headed for lunch, I knew that my whole case was now
on the table. I had managed to hold it until my last scheduled
witness was on the stand. In doing so, I had maximized the element
of surprise for the prosecutor, but also greatly increased the risk.
If the judge found us wrong on the law, we were back to pleading
mitigating circumstances. The legs of the defense would be cut
from under us.

When we returned to the courtroom, the judge was still undecided. He asked Dr. Unger to return to the stand, and this time he
asked the questions.

Judge Maine's interrogation went on for more than an hour. He
seemed to struggle with and weigh carefully the evidence as Dr.
Unger explained his opinion that Norma had been influenced by
a posthypnotic suggestion when she had met with Pappas and
Hanscom, that her will had been acting *against* the suggestion, but
that her will had not been strong enough to block it.

"Do you think any one of us might be capable of acting involi-
tionally by some type of posthypnotic suggestion without the concurrence of these other factors—that is, the use of amphetamines
and a traumatic personal emotional experience?" the judge asked.

"I think ordinarily, if the suggestion were rendered by a relative
stranger on a given day, and it were not on fertile ground with long
rapport and a disabled person, I don't think a person would accept
it. Which is why, I guess, the sum total there that makes me feel

strongly that it had to be looked at in the totality."

Dr. Unger and the judge also covered the meetings with Hanscom and Unger expressed the opinion that Norma's behavior showed her struggling against the posthypnotic suggestion.

"I also have a question relative to her again returning the second time after the first meeting at Denny's Coffee Shop," the judge continued. "I suppose that she had the ability to be able to back away from it between the first meeting and the second meeting, but she chose to bring pictures and the hundred dollars and the map to Officer Hanscom. Do you feel she was in a position constitutionally to be able to back away from it, or do you feel that she was operating as an automaton, in effect?"

Unger thought for a moment. "I believe she brought the picture and the map to the first meeting also, but did not give them to him."

For the first time in his interrogation of the doctor, the judge paused and looked up for a minute in thought. Then he turned back to the witness and nodded.

"I think you are correct," he said.

He asked just one more question of Dr. Unger, and I barely heard the answer. The judge seemed to be impressed in the last exchange with the depth of Unger's understanding of the details of the case and with his candor in rendering an opinion. I was hopeful that he would rule in our favor.

With the jury still out of the courtroom, Morrison asked Dr. Unger several questions, including whether his "medical" definition of "unconsciousness" matched the "legal" definition in the CALJIC instruction. Dr. Unger said it did not. Morrison renewed his objection to all of Dr. Unger's testimony.

"Until his definition fits within the legal definition, I would submit that his opinion is irrelevant, and if his opinion is not one that she was unconscious, this business about her laboring under some posthypnotic suggestion does not constitute any legal defense that I can find."

"Well," the judge said, "my understanding of this doctor's testimony is to the effect that she was incapable, even though a part of her mind told her not to go through with this, that she was incapable of not going through with it, and—"

"I think that might go to diminished capacity, Your Honor," Morrison interjected, "but not to unconsciousness."

"Well, what about a somnambulist who does certain things? His mind is telling him to do certain things, but he is incapable of doing anything about it.

"In effect, the doctor has stated that she was in about the same situation as in the *People* v. *Baker* case," the judge said, holding up one of his law books. "They say in that case there was ample evidence of involuntary intoxication, and there was also evidence that the defendant was unconscious at the time of the offense, because he was in the clouded state of an epileptic attack. And in this case, this witness is contending that she was in this state, imposed or brought about by the use of amphetamines and emotional traumatic experience and posthypnotic suggestion. I would think that under those circumstances, that he should be able to testify to that effect."

Morrison sighed. "Very well, Your Honor."

It was a crucial victory for the defense. Not only was the judge allowing Dr. Unger's testimony, but he was indicating that he would change the CALJIC instruction to the jury so it would fall in line with the issue of volition mentioned in the cases. The absence of volition—the profound compromising of will—was the guts of our defense.

We took another recess, and Gene Tucker, who had been in the courtroom and had witnessed the arguments, said, "I'm not sure what that was all about, but it sure sounded good to me."

I looked at him, almost beaming. "Gene," I said, "we just won the case."

It was an overconfident remark. We had won a battle, not the war, and I still had a long way to go in detailing Unger's testimony in the courtroom. But the ruling meant that the culmination of five months of work could be presented to and considered by the jury.

The legal argument had consumed much of the day. At 3 P.M. the jury filed back into the courtroom for the first time since 10:30 that morning. The judge's questioning of Dr. Unger had been particularly effective, I thought, and since he had asked the questions, I assumed he would have a difficult time sustaining objections to them. Using them as the backbone of my questioning, I proceeded.

"Doctor, we left with the question of whether you had formed an opinion as to whether Mrs. Winters was suffering from a post-hypnotic suggestion on the occasion of her visit to Anthony Pappas's office."

"I felt that she was under the influence of posthypnotic suggestion at the time of her visit to the office."

He told the jury that the amphetamines, the thyroid, the weight loss, and the news of the incest upon her daughter had made her more susceptible to suggestion, and that the news of the incest had been an extreme shock and had added to the amount of anger she felt towards her husband. "I have no doubt that she has had murderous feelings toward him," he said.

"Now, with relationship to the visit to Anthony Pappas's office, is it your opinion that Mrs. Winters was constitutionally incapable of resisting the posthypnotic suggestion which had been given to her?"

"Yes, because of her particular circumstances."

"In your opinion, are those particular circumstances singularly unique?"

"In my experience it would be terribly unusual to find all these factors converging together in one patient—that is, the history of high amphetamine use, the history of thyroid administration, the possibility of some clouding of consciousness during the time of a fifty- to sixty-pound weight loss, and what appeared to be a post-hypnotic suggestion given by an old and trusted friend."

Then I asked, "Do you have an opinion as to whether the posthypnotic suggestion that had been provided on the prior week was still operating during the period of time that she engaged in conversations with Mr. Hanscom?"

"Yes. I believe it was."

"Would you explain the basis of your opinion?"

"I think that because of the extremely weakened state Mrs. Winters was in, the suggestion, and the conditions of the suggestion, it took a much stronger hold than it might ordinarily have. In such a case I would expect a person who received such a suggestion to act in a very highly ambivalent manner. That is, they might be acting on the suggestion while at the same time, part of them, perhaps their own will, was opposing it. I believe that is the reason that she appeared to have acted so automatically upon occasion, as with Mr. Pappas. And in the case of Officer Hanscom, it appeared that she was continually throwing things in his path, as a block."

The doctor testified that, in general, persons would not do under hypnosis what they normally would not do, but when I asked whether that was true in this case, he said, "I think that there would be exceptions, depending upon the conditions that that occurs under. The most important would be the distancing of the suggestion from the actual act. There would be an enormous difference on how a person might respond, for example, if they were asked to shoot a person than if they were asked to ask someone to shoot a person. The farther the distance is from the patient, the easier it is to depersonalize the suggestion. . . ."

"In this case, Mrs. Winters was not commanded to kill someone, was she?"

"No. She was commanded to ask something."

In her meeting with Pappas, he said, "it appears that this was almost like carrying out an order with the express purpose that it fail."

"She was technically complying with the directive or the order?"

"Yes. I don't think that she was aware at any time that she might be carrying out something with perhaps a struggle going on that it might fail, but I think that is indeed what was going on."

"Can you explain that—how she might be unaware of that?"

"Well, I think the posthypnotic suggestion would be operating outside of awareness, and if it were in a person who, because of this rather unique set of circumstances, was very susceptible to suggestion, it would probably operate in that the suggestion was pushing them toward an act while another part of their mind—another part of their own volition, was opposing this."

Unger then testified that a posthypnotic suggestion can last several weeks or months.

"You have stated," I continued, "that it is your opinion that on the occasion of Mrs. Winters's visit to Anthony Pappas's office, that she was constitutionally incapable of resisting the hypnotic suggestion, is that correct?"

"Yes."

"Similarly, is it your opinion that on the occasion of her conversations with Al Hanscom, that she was constitutionally incapable of resisting the hypnotic suggestion which had been set approximately the week before, or a few days before?"

"Yes." He said Norma's resistance to the suggestion was greater, but that she was still incapable of actually resisting it.

"Would it be fair to say that at the time the crime relating to Anthony Pappas was allegedly committed, the defendant was suffering from some abnormal mental or physical condition—however caused—which prevented her from forming the specific intent or mental state essential to constitute the crime of solicitation to commit murder?"

"Yes. I believe the mental state she was in could have seriously hampered her ability to form any intent."

"Would that also hold true with relationship to her conversations with Al Hanscom?"

"Yes."

I looked at the judge. "I have no further questions."

It was Morrison's turn to question Dr. Unger. How well he did could well determine the outcome of the case.

Morrison's initial cross-examination was an effort to undermine Dr. Unger's definition of intent and awareness, and an effort to establish that Norma had indeed known to some extent, what she was doing during her meetings with Pappas and Hanscom.

"When Mrs. Winters told Anthony Pappas, 'I want you to help me kill my husband,' was her conscious mind working at that time?"

"Partially."

"Partially?"

Unger nodded.

"And, doctor, was she, in fact, aware of what was going on at that point in time?"

"I don't think you can say that from what has gone on."

"Are you saying, doctor, that she didn't know what was happening?"

"No. I'm saying that she was not aware of the force pushing her in that direction, I don't see how you can say she was aware of what was going on at that time. . . . I think she was acting under the influences of forces outside her awareness."

"And when she got there [to Pappas's office] and began the act, the actual statement to Mr. Pappas about 'would you help me find someone to kill my husband?'—did she know that she was making that statement?"

"Yes."

"Would it not be fair to say, then, doctor, that she was in fact aware—very aware—of what was going on at that point in time?"

"No."

"In other words, she didn't know what was happening?" Morrison's voice was impatient.

"No, it would not be fair to say she was aware of what was going on at that point in time."

"Would it be fair to state, doctor, that she knew that her mouth was moving and some air was passing through her vocal chords and she was mouthing the words, 'Mr. Pappas, I want you to help me kill my husband'?"

Dr. Unger paused for a moment and answered the question carefully. "At that point in time, her motions were so automatic that I am not sure of anything except the fact that she carried out the suggestion."

Morrison's questions continued in similar fashion, as if he were laying out traps, hoping to snare Dr. Unger in at least one of them.

"I believe you said she didn't know what was going on because she didn't understand the motives, is that correct?"

"I said she was impaired and that would have hampered her ability to know what was going on."

"Would it have hampered it to the degree that she did not know what she was saying at the time she said it?"

"By that, do you mean that she perceived her words?"

"Right."

"She heard them, I believe."

"They probably registered in her mind, would that be correct?"

"I believe that is right."

"And, doctor, wouldn't that indicate to you that her ability to do that means that she was aware of what was going on?"

"They are not necessarily correlated."

Morrison backed off that attack. He set up an analogy between Unger's use of hypnosis in the treatment of pain and the use of anesthesia. Unger agreed that a person given a spinal anesthetic would not feel stimulus to parts of his body, but he stressed that he did not equate hypnosis with spinal anesthesia.

"In other words, let me put it this way: If a person had spinal anesthesia to the point where he could not move any portion of his lower part of his body, I mean, that happens, isn't that correct?"

"Hopefully not," Dr. Unger replied.

"I mean while they were under the anesthetic."

"The idea is not to feel pain; not to be paralyzed."

Morrison was searching for a weakness. But despite Unger's repeated indication that the analogy was off, Morrison stuck with it, and instead of merely failing to breach the defense, he seemed to stumble in front of the jury and inflict damage on himself.

"Now, let me ask you this: If I had some form of anesthesia wherein I could not move my lower limbs . . . I would still be able to see them and observe that they were there, isn't that correct?"

"Yes."

"I may not be able to control them, isn't that correct?"

"Yes."

"All right. Now, isn't that what you were telling us about Mrs. Winters—in essence, that she knew, she understood and knew what was taking place, but was unable to control it because of this first hypnotic suggestion that you have been telling us about?"

"No. You are equating the giving of anesthesia and deadening of pain with hypnosis, and I am not sure they have anything in common."

Finally, Morrison abandoned that tack and asked about Norma's passive-dependent personality.

Dr. Unger acknowledged that passive-dependent people were manipulative and might try to use symptoms or circumstances to suit their own ends.

"Such as being found not guilty in a criminal trial?" Morrison asked.

"I'm going to object to that as being argumentative," I said.

"Overruled."

"They might," Dr. Unger said.

"And Mrs. Winters had this passive-dependent personality disorder when you were conducting these interviews upon which you base your opinion, isn't that correct?"

"Yes." He noted, though, that manipulation was characteristic of most personality disorders.

"Doctor, did Mrs. Winters appear to you to be attempting to manipulate you when she was talking with you?"

"I do not believe so."

"Would it be fair to say, doctor, that during all of the conversations you had with Mrs. Winters, she had selective recall, that is, she only recalled certain items and not others?"

"No."

"Did she recall everything?"

"I don't think I would use the words 'selective recall.' She appeared to have some amnesia. Selective recall, I think, implies some voluntary aspect."

After a few more questions, court adjourned for the day. Few of Morrison's questions had damaged the defense, but he had managed to eat up time to give himself an evening to prepare for a more rigorous cross-examination the next day. He seemed significantly more prepared when he began his questioning the next morning.

In his first questions Morrison acknowledged Unger's opinion that Norma's will had resisted the posthypnotic suggestion, and he asked, "It was her desire not to have her husband killed, in your opinion, is that correct?"

"I think that was the main thrust of her will," Dr. Unger answered. "I have already stated that I thought she had murderous thoughts toward her husband, and she was feeling ambivalent toward him for a long time, but the principal thrust of her will, I believe, was against doing anything of that nature."

Morrison seemed to gain confidence when Unger referred to "murderous thoughts," thinking, perhaps, he'd found a dent in the doctor's hitherto resistant armor. It was a term that seemed to intrigue the jury as well as Morrison.

"And these murderous thoughts, doctor, the ambivalence which you described as murderous thoughts, are murderous thoughts, doctor, by definition, thoughts involving the murder of another human being?"

"I characterized them as rage and harboring murderous thoughts. Murderous thoughts on occasion of anger directed at someone else, including oneself, are very common."

"Did she or did she not harbor murderous thoughts on occasion, doctor, toward her husband?"

"She did."

"Does that not mean, doctor, that Mrs. Winters then desired her husband's death prior to any hypnosis that may or may not have occurred in this case?"

"No, that can't be equated. You are equating the harboring of murderous thoughts and desiring a person dead. The one is an internal fantasy which may be carried no further than a vague fantasy and not be specifically formed into anything."

Morrison asked whether Mrs. Winters's murderous thoughts didn't mean she had been fantasizing that she wished her husband dead.

"No, I am saying that she was fantasizing murderous thoughts."

"And by 'murderous thoughts,' do we mean a desire to kill somebody?"

"No."

"What do we mean by 'murderous thoughts'?"

Dr. Unger paused a moment and shrugged. "Murderous thoughts are murderous thoughts. A desire to kill somebody is a formed opinion."

Dr. Unger also testified that Mrs. Winters's statement to Hanscom that she had been wishing her husband dead off and on for the past ten years would not alter his clinical opinion of her intent. Then he clarified that Norma had not been under hypnosis, but under the influence of a posthypnotic suggestion when she had met Hanscom at Denny's Coffee Shop.

"In what way is that different, doctor?"

"A person under hypnosis is more likely to be in a trance state, and the hypnosis is still in effect. It usually means that the person who is performing the hypnosis is close by and the person is much more controlled and much more susceptible to influence."

"And the person who is under posthypnotic suggestion is not as susceptible to influence, isn't that correct?"

"Somewhat less."

"How much less, doctor?"

"That depends on the individual. You can't make generalizations."

"Doctor, aren't your opinions in this trial generalizations?"

Unger paused a moment, then replied, "My opinions are opinions."

His response was neither haughty nor condescending. It was low-key but firm, and, like several of his other answers, it seemed to knock Morrison off stride. Another of the prosecutor's blows, directed with confidence at the witness, had glanced harmlessly away. But Morrison kept coming at him, and now he sought to undermine the heart of the case.

"Doctor, isn't it true," he asked, "that all of this business about hypnosis, or your opinion about all of this business about hypnosis, is based on what Mrs. Winters and what her daughter had told you?"

"It is all based on my clinical examination," he replied.

"But that was primarily interviews with Mrs. Winters and her daughter, right?"

"Correct."

"Now, you did not, under hypnosis, examine Mrs. Winters concerning the incident in El Centro, did you?"

"No."

"So, doctor, you were not able to determine through hypnosis whether or not Mrs. Winters was under a posthypnotic suggestion at that time, were you?"

"That does not necessarily follow."

"Well, you did not talk with Mrs. Winters about any of those incidents over there under hypnosis, did you?"

"No."

"So would it be fair to state, then, that your opinion that Mrs. Winters was suffering from a posthypnotic suggestion in El Centro is based solely upon what she told you about those incidents when she was not hypnotized?"

"No. During hypnosis, she told me about the episodes involving

Ellie and the period that there was a very strong possibility or probability of a posthypnotic suggestion, and this could have easily lasted through the period in El Centro."

"But that is speculation on your behalf, isn't it?"

"No, it is the nature of posthypnotic suggestions."

"And, doctor, isn't your opinion that she was still laboring under this posthypnotic suggestion nothing more than educated speculation on your behalf?"

"It is my clinical opinion."

"And isn't that opinion based on speculation that she was laboring under posthypnotic suggestion in El Centro?"

"It is my clinical opinion."

"That clinical opinion is not based on any interviews with Mrs. Winters conducted under hypnosis, is it?"

"No. My clinical opinion is based on my knowledge of hypnosis, what she told me, and what she revealed under hypnosis, and the deductions thereof."

Dr. Unger said he could not express his opinion in any quantitative degree of certainty, but that his conclusion was that Mrs. Winters had been hypnotized and had committed the crime under hypnosis or posthypnotic suggestion.

"And it is your opinion that all of this is a product of posthypnotic suggestion, is that correct?"

"I believe I have stated that I thought all of this was a product of a complex series of events that includes posthypnotic suggestion."

"But the posthypnotic suggestion was the trigger, wasn't it?"

"I don't know that one can even say that. It may have been that the traumatic event with the daughter was the trigger that allowed the posthypnotic suggestion to work. It may have been the clouding of the amphetamines, together with the traumatic situation, that allowed the posthypnotic suggestion to work."

Dr. Unger also testified that Mrs. Winters's request that Hanscom deliver a message before killing her husband and her concern about screwing up her weekend with Wayne Connors if Bruce was shot on a Saturday were consistent with Norma's ambivalence and with his opinion that she had been under a posthypnotic suggestion when she had committed those acts.

"The ambivalence would be operating in a manner outside of awareness," he explained, "and had postponing been done in pushing to a certain night, the patient would not have been aware of why she was doing it, just the fact that she was."

Wanting to keep her meeting with Connors a secret and the ambivalence she had indicated in her approach to hiring the hit man were "not mutually exclusive," he said.

Similarly, Dr. Unger testified, Norma's fears of getting caught —her worrying about paying the hit man a large sum of money, her Xeroxing the photograph, her typing out the license numbers rather than giving them to Hanscom in her own handwriting, and her concern over what would happen to her if Hanscom got caught —were "the verbal expression of a person who would still be operating under posthypnotic suggestion."

Morrison had tried in vain to undermine Dr. Unger's testimony, and now he resorted to hypothetical questions.

"Doctor, Mrs. Winters and her daughter told you that Mrs. Winters had been hypnotized, is that correct?"

"It was my understanding that the daughter told Mrs. Winters about it and Mrs. Winters didn't remember it."

"Yes, but I mean, you gleaned all of this from talking to the two of them, isn't that correct?"

"Correct."

"Now, if those statements were wrong—untrue—would your opinion change?"

"If those statements were wrong or untrue, my opinion would change. They would have been deemed wrong or untrue under my clinical examination."

"In other words, what you are telling us is that there is no possibility that those statements are untrue?"

"No. What I am telling you is my utmost reliance was on my clinical examination."

"Doctor, you just—no, never mind." Morrison paused, then looked back at Dr. Unger. "Could you be mistaken in this case?"

Unger nodded. "It is conceivable."

"Would it be a fair statement to say, doctor, that you have arrived at an opinion and you are not willing to change it?"

"No. I would say it would be a fair statement to say that I am as certain as I can be within the limits of my medical science."

Morrison asked only a few more questions, wrapping up what had become nearly two full days of testimony from Dr. Unger. Not once, I felt, had Morrison's persistent and often carefully plotted cross-examination significantly weakened Dr. Unger's testimony or Norma Winter's defense. I decided I didn't need to ask the doctor another question. His testimony was before the jury. The judge had indicated clearly that his instruction at the close of the case would allow the jury to consider it as they would the testimony of any other witness. Our defense was now fully before the court and before the twelve men and women who would decide Norma's fate.

"Your Honor," I said after Dr. Unger had been excused from the witness stand, "the defense rests."

CHAPTER 31

To challenge Dr. Unger's testimony, Morrison called as a rebuttal witness Dr. William Samuelson, a psychiatrist who testified frequently as an expert, usually for the prosecution. Like Dr. Unger, he had a long list of credentials, which he recited for the jury, and, in response to a question from Morrison, he testified that he had seen police reports, medical records, Dr. Ellison's psychiatric evaluation, and some of the trial testimony, including Norma's cross-examination, in reaching his opinion on the case.

"Have you read the material, doctor?"

"Not word for word. It was much too much, but I certainly perused as much as I could."

Samuelson testified that, contrary to what Dr. Unger and Dr. Ellison had maintained, amphetamines and thyroid would not make a person more susceptible to suggestion.

"They would, in essence, do the opposite," he said. "When you talk about amphetamines and thyroid drugs, you are talking about drugs that essentially stimulate and heighten one's awareness and certainly, in my opinion, would not, therefore, increase suggestibility."

He also said that in a healthy person the thyroid gland produced only as much as the body needed. Since Norma was taking four grains of thyroid per day, the gland, which normally produced only three, would produce no additional thyroid.

Under Morrison's questioning he then testified that a person had to be specifically programmed during hypnosis with the directions he or she would follow under a posthypnotic suggestion. The implication was that in order to have successfully planted the suggestion, Lovell would have had to know, for example, that Hanscom was going to call and meet with Norma and what they would do at the restaurant and the hotel room. Lovell certainly could not have known all that.

Samuelson said the hypnotist would have to give the subject a signal to induce the suggestion, and that it was "possible, but highly unlikely," that a signal could be transferred to a third party. That would rule out Ellie's involvement.

He also testified that Norma's passive-dependent personality might have made her more susceptible to hypnosis, but that neither the drugs nor the news about Beth would have affected that. And he said that, usually, a person under a posthypnotic suggestion could perform only simple, straightforward acts, not complicated ones involving conversations and responses from other people— acts he called "multiple related behavior contacts."

"If we were to talk about, say, a posthypnotic suggestion that you kill somebody," Morrison said, "that is, say, pick up a knife and, at a given signal, stab somebody, is that the type of multiple related behavioral contact we are talking about?"

"No," Samuelson replied. "Although it is a serious social behavior, it is really a simple act to do. . . . ."

"What about, though, the posthypnotic suggestion that you contact someone else to arrange for the . . . killing of a given person. Is that a multiple related behavioral contact?"

"It would depend. . . . If you were asked to, say, just make a phone call and say to someone who answers on the other end, 'I want you to do this,' that would be the essence of what I would classify as an acceptable posthypnotic activity. Now, to go into more complicated behavior discussion, other manifestations of what to do, where to do it, et cetera, embellishments of such a contact, in my opinion, no."

The answer was surprising. Samuelson had just described almost exactly what had occurred in Lovell's office—a phone call. I was certain he didn't know that—he had, after all, perused only some of the evidence. That was a point to bring home in cross-examination.

Morrison mentioned the phone call Norma had received from Hanscom and asked, "Now, would you expect Mrs. Winters's behavior with regard to the phone call to be the result of posthypnotic suggestion?"

"No, counsel."

"And would you tell the ladies and gentlemen of the jury why?"

"There is just too much higher thought process involved—independent thinking, interpretation, perception." He paused for a moment and looked at the transcript of Norma's meeting with Hanscom in the coffee shop.

"This is just very complicated," he said, "I am just looking at some of the transcripts here, when she makes the statement, 'No, you're probably having me watched. You're probably a cop.' And then the officer says, 'I do this part time, you know, you have to make a little side money, you know.' And her answer is, 'That is probably what is going to happen. I'll probably end up in jail.' . . . That kind of thinking, in my opinion, does not conform or coincide with a posthypnotic state."

Samuelson agreed with Dr. Unger that ambivalent feelings could occur under a posthypnotic suggestion, especially if the suggestion was unacceptable. And he acknowledged that under special circumstances persons could do in a posthypnotic state something that was unacceptable to them in their normal states of consciousness. Thus, in some important areas he seemed to support the defense. But I knew I'd have to find a way to undermine his contention that Norma's actions in her meetings with both Pappas and Hanscom had been too complicated to have occurred under posthypnotic suggestion.

Then, perhaps to cover the possibility that Norma *had* been under a posthypnotic suggestion, Morrison asked a question that indicated he thought it wouldn't matter, anyway.

"Would posthypnotic suggestion, doctor, in your opinion, diminish one's capacity to form a specific intent to commit the crime of solicitation of murder?"

"Would posthypnotic suggestion do that?" the witness responded.

Morrison nodded.

"Yes," Samuelson said. "A person laboring under a posthypnotic suggestion if, in fact, that is the case, yes, very definitely. In fact, it would be, in my opinion, totally exculpatory."

Morrison appeared surprised by the answer. He had argued before the judge that, at best, the posthypnotic suggestion might be a "diminished capacity" defense; now his own expert had said it was more than that. But Morrison continued without hesitation. "And would that be because it has diminished that person's capacity or because that person would be unconscious at the time?"

"In my opinion, he would be unconscious at the time," Samuelson replied.

"If a person is in, truly, in fact, laboring under posthypnotic suggestion, is that person in an altered state of consciousness?"

"Yes."

"And it is not, their capacity would not merely be diminished, but rather, they would be unconscious. They might be diminished by virtue of being unconscious but—" Morrison paused, appearing confused.

"It would be fully diminished," Samuelson interjected, "because unconsciousness, as I said, is totally exculpatory."

But he testified that nothing he saw in the evidence indicated Norma had been in an altered state of consciousness when she had committed the crime. And he said that Norma's "murderous thoughts" showed that she had indeed thought about killing her husband. Morrison asked one last question.

"Doctor, do you see anything in the data which has been presented to you that leads you to form the opinion that, at the time of the acts in question, Mrs. Winters did not possess the capacity to form the specific intent to commit the crime of solicitation of murder?"

"No, I find no data to support that conclusion."

It was my turn for cross-examination.

Samuelson's testimony puzzled Norma. "How does he know all that stuff, Milt?" she asked during a recess. "He didn't even talk to me."

"You're right, and I hope he's going to regret that," I said.

On the surface Samuelson had damaged the defense; he had contradicted Dr. Unger on two key points, saying Norma couldn't have been under the influence of a posthypnotic suggestion while involved in such a complex crime—that she couldn't have been programmed to do what she did—and that she had been able to form the intent to commit it. His definition of "murderous thoughts" clashed significantly enough with Unger's to raise a third doubt in the minds of the jurors. It was his word against Unger's, and I didn't think our defense could withstand such a severe difference of opinion.

But we had two advantages, I thought, in challenging Samuelson's position. A battle between expert witnesses is often as much a clash of personalities as of expertise, and Barry Unger was well received by the jurors. There was no doubt in their minds, I thought, that he was putting his professional reputation behind his opinion and not just selling his services. Although he was testifying at the request of the defense, he wasn't an advocate for Norma; he was representing his profession.

Second, he'd been far better prepared to testify. Samuelson was unfamiliar with a lot of critical evidence. His direct testimony seemed solid, but the key areas of conflict, I thought, were where he was not aware of Unger's findings.

Over my objection Judge Maine had ruled early in the trial that the prosecution had the right to examine Norma, but Morrison had not taken advantage of it. He apparently thought the case was too straightforward to need it. I hoped he had opened the door for me with that oversight.

"Do you see the defendant in the courtroom?" I asked Samuelson when testimony resumed.

"I have never met her, but I assume she is the woman to your right."

"This woman sitting here?" I asked, pointing to Norma.

"Yes."

"Do you know if that is Norma Winters?"

"Not by personal knowledge, no."

"Have you ever talked with her, interviewed her, or anything along those lines?"

"No."

"She has been available for an interview, has she not?"

He said he was not aware that he could have interviewed her, and then acknowledged that "direct interview is always the manner in which you try to make direct evaluations and judgments." Morrison, however, had not indicated to him that the judge had ruled that Norma would be available for a psychiatric examination. He also said he had read Dr. Ellison's testimony in preparing his opinion, but that he had seen none of Dr. Unger's and that he had not discussed the case with Dr. Unger.

"Other than what Mr. Morrison has told you," I asked, "do you know what Dr. Unger's testimony has been here in court?"

"Not directly, no, counsel."

He also was unaware of David's testimony that his mother had told him to tell Bruce that she loved him—key evidence, I thought, in establishing Norma's ambivalence. He had not interviewed Beth or Norma's mother, and he didn't know that Mrs. Holden had lived with Norma from March to August of 1974. Those interviews, he acknowledged, might have been helpful to him in reaching his opinion in the case. I hoped the jury was getting the message that despite his professional credentials, the validity of Dr. Samuelson's conclusions in the case depended on his knowledge of the facts in evidence.

Then I moved to the signal that a hypnotist might use to trigger a posthypnotic suggestion and asked Dr. Samuelson whether rubbing the neck might be such a signal. He said it would not be a good signal, because in medical hypnosis the doctor would minimize any "physical touching and closeness that might be misinterpreted, particularly in a person with altered states of consciousness. And if touching were indicated," he continued, "certainly it would not be in an area that I would consider intimate, which is the neck, for instance, that you described."

However, the doctor added, under my questioning, that rubbing the neck could be used as a signal by hypnotists who were not concerned about the implications of touching.

"And might there even be further motivation for tactile contact," I asked, "if that individual, in fact, had expressed a romantic interest in the subject?"

"Oh, if that were one of the motivations for that kind of behavior, obviously, that could apply. Yes."

Clearly, Samuelson was not aware of Lovell's sexual interest in Norma.

"Would it be fair to say that in determining susceptibility to hypnosis, and particularly in this case, that there are a number of factors to consider?"

"A number of factors you would consider in any individual, yes."

"Those might include the ingestion of drugs?"

"Yes."

"Those might—might they even include the question of the recently learned traumatic event or the reception of a traumatic experience?"

"No, I wouldn't agree with that."

I referred to his testimony that in exceptional situations, someone might be compelled to do something out of his or her moral character under hypnosis. I then asked, "If a person is told under hypnosis of a darned good reason why that person should act in a manner which might otherwise be inconsistent with that person's constellation of emotional responses, might that be utilized to advantage in convincing that person that it was proper to take a course of conduct differing from that which the individual would normally take?"

"Yes."

"Might such a motive be supplied in circumstances where a woman has just been informed that her minor daughter, since the age of twelve had been the victim of repeated sexual attacks, might that be maximized?"

"If that is information given during the hypnotic trance, yes, it could be used to maximize an effect."

In further testimony Samuelson conceded that Norma could have been following directions when she had approached Anthony Pappas. But he held his ground when I asked whether it wasn't possible for someone under a posthypnotic suggestion to carry out "multiple related behavior," which he defined as contact that involved dialogue, communication, and unpredictable behavior that required responses from another person.

"When you include behavior with another individual," he said, "you are expanding that situation, and you are not in control of the third party, who may, in fact, not provide you with the proper environment to achieve your goals. And so a multiple related incident would be sufficiently complex that it is beyond the scope of a hypnotic trance and a posthypnotic suggestion."

He also said a posthypnotic suggestion generally lasted only a few hours. In Norma's case we were talking about a week.

Temporarily thwarted, I went back to the question of Ellie's having planted the suggestion in Norma's mind. Samuelson had already testified that it would be more difficult to successfully plant a posthypnotic suggestion if someone other than the hypnotist was the conduit for it.

"Does that hold true," I asked, "in circumstances where the person who acts as the conduit, in fact, enjoys a much closer relationship to the subject than the hypnotist himself?"

"In my opinion, yes."

"Would it matter whether the hypnotist and the conduit were present—both present, during the hypnotic induction?"

"During the initial induction?"

"Yes."

"I don't believe so."

"What about a suggestion from the sister of the man who was the subject of a discussion relating to murder, the sister who enjoys a very close and deep relationship with the subject? What about circumstances such as that when the suggestion may be used in a manner that utilized that sister as a conduit?"

Morrison objected and was overruled.

"Counsel," Dr. Samuelson replied, "I think that is grasping at straws."

There was a hint of mockery in his voice as he answered that seemed almost a challenge to me. He was an experienced witness, and it showed. Despite his lack of information on the case, I'd failed to shake him on the major issues, and he knew it. Now he was saying, in effect, "Counsel, you can't touch me." I felt the urge to fight back, to ask, "Doctor, just what do you mean by 'grasping at straws'?" But to respond emotionally to an expert witness without the information to back him down is foolish. If I got involved in a sparring match with him now, I told myself, I'd lose—and I might lose the case, as well. I took a deep breath, asked a few more questions, then looked at the clock. It was late in the day.

"I'm not going to finish, Your Honor," I said.

Samuelson would have to come back for another day.

As we left the courthouse that afternoon, I wondered whether I should have completed my questions with Samuelson. Maybe I could make a strong enough argument in summation to encourage the jury to overlook his testimony. Why did I want him back on the stand the next morning if he was only going to knock me back with comments like "grasping at straws"? I still thought Unger's was the stronger testimony, but the jury, too, had to believe that. I didn't know what more I could do about Samuelson's testimony.

For the first time in two weeks of testimony, I felt pessimistic. After so much promise, the whole defense, it seemed, was about to collapse.

I was sitting at home alone, replaying the day's testimony over and over in my mind, when the telephone rang at about ten that night. It was Unger, wanting to know how Samuelson's testimony had gone.

"Not well," I said, filling him in on the details.

Dr. Unger, however, was not perturbed. He challenged the assertion that posthypnotic suggestion rarely lasted beyond a few hours.

"Yeah, Barry, but it's your word against his."

"No it's not," Unger replied. "It's his word against the literature of hypnosis."

He also disputed the statement that Norma's actions were too complex to work under posthypnotic suggestion. And murderous thoughts did not mean, as Samuelson had maintained, that Norma had planned to have her husband killed.

"You get some sleep," Unger said, "and you come over to my house at six o'clock in the morning. I'll have some coffee on and some books here, and we'll get you ready for Samuelson."

When I arrived at Unger's the next morning, it was clear he had spent most of the night in his library. The coffee was brewing, and the kitchen table was stacked to overflowing with thick medical texts and numerous periodicals, all of which were scientifically indexed and marked where they contradicted the points raised by

Dr. Samuelson. Within a couple of hours I was ready for the witness.

Samuelson's flight into San Diego was delayed, and it was after lunch before he resumed the stand.

"Would you distinguish for us, please, the difference between a specific and nonspecific hypnotic suggestion?" I asked.

"Well, it is almost self-definable," he replied with an air of self-confidence. "When you give a specific hypnotic suggestion you direct someone to do something, and in a nonspecific suggestion you are giving him an open order and finding out what he would do in response to it."

"Might . . . an example of a specific suggestion be directing a person that at the conclusion of the hypnotic session, they would move to the window and open the window?"

"That is correct, yes."

"Might another way of accomplishing that be simply informing the person that at the conclusion of the examination that person would feel very, very warm and very, very stuffy?"

"That would be nonspecific, and ask him to do something about it."

"And it would not be surprising, in the circumstances where a nonspecific posthypnotic suggestion was provided, that the person might, in fact, act essentially on his own in terms of opening the window without a specific directive that he do that?"

"That is correct."

"Similarly, if I were to plant a nonspecific posthypnotic suggestion that a person would feel extremely cold at the conclusion of the interview, might we expect that that person might put on a coat?"

"Yes."

"If we asked that person why he put on the coat, might we expect that person would respond, perhaps, that he wanted to see how it fit?"

Samuelson said a person might use a wide variety of reasons to logically explain "silly" or "unusual" behavior.

"You stated that in your opinion and from the data that you have available, that . . . the reasoning process and so forth exhibited by Mrs. Winters militates against a conclusion that she was suffering from a posthypnotic suggestion, at least at the time she was talking to Al Hanscom."

"That is one of the reasons. There are at least two others that I could enunciate."

"Let's stick with that one for the moment," I said. I referred to the package of documents he had in front of him—the police reports, psychiatric reports, and trial testimony Morrison had provided him with.

Those reports, he testified, did not include the exact language of the conversation between Norma and Anthony Pappas.

"Yesterday, when we were speaking in terms of the compliance with a specific hypnotic suggestion, you indicated that it, one example of a specific response to a specific directive might be the act of a person in picking up a telephone and making a phone call."

"The act of the subject?" he asked.

"Yes, the act of the subject."

"Yes."

"Are you aware of the substance of the testimony which occurred between Mrs. Winters and Anthony Pappas?"

"I have so stated that I was not. . . . If Mr. Pappas has testified, I am not familiar either with the transcript or the testimony."

"All right. Do you know whether Mrs. Winters called the offices of Anthony Pappas on an occasion prior to her meeting with him?"

"Yes, I—she had had previous contact with him." He said it would not matter when the prior contact had occurred.

"Do you know whether Mrs. Winters was alone or in the company of other individuals at the time that she made these initial contacts with Anthony Pappas?"

"No, I don't know specifically as to what other individuals were present," he said.

That wasn't just superficial information. It was critical to the case. Such gaps in his knowledge had to seem significant to the jurors, I thought. After all, they knew the answer to the question. If this expert didn't, why should they listen to him?

"Would it be significant to you if the person whom we must assume from the evidence was the hypnotist was present on the occasion of those phone calls?"

"I would have to know more than that, but that could be a significant factor."

Samuelson had finally conceded an important point. The more he learned about the case from my questions, the more he seemed to make room for our defense. I grew more confident.

"Now, if I may, I'd like to grasp for straws in my next questions," I said. "You indicate that third-party or conduit hypnosis is extremely difficult to achieve?"

"Yes."

"What statistical methodologies have you referred to in arriving at that conclusion?" I asked, glancing at the stacks of books on my table.

He paused. "I have specifically not done so. It is just a matter of my own experience with my past recollection and reading of material in the field."

I had to close one more door before confronting him directly. "Have you ever conducted an experiment of such a nature?"

"To attempt to get a third party involved?"

I nodded.

"No."

I proposed a hypothetical case depicting the circumstances of Norma's hypnosis when she called Pappas. "Now," I asked, "have there been any two-party statistical studies of the likelihood of success or failure of that particular kind of communication?"

Samuelson eyed the books in front of me. "Specifically, I know of none. But I would guess there have been statistical studies on everything, counsel, so I wouldn't be surprised if there were one on something like this."

I referred to the previous day's testimony when I asked whether a normally unacceptable hypnotic suggestion might be accepted if its source was the subject's closest friend and also the sister of the man who was supposedly going to be killed. "You indicated that you felt I was grasping at straws on that question, is that right?" I asked.

"I believe so, yes."

"And the reason for that would be because of certain unspecified studies and your own reading have caused you to hold the opinion that, as a general matter, third-party transmission of hypnotic suggestions are destined to fail?"

"That is correct."

The implication was clear: he had performed no experiments, had no personal experience in the area, and although he claimed to have remembered something about the subject in the literature, he couldn't recall what it was.

"Now, with relationship to your operational definition for 'murderous thoughts,' have you had occasion to read Manfred Guttmacher's book *The Mind of the Murderer?*"

"I have looked at it. I don't believe I read it from cover to cover, but it has been a minimum of ten years."

The late Manfred Guttmacher, Samuelson knew, had been one of the foremost forensic psychiatrists in the world. What Samuelson didn't know was that Dr. Unger had trained under him.

"And do you know," I asked, "if in that book, whether Manfred Guttmacher uses the phrase 'murderous thoughts'?"

"Not—I don't have any independent recollection."

"And if the party who had testified and had utilized that phrase might have been trained under Manfred Guttmacher, might that not perhaps account for his operational definition, if it, in fact, coincided with that of Manfred Guttmacher?"

Morrison objected, but was overruled. Samuelson studied me a moment. "You are correct. You tend to use the terms as you have learned them in your training."

Then I asked him again about using Dr. Unger's report and testimony in reaching his opinion in this case.

"Do you have his testimony?" I asked.

"Not in writing, no. I was just advised of the testimony."

"By the district attorney?"

"Yes."

I noted his conclusion that Norma could not have been in a posthypnotic state when she had talked with Al Hanscom, and I asked, "What, if any, active role did you take in acquiring information deemed by you to be essential to the rendering of your opinion?"

"Only to suggest to the district attorney, Mr. Morrison, certain information that would be of benefit, that if there were psychiatric evaluations, [they] would, in my opinion, be important to peruse.

And he said that he did not initially have it available, but when it became available, he would forward it. I was primarily interested in that aspect in order to, at least indirectly, best assess the character structure and the diagnostic category that Mrs. Winters was placed in."

"Is there anything in any of these reports other than a brief mention of the subject by Dr. Ellison—referring to Dr. Unger's report—about hypnosis . . . ?"

"No. I believe that Dr. Ellison's typewritten report was the basis for the definitive information that I have."

That report contained just two sentences, the witness acknowledged, regarding Dr. Unger's conclusion that Norma might have been under a posthypnotic influence.

"And you, of course, considered those statements, I take it, in rendering your opinion here yesterday?"

"Very definitely, yes," he said.

"Wasn't your curiosity aroused as to what Dr. Unger might have to say?"

"I did suggest that if it were available, I would like to see it, but I was told it was not available."

By now, I felt, Samuelson's opinion carried less weight with the jury, no matter how impressive his credentials.

"All right, you have testified that you might characterize yourself as a forensic psychiatrist?"

"Yes. That is basically what I do."

"I take it you have testified on many, many occasions and have been qualified on many occasions as an expert witness?"

"That is correct."

"In your opinion, is the expert testimony of an individual characterized as a forensic psychiatrist entitled to greater weight than the opinion of just a plain old professor of psychiatry at the University of California?"

"I would leave that up to the trier of fact, counsel," Samuelson replied.

I nodded. So would I.

Morrison asked several more questions. In answering them, Samuelson testified that Norma would not have made repeated attempts to carry out the act of solicitation of murder unless she had been hypnotized more than once, or unless she had been given multiple suggestions during the initial hypnotic session. Then I had another turn.

I presented Dr. Samuelson with the situation of a woman who was told under hypnosis that she would have no desire to drink alcohol and would not drink alcohol, but who, once out of the trance, was at a party where someone forced a drink down her throat.

"Might you not expect to find an acute anxiety reaction on that person's part?" I asked.

"Yes. . . . You could expect to find it more serious than acute anxiety," he said. "You might precipitate psychosis."

"Now, would it be of interest to you if you were to learn that Dr. Unger, when he had Mrs. Winters under hypnosis—and let us assume that he did—that at the time he began to question her relating to the phone call that was placed to the offices of Anthony Pappas, he became extremely alarmed at the response of Mrs. Winters, and that he was afraid that she might suffer either an anxiety reaction or an outright psychotic episode?"

The doctor paused. For the first time, he seemed genuinely surprised by something he hadn't known. "That would be a very significant piece of data, yes," he said.

Then I referred to his earlier testimony that a posthypnotic suggestion, though usually lasting only a few hours, might last as long as a month.

"I said I would be surprised if it did," he explained, "that it would be contrary to the evidence available."

"Now, what statistical or methodological data did you refer to in arriving at that conclusion? What specific study?"

"Again, it is really more a matter of experience."

"Now, are you aware of an article by Kellogg in the *Journal of Experimental Psychology* on the subject of the duration and effects of posthypnotic suggestion?"

"No."

"Are you aware of an article by Erickson in the *Journal of General Psychology* entitled 'Concerning the Nature and Character of Posthypnotic Behavior'?"

"No."

"Are you aware of a specific study by Fisher in the *Journal of Abnormal and Social Psychology* entitled 'The Role of the Psychiatrist in the Performance of Posthypnotic Behavior'?"

"No."

"Are you aware of a study by Gurney," I said, picking up yet another book, "entitled 'The Peculiarity of Certain Posthypnotic States'?"

Samuelson squirmed in his chair. A couple of the jurors smiled.

"No," he said.

I had even more ammunition on my desk, but the point was made. "Would it surprise you if the consensus of those articles was that the average duration and effectiveness of a posthypnotic suggestion was a period of two months?"

Samuelson took a deep breath. "No," he answered.

"Thank you, doctor," I smiled. "I have no further questions."

Neither did Morrison. Samuelson stepped down.

The prosecution announced it had no further evidence to present. During a short recess I spoke with Dr. Unger, whom I had earlier asked to come down, in the event Samuelson's testimony did not go well for us. But several colleagues who had witnessed the cross-examination agreed that there was no reason to recall Dr. Unger. "Samuelson helped you," one of them said. I informed the court the defense had no surrebuttal.

We were ready for final argument.

CHAPTER 32

The closing arguments are the climax of a jury trial. While the criminal justice system is based on the premise that the evidence, and only the evidence, presented in a trial should determine a defendant's fate, it is widely acknowledged that cases can be won or lost in summation. In complex cases that run for months and involve dozens of witnesses, and in bizarre or unusual cases, such as the trial of Norma Winters, the summation can be even more important. Although the arguments themselves are not evidence, they are the lawyers' only opportunity to explain the evidence to the jury—to make the connections, to raise the unanswered questions, and to frame the evidence in a context that suggests the defendant's guilt or innocence.

Under California law the People make the first statement to the jury; the defense follows. Then, because the People bear the responsibility of the burden of proof, they get the final word—the final argument to the jury before it begins its deliberations. Just before Morrison rose to address the jury, the judge, at my request, reminded the jurors that Norma had been available to the prosecution for a psychiatric examination since March 10. Samuelson's testimony had raised questions about that, and I wanted to make sure the jury understood that the People had had access to her.

"Mr. Morrison," the judge said, "are you ready for your final summation?"

"We are, Your Honor."

"You may proceed."

It was late Thursday afternoon, and since the judge did not hold trial on Fridays, both Morrison and I were under pressure from the clock. It was either finish the arguments today—after which the judge would meet the next day to instruct the jury—or finish on Monday, which would mean an interruption of three days. Such a delay could have a troubling impact on the logic and effectiveness of a summation.

Morrison walked up to the lectern, took his watch from his wrist, and placed it in front of him.

"May it please the court, counsel, ladies, and gentlemen," he began. "As you see, when I walk up here, I take my watch off and put it up here. Unfortunately, it is not as big as the clock behind me, and I hope that what I say and what I don't say will at least distract your attention somewhat from the clock in hopes that what I say is at least interesting enough to gain your attention."

He didn't need to ask for their attention. The concentration in the jury box was intense.

"When you think about this case," he said, "and you think about the evidence in this case, you may wonder what I am doing here, because this is one of those once-in-a-lifetime cases where argument is unnecessary. This case is open and shut.

"The evidence of Mrs. Winters's guilt in this case is overwhelming. We have got everything but moving pictures of the crime in progress in this particular case."

He noted that his responsibility was to prove Norma's guilt beyond a reasonable doubt. "But we have done more in this case. We have proven her guilty beyond all shadow of a doubt and beyond all imaginary doubt."

He described our defense as a "smoke screen" established to hide Norma's guilt and an "unadulterated pitch for sympathy."

"All that has been presented by the defense, ladies and gentlemen, may give someone—some one of you—an excuse to attempt to render a not guilty verdict in this case, but, ladies and gentlemen, there is no reason based upon the evidence or founded in logic or law for doing anything but finding Norma Winters guilty of the crime of which she is charged." The evidence, he maintained, left no doubt that she had solicited the murder of her husband, and that she had intended to do it.

Then he recited that evidence for the jurors—the contact and meeting with Pappas and her telling him, "I want you to help me find someone to kill my husband."

"The evidence did not show that she was behaving as an automaton, that she was in any sort of trance," he argued. "The evidence showed that she went in there and solicited the murder of her husband."

He pointed out that just because she had been unsuccessful in having her husband murdered by her meeting with Pappas, it did not mean she was innocent of the crime. "All that is required, ladies and gentlemen, is the intent to solicit murder and the words or the utterance of the words themselves."

And he reviewed the phone call and the meetings with Hanscom.

"When Officer Hanscom said to her, 'This is Al from San Diego. I understand you have something you want to get rid of,' " Morrison said, "what was Mrs. Winters's response? 'No. I don't know what you are talking about. Who are you? What is this?' " He paused.

"That was not her response. Her response was, 'Huh? Yeah.' " Not that of an automaton, he argued.

He noted that she had also solicited Manny Lopez and that she had asked him to go to Denny's to keep an eye on her during that meeting with Hanscom.

Why did she do that? he asked the jury. "Again, a concern by Mrs. Winters for her own well-being, not the act of somebody laboring in a posthypnotic state."

Similarly, he argued, Norma had typed out a list of license numbers, so that a handwritten list could not be traced to her. "I submit to you, ladies and gentlemen, there is no evidence of a posthypnotic suggestion in this case. No evidence that can be accepted by you as a trier of facts in a court of law."

Then he asked the jury rhetorically, "What else did Mrs. Winters do at that point in time?" He paused dramatically and looked over at Norma at the defense table.

"Norma Winters, the shrinking violet we have heard so much about," he continued, his voice rising almost in anger, "Norma

Winters with the passive-dependent personality who won't do this, who was abused by everybody who came in contact with her—ladies and gentlemen, Norma Winters at that particular point in time told Officer Hanscom, 'Don't do it before this weekend.' And when we were talking with Mrs. Winters about that when she was here on the witness stand, and we said, 'Gee, Mrs. Winters, why didn't you want that done?' she said, 'Gee, my husband was going to take two days of annual leave.' " He paused again.

"What was she trying to tell us, ladies and gentlemen? That she was concerned for her husband in his last two days on earth at that point in time? Is that the feeling that Mrs. Winters was attempting to convey to us?" Again, he looked over at the defendant, then back at the jurors, some of whom were studying Norma closely.

"Well, ladies and gentlemen, if that was the feeling she was attempting to convey to us, I submit to you right now that that was a sham. Because we later found that the reason she didn't want her husband killed was so that her weekend or her meeting with her old boyfriend, Wayne Connors, in San Diego on Saturday night, would not be disturbed, upset, or found out about.

"Now, is this the person who is laboring in a posthypnotic state, who is goal directed, who is acting like she wants her husband killed as a result of somebody else's suggestion? . . . I submit to you that it is not."

Then he reminded the jury of Norma's statement to the police after her arrest in which she had insisted that Pappas and Hanscom were the only people she had contacted and of how Ryan and Hanscom had tripped her up on Manny and forced her to admit to a third contact.

"It is on tape," he said. "That is one thing that she can't deny. She cannot deny that. And I would submit to you that, well, let me put it this way: generally we are not fortunate enough to have that type of evidence."

In addition to the tape, testimony from Sergeant Ryan, Pappas, and Pappas's secretaries, he said, stood as "uncontradicted proof of the fact that Mrs. Winters solicited the murder of her husband."

Then Morrison moved for a moment to Dr. Unger's testimony.

"Now, Dr. Unger . . . testified that all these things she was doing showed ambivalence. Of course, he couldn't pick any one of them out as showing ambivalence, just his gut feeling that the whole thing showed ambivalence."

Morrison argued that Norma's hedging on the payment to Hanscom—both spreading the $10,000 payment out over ten months and dickering over $500 or $100 in front money—was evidence that she had been worried about getting caught.

"And now she claims that this is just some kind of ambivalent feeling that she was having. All of these acts, ladies and gentlemen, were done not by the shrinking violet that they would have us believe that Mrs. Winters is," he said, wrinkling his brow for emphasis, "but rather by an individual, coldly and in a calculated manner, who planned the death of her husband."

Then Morrison talked about motive—something I didn't think he'd ever established. He told the jury that Norma herself had disclosed her motive on the tape with Hanscom.

"He said, 'What about the insurance?' She said, 'I don't care about the insurance. The reason I am doing this is because I just found out that my husband has molested my minor child.' "

Whether her husband had molested Beth or not was not at issue in the trial, Morrison said. "The only thing we have to concern ourselves with here is whether or not Mrs. Winters solicited the murder of her husband, and I submit to you that the evidence shows that she has, that Mrs. Winters made up her mind, according to her, that Mr. Winters wasn't entitled to the same due process of law you have seen her benefit from in this trial. She was going to act as a vigilante and take the law into her own hands, if that was her motive."

It was a strong point, I thought, but Morrison didn't stop there. He suggested that Wayne Connors's involvement could be another motive. "Was she looking for a less expensive way to get rid of her husband than perhaps going through a divorce action where there would be a division of property? I don't know. That's a possible motive. Just as the insurance money is a possible motive." And he reviewed the arithmetic that showed that her total loans—$55,000 —had been almost identical to the proceeds of her insurance policies—$57,000.

Norma wept softly as Morrison continued.

"The court is going to tell you that the presence or absence of a motive is one of the things that you may consider," he said, "and all of these things, ladies and gentlemen, point to a motive, not to an excuse, but to a motive that Mrs. Winters possessed on the dates in question wherein she wanted to have her husband killed."

The evidence against Norma, he reiterated, was overwhelming.

"What does the defense do, then, in the light of this overwhelming evidence?" he asked. "They submit to you basically two possible legal defenses, and I call them possible, but I would submit to you really that they do not exist. But in the law they are permitted to argue she was unconscious, or on the other hand, that her capacity to form the intent to solicit her husband's murder was so diminished that she was incapable of doing so. So what do we do?

"They don't have enough by itself from Norma Winters, so she now claims she has been hypnotized, and this is all as a result of a posthypnotic suggestion. What do they do with regard to this crime? Do they call the alleged hypnotist, Walter Lovell, her brother-in-law?" His voice was rich with sarcasm. "Do they call him down here and put him on the stand and have him either admit or deny it, or take the fifth?" He paused, letting the question hang.

"No, they do not. Whose word do we have for this? Norma Winters's, and, of course, Dr. Unger's testimony, based upon what Norma Winters told him. But they never attempted to corroborate the claim that there ever was, in fact, a hypnosis."

He noted that Dr. Ellison had testified that Norma was susceptible to hypnosis, and he added, "Ladies and gentlemen, the prosecution in this case has never for one instant contended that Mrs. Winters is not susceptible to hypnosis. She may be. But that is all they wanted us to know."

From the cross-examination of Dr. Ellison, he said, "we learned some other things," and he read from the court record Dr. Ellison's testimony that there had been a functioning of Norma's conscious mind between August 6 and 14, and that, in his view, Norma's capacity to solicit the crime of murder had not been impaired.

"Dr. Ellison, we find out," Morrison said, "when we get a chance to ask him some real questions about the real issues in the case, testified that this defense as raised by Norma Winters is just that, a bogus defense."

Morrison neglected to mention that Dr. Ellison wasn't asked to consider Dr. Unger's findings when he rendered that opinion. But Morrison wanted to discredit Unger's testimony.

"Ladies and gentlemen," he continued, "[Dr. Unger] testified in a manner which I regret to say can only be characterized as the rankest form of speculation. He can be forgiven, I submit, as can any expert, for voicing an erroneous opinion, but he cannot be forgiven for his failure to concede that he might be in error."

Unger, Morrison contended, was not an expert witness testifying as a physician, but an advocate for Norma's cause, and his credibility was therefore "extremely suspect." He maintained that Dr. Unger had avoided some questions and been unresponsive to others.

"Now, in addition to the testimony of a psychiatrist," he continued, "Mrs. Winters testified herself, and if you were to disregard all of the psychiatric testimony that has been put before you in this trial, you are left with this: Mrs. Winters herself testified that during these acts and during the times that she was preparing to furnish Officer Hanscom with some of the documents necessary for him to kill her husband, that she had the specific intent to do so."

He read again from the court record, the testimony in which Norma had acknowledged typing the license numbers.

" 'And would it be a fair statement, ma'am, to say while you were performing that act, it was your intention at that time to have your husband killed?' Answer from Mrs. Winters: 'Yes.'

"Now shortly after that there was a recess, and, of course, when the same questions were posed to Mrs. Winters, after a long time, she all of a sudden drew a blank. Selective recall came into play, and Mrs. Winters began to shift on the stand."

In determining whether witnesses were credible, he explained, the jury could consider "their demeanor on the stand, that is, the way they look, the manner in which they testify. Do they appear to you as if they are telling the truth? Well, ladies and gentlemen, I submit that Norma Winters wasn't telling us all she knew."

He paused, then began his conclusion.

"Deep in the heart of every criminal defendant lurks the hope, no matter how remote, that some jury, or some juror, may disregard the evidence against them," he said, "and I submit to you that that should not be done in this case. For whatever reason of her acts, the fact remains that she did what she is accused of doing, and she intended to do so.

"These trials are conducted, ladies and gentlemen, in an effort by our system to arrive at what we sometimes refer to as justice. Justice means many things to many people, but I think that it might be characterized in this case as truth.

"In view of that, I would submit to you that the only just verdict in this case—the only true verdict in this case—is a verdict of guilty on both counts, and to find otherwise at this point in time, I would submit to you, would be to perpetrate fraud upon the very system which protects all of us."

As Morrison gathered his notes and stepped back from the lectern, I wondered what the jury was thinking. His statement, although at times grating in its delivery, had been very effective, especially when it had maintained that the defense was just an elaborate smoke screen. How many jurors were now asking themselves, "Are we being snowed? Is this for real?"

The defense, if nothing else, was bizarre. I believed that in presenting it, we had done a better job than Morrison had in winning the hearts of the jurors. Now, Morrison was saying, don't forget your minds. Don't get swept up in sympathy for this woman; just look at the facts.

I wanted them to look at the facts, too, but I had to dispel Morrison's insinuation that they were too bizarre for the jury even to consider. And I had to dispel it immediately, I thought, or the case could be lost.

"Mr. Silverman, are you ready for your final summation?"

"Yes, Your Honor."

I stepped up to the lectern.

CHAPTER 33

"**M**ay it please the court, ladies and gentlemen of the jury," I began. "I want to begin by clarifying what I view as my position here. There has been allusion by the prosecution to 'smoke screens' that have been presented to the jurors. There have been allusions and, in fact, repeated references to Mrs. Winters's 'having you believe' certain evidence, and, frankly, it sounded to me like the prosecution thought that Mrs. Winters was in control of the destiny of her defense, and she is not. I am.

"If certain evidence is unbelievable to you, then so be it. But I view my role here in a court of law as being a person who presents evidence. I don't view my role as being one of an advocate in the sense of by rhetoric or other means to convince you that a certain set of facts is true or false.

"You promised me at the beginning of this case that you wouldn't make up your minds until all the evidence was in, and there is not a man or a woman sitting on this jury that I did not believe, and so I am going to make a promise to you. I promise that if you decide this case in accordance with the evidence and consistently with your own consciences, that I will be pleased with the outcome of this case, regardless of what the verdict may be. And I say that as sincerely as I ever spoke a word."

I felt the jury relax; it was almost as if they had given a collective sigh of relief. I felt they would listen to my argument with open minds.

"This started out as an insurance case," I said, leaning over the lectern. "And the prosecution's opening remark—you may recall that the first words out of his mouth were that 'the prosecution will prove'—and he said so in a strident tone, which in a sense communicated a quality of importance to the statement—'that Mrs. Winters had insurance on her husband's life in the amount of \$57,000. . . .' It looked for a while that the evidence was going to show that the motive in this case was that Mrs. Winters was going to seize certain funds and benefit by them.

"That was, of course, an opening statement. What became of that? What became of that statement in opening remarks later down the line?"

I reminded the jury that each time Hanscom or Ryan had mentioned insurance, Norma had immediately stated that she hadn't thought about it, that she hadn't been in it for the insurance. I noted that comparing the total proceeds with the amount of Norma's outstanding loans, which seemed troubling at first, was misleading, since one loan was to be paid off with another and since the total would not come close to the life-insurance benefits.

"Well, after the prosecution had presented that evidence, it was later learned, of course, that these insurance policies had been taken out in 1966. One of the policies, as a matter of fact, was one over which she had . . . no control. It was by virtue of her husband having worked at the, with customs, which is automatic.

"The inferences that were created by the prosecution's evidence, I think, were disturbing," I said. "But, I think, ultimately we were not disturbed. We explained." I paused for a moment, before elaborating on one aspect of the insurance policies I considered very significant.

"It is important to note," I said, "that the testimony has been that Norma Winters didn't even have physical possession of those policies and that they were physically in the possession of another person by the name of Walter Lovell."

Then, I said, Wayne Connors, the boyfriend, had become an issue. Again, the implications had been disturbing. But we had demonstrated through telephone records that Conners had called

Norma *before* she had talked to Hanscom. I noted that Connors had testified under oath that he had not seen Norma since 1970. I conceded that unless the jury believed him and Norma, there would always be some room for doubt about his involvement in the case.

"The case, as I mentioned in my opening remarks, would appear overwhelming," I continued. "I am in agreement with the prosecution. I am not in agreement that moving pictures would help, because there is no moving picture that can transgress the internal processes of the mind." I paused. There was not a sound in the courtroom.

"And in our criminal law, persons are not punished for acts unless they are accompanied by specific intents. Persons are not punished in our law for conduct that is not the product of their own will."

I took a deep breath. The jury seemed to be warming to my argument.

"The defense, I will concede, was of an extremely bizarre and unusual character," I continued. "It occurred to me that the evidence was bizarre. It occurred to me that it was unusual. It occurred to me that it might not be believed. But that didn't alter, in my view, my responsibility to present it."

I told the jury about the meeting in my office on January 17, the day we had discovered quite by accident that Norma had been hypnotized. It had been out of desperation over her inability to remember certain events, I said, that she had asked, "Why can't I remember that?" And in free-floating thought I had responded, "Amnesia, hypnosis—" which had brought the immediate reply from Beth: "He was always doing that to us."

"Now," I said, "if there is a certain calculation to the manner in which that information was given to me, then I think that the level of sophistication on the part of Norma Winters has to be something to behold. She doesn't say, 'Yeah, I was hypnotized by so-and-so on such and such a date, and that is going to be my defense in this case.' She says, 'I wasn't hypnotized.'

"Now, she has to be pretty smart to say that. She has to know that if she tells that to a doctor, he is not going to say, 'Okay, forget it, you weren't hypnotized.'. . . She has to have at least that level of sophistication, in order to even know that by some kind of remote process of conviction, the doctor isn't going to be fooled by that statement."

I reminded the jury that Norma herself had testified that if you had asked her between August 6 and August 14 whether she was hypnotized, she would have said no.

And I noted that the prosecution had portrayed some of Mrs. Winters's testimony as believable and other parts of it as unbelievable. "They rely on the testimony as far as incriminating matters are concerned," I said. I wondered aloud to the jury about Morrison's characterization of Norma's testimony as "selective recall." "I am wondering," I said, "if a person really wanted to be selective about the recall of the events, how it would be that they would select the specific material that can't be recalled in this case, and for what reason? For the reason that it would somehow result in their acquittal?"

Then I talked about Dr. Unger's credibility as a witness, characterizing him as a man with pride in his work and concern about the quality of his testimony. "It is true that he doesn't make his living by testifying," I said. "It is true that he doesn't characterize himself as a quote-unquote forensic psychiatrist, which apparently is defined as a person who testifies a lot in court. It is true that he is none of those things, but he is experienced in the area of hypnosis. He has testified that he has hypnotized well in excess of a hundred patients. . . . And he testified that he performed a certain clinical procedure, and that clinical procedure consisted of intensive interviews, both under and not under hypnosis, of Norma Winters, and as a result of those sessions, he formed a certain opinion.

"Now, it is said that the only evidence of hypnosis in this case is the testimony of Norma Winters," I said. But Beth had testified that she had seen Walter Lovell place Norma under hypnosis and that she remembered things about the session that her mother did not.

"The prosecution has asked why I haven't called Walt Lovell," I continued. I looked over at Morrison, sitting at his table. "I have a more interesting question: why haven't they?"

Several jurors seemed to nod slightly.

I said if Lovell were called, it was doubtful he would admit to having placed Norma in a hypnotic trance and having planted a hypnotic suggestion to murder her husband.

"I rather think that the reason that Walter Lovell hasn't been called is that the prosecution is afraid to call him. I rather think that the prosecutor is a little bit afraid of what might happen to Walter Lovell on cross-examination."

By now I was pacing slowly back and forth in front of the jury box. I told the jurors I had reluctantly called Dr. Richard, and only to identify the medication Norma had taken, but that the judge had allowed the prosecution to question him out of order as a rebuttal witness.

"Dr. Richard was a very interesting witness. He apparently expected the patient to know the nature of the medications that the patient was taking without being aware of them himself."

I reminded the jury that he had ignored Norma's symptoms of itchy skin, tiredness, and nervousness and that he had commented cavalierly that if she were really bothered by such problems she should see her family doctor. And I noted that he had been administering drugs to her that were classified as dangerous by the federal Food and Drug Administration and that he had taken no steps to monitor their effects on her system.

"We have Norma Winters at the time of this incident under the combined effect and influence of dextroamphetamine—a dangerous drug within the meaning of federal drug laws—and thyroid—four grains a day—and a whole panoply of other pills . . . the purpose being with the amphetamines, bring her up in the morning, and barbiturates, bring her down at night."

And I noted that Dr. Ellison had testified that these drugs had had a significant impact on Norma's basic personality and that it had been "out of character for Mrs. Winters to go to the offices of Anthony Pappas and to engage in the conduct in which she did."

I remarked that Morrison had made a big point with Ellison's testimony that Norma might have been capable of forming the specific intent to solicit the murder of her husband, but I pointed out that the questions and Dr. Ellison's answers had been based only on Dr. Ellison's examination of Norma Winters.

"Was he asked to consider the opinion of Dr. Unger?" I asked.

"No."

I told the jury that Morrison had tried to impugn Beth's credibility as a witness by questioning whether her mother had really been upset during the car ride and the visit to the banker's house.

"It is true in this case that it doesn't matter whether Beth Winters was sexually assaulted or incestualized by her father. The question is really whether, upon receipt of that information, Norma Winters believed it. I would submit that in this case that seems fairly certain.

"Beth described what her mother did. She described that, and she wept. She described in her own words that she had never seen her mother more upset than that. Perhaps Beth is lying, or perhaps Norma Winters is such a good actress that she can convince her own daughter that she is upset when really she is not."

And I mentioned David's testimony, about his mother's asking him to "tell your Daddy that I love him too." Morrison's cross-examination, I noted, had tried to portray young David as a liar.

"Every witness, all the way to David, was potentially a liar in the prosecution's mind," I said. "Beth might be lying to protect her mother. She might be lying about the molestation. Norma is lying because she has selective recall. David is lying because his mother is telling him to forget or remember things about conversations that didn't exist."

Then I reviewed the key evidence in favor of my client.

"We have a woman with a basic personality structure of passive dependency," I said, "a basic personality structure that had accepted the act of being held at gunpoint over a weekend. We have a woman who has accepted the act of having the Bible ripped apart and thrown at her. We have a woman whose response when she . . . sees Wayne Connors and knows that her husband is there—whose response is to go and hide in the bathroom.

"That is the type of personality structure we have in Norma Winters: a structure that is completely consistent with passive dependency. And then we have something that is completely incongruous. We have this woman doing things that are out of character, that require some explanation.

"Whether any of these factors—the incest, the pills, or the hypnosis—alone would have been sufficient to occasion what occurred here, I don't know, and I don't think that anybody does. But I do know that Dr. Unger testified that he placed Mrs. Winters under hypnosis, that he regressed her, and that he asked her about the events leading up to the phone call of Anthony Pappas."

I took the jury through that testimony once again, including Norma's statement while under hypnosis that it had not been in her mind to make that phone call when she had walked into Walt Lovell's office. I talked about the letter that Lovell had known about because he and Ellie had arbitrated a dispute between Norma and Bruce over what Pappas had intended with the letter and the flowers. I talked about Norma's nearly coming out of the trance when she had said that Ellie had suggested she make the phone call, and finally, about Lovell's sitting in the background, nodding.

"Maybe," I said, "maybe that is hard to believe. But then we have an additional fact. We know that on the next day, the day when she goes to see Anthony Pappas, that she is driven there in a car, and that she is driven in the car by Walter Lovell. . . . That is the testimony. If that were untrue, then I would think that the prosecution would be interested in calling Walter Lovell and having him deny it."

Then I recalled that Norma had walked into Pappas's office and that the first words out of her mouth had been, "I want you to help me kill my husband."

"I am wondering," I said to the jury, "if Mrs. Winters were as cold and diabolical and as calculating as the prosecutor has characterized her, if that would be the manner in which she would have approached Anthony Pappas?"

We broke for a short recess. When the jury filed back in and was seated, I talked about Dr. Samuelson's testimony. I pointed out that he hadn't known what had been said during the meeting between Norma and Pappas. He had said he wasn't interested in knowing of any telephone contacts between Norma and Pappas before their meeting or whether they had occurred five minutes or three months before the meeting.

"So then he was asked, would it make any difference when the phone call was made if the person who was supposed to be the hypnotist was present in the room? 'Yeah, that might.' Did he know about that fact? No.

"He was asked if the response of Mrs. Winters under hypnosis to having to retell that story might be significant, particularly if Dr. Unger feared a danger of anxiety reaction or perhaps even a psychotic episode. 'Yes,' he said, 'that might well be significant.'

"Was he provided that information by the prosecution? No.

"It is not surprising to me, ladies and gentlemen of the jury, that the doctor would respond in the manner that he did and render an opinion in the way he did on the basis of the evidence that had been submitted to him, because there wasn't anything relating to what Dr. Unger's clinical findings were in his direct testimony yesterday."

I pointed out that when Dr. Samuelson had used the example of picking up a telephone as an automatic act, it had been significant because he hadn't known at that time that picking up a telephone was precisely what had happened in this case, in the presence of Walt Lovell and Ellen Harris.

"He didn't know that yesterday," I said, "but he described it. He said, 'Yeah, that type of act, you could probably get that kind of response.'

"Dr. Unger testified that he was of the opinion that when Mrs. Winters walked into [Pappas's] office, she was suffering from a posthypnotic suggestion. Dr. Unger testified that that was his opinion, based on seven hours of clinical findings. Dr. Unger reviewed all of the evidence that was available to him. He stated at the time Mrs. Winters made that statement, that in his opinion, she was constitutionally incapable of resisting that suggestion. . . .

"You will recall [Dr. Samuelson] was asked extensively about the tapes of the conversations on the next Tuesday with the police officer. But in description and in detail, without even knowing it, he specified the precise sequence of procedures that would be utilized by an individual who was attempting to achieve that result. He said, 'Pick up the telephone,' before he knew whether a telephone had been picked up. He said, 'Physical proximity,' before he knew, and I don't even know if he knows now whether Walt Lovell was present on the ground floor on the day that that solicitation was made."

I said the prosecution had tried to impugn Dr. Unger's testimony by suggesting that "Norma Winters from Holtville" could "fool Dr. Barry Unger, a professor of psychiatry at the University of California."

Then, I said, "Dr. Unger won't testify as to a certainty any more than Dr. Samuelson would. They use 'usually.' Dr. Unger says, 'Within the limits of my discipline, within the limits of what I know about psychiatry, within the parameters of my ability to express an opinion as a psychiatrist, I am certain.' Can he be wrong? Yes. He can be. Has Dr. Samuelson's testimony in any way challenged his findings? No."

He hadn't in relation to the Pappas count. But Samuelson had challenged Unger on the meetings with Hanscom, and that matter remained for me to address.

I reminded the jurors of the difference between a specific hypnotic suggestion—go open the window—and a nonspecific suggestion—you are going to feel very warm—and I pointed out that in a nonspecific suggestion a person could invent any number of schemes to explain unusual behavior.

Then I noted that Hanscom had asked Norma for the picture, the vehicle, the addresses, and the money. And I took the jury through the evidence—that Norma had had enough money to pay Hanscom $500 that day; that she'd told him to kill her husband on the way to work on Sunday night, when he wouldn't be working; that she'd given Hanscom a photograph that hadn't looked like her husband and a map of his route to work that she'd never known him to take; and that one of the cars she'd described hadn't even been running.

I conceded that some of this evidence was open to other interpretations—that perhaps Norma Winters had been trying to avoid detection. But I suggested, for example, that if she'd really wanted to avoid detection in typing out the license numbers, she would simply have given them to Hanscom orally.

"It is possible," I said finally, "that Norma Winters is [such a] diabolical person that she'd be able to figure that out. But it is also susceptible to another interpretation, and that is the interpretation that has been given to you by Dr. Unger—that all of these acts manifested ambivalence and that type of ambivalence is of the kind and character that we would expect to appear in a person who had been given a nonspecific posthypnotic suggestion.

"It is not contended in this case that Walt Lovell, by some miraculous foresight, knew that Norma Winters was going to be contacted by Al Hanscom and then programmed her to give him a picture, a map to work, and everything else, because he didn't have to. Just as I wouldn't have to program any of you if you were placed under hypnosis and I said, 'You are going to feel hot.' I wouldn't have to tell you, 'When you come out of a trance you are going to have to take your coat off.' I wouldn't have to tell you, 'You're going to have to turn the air conditioning up.'" They would do it themselves, I suggested.

I stopped for a moment to gather my thoughts and glanced at my watch. It was getting late. Morrison and I had agreed to limit our summations. If I didn't finish soon, he would be allowed to conclude on Monday, and he would have three days to prepare a rebuttal I would be unable to answer. I had touched all the bases, I thought. I was ready to turn Norma's fate over to the jury.

"There are two defenses in this case, and they are unconsciousness and diminished capacity," I said. "Unconsciousness, as you will recall, is the state where there is no conscious activity of the brain. The judge will instruct you that those types of acts are the types of acts that are committed without volition, and I think everyone is agreed in this case, even Dr. Samuelson, who was called by the prosecution, that if Mrs. Winters was suffering from a posthypnotic suggestion at the time that that occurred, she would be innocent. That was his testimony. In fact his word was 'exculpatory.' It would be 'completely exculpatory.'

"So finally, I guess what we have to do in this case is consider whether Dr. Unger's testimony is so inherently incredible that it is unworthy of belief. If you feel in this case that Dr. Unger might be wrong, that he might be right, or that it is reasonably possible that he is right, then you have to acquit her. The reason for that is because in a criminal case, the prosecution bears a certain burden, and the burden is proving the defendant's guilt beyond a reasonable doubt and to a moral certainty, so that at the conclusion of this case you can say with a sound and steadfast mind, not only that the state of facts that you have decided are consistent with guilt, but they are irreconcilable with any other rational conclusion.

"I don't know how you can do that with relationship to the Pappas contact. There has been hardly anything, in my view, to rebut, on the part of Dr. Samuelson, the testimony of Dr. Unger.

"If you merely find with relationship to the phone call from Al Hanscom and the subsequent events that Mrs. Winters's capacity was so severely impaired that she could not formulate the specific intent to solicit murder, then you must acquit her."

I paused one last time. The jury was as attentive as it had been at the opening of my argument.

"This has been a long and difficult and complex and bizarre case," I said. "And I will be the first to concede that these facts are bizarre. I would be the first to concede that they are unusual. That doesn't necessarily mean that they are not true.

"I ask you to decide this case on the basis of the evidence, using your sound judgment and weighing the evidence. . . . It is really beyond your province to exercise compassion or punishment in this case, or anything else. I don't want Norma Winters acquitted because you feel sorry for her. I want you to acquit or convict her on the basis of the evidence alone, and in accordance with your own convictions."

Morrison's closing argument seemed repetitive and, I hoped, slightly wide of the mark. More than in his earlier statement, his tone was harsh and aggressive and appeared to put the jury off.

He maintained that he hadn't tried to establish any motive for Norma's crime, but had only suggested that the attacks on her daughter, the insurance money, or Wayne Connors could have been the motive "behind the acts of Norma Winters when she solicited the cold-blooded killing of her husband."

He told the jury he didn't have to prove a motive and that it didn't have to agree on one. That was technically true, but by now the jury knew that he'd begun with a single motive, abandoned it, seized another, abandoned it, pursued yet another, and abandoned that one. If he wasn't required to prove a motive, why had he addressed the issue at all?

He reiterated his position that Norma had had Hanscom put off the killing till Sunday only to avoid spoiling her weekend with Wayne Connors, and not out of some ambivalence resulting from a posthypnotic suggestion. But he still didn't explain why she had pushed so hard for a day on which she had known he wouldn't be working.

And then he reminded the jury that he'd asked Norma if she had read the book *Anatomy of a Murder.* He outlined its plot for the jury—telling them how a defendant and lawyer had concocted a defense after all other possibilities, including self-defense and insanity, had seemed out of the question.

"Now, whether that is the case here, or not, I don't know," he said, "but I submit to you that this defense is contrived."

That Morrison would suggest that surprised me. Did he really think the jury would believe that?

Morrison said he had felt no need to have Dr. Samuelson examine Norma, because Dr. Ellison, Norma's own psychiatrist, had already testified that she had not been unconscious at the time of the crime and that she had been able to form the intent to commit the crime.

And then he addressed my contention that he had characterized Norma as a liar.

"That is not my decision to make," he said. "That is your decision to make, and if you find after this action that Norma Winters has lied in this trial, that she lied to Dr. Unger, then I would submit to you that it would be a travesty of justice to allow those lies to serve her purpose.

"You know, I used the term 'shrinking violet' before, and that is exactly how the defense has attempted to characterize her. But take a look at her," he said, glancing at Norma, who sat next to me at the defense table. "She is a business woman. You know, I'm not opposed to women's lib and to women going out and going out into business and getting jobs, and so forth. Well, my wife would like to hear me say that. But my point is that Mrs. Winters was out in the tough world, ready to compete. She was no shrinking violet, and she was able to take time out to pause to tell Officer Hanscom, 'Hold it just a second; you're going to screw up my weekend.'

"Now, at the time, she didn't tell Officer Hanscom what she had in mind. It took a little digging. She didn't want to tell us about it initially, either. But folks, this is not the person that the defense has attempted to portray for you."

Morrison talked briefly about the law in the case, particularly about the unconsciousness instruction that the judge would give them.

"The state of unconsciousness, you will be told, contemplates a person of sound mind who suffered from some force that leaves their acts *totally without volition,* not partially without volition, not a little bit of volition over here, but totally without volition, and Dr. Unger testified that she was not acting totally without volition.

"Remember, he talked about her trying to fight it off; so even if you believed Dr. Unger, she wasn't acting without volition, and her defense fails."

Then he completed his argument: "Nothing that has been said or done during this trial by the defense changes the facts, and the facts are that this woman on August ninth and August the twelfth through thirteenth did on two occasions—the two occasions charged—solicit the murder of her husband in a cold-blooded manner.

"Now, you don't have to prove it is cold-blooded, only that it was solicited, but I am submitting to you now that she did solicit the cold-blooded murder with the intent that her husband be killed. And for what reason? We don't have to decide that, but nothing that has been said or done in this trial changes that fact. And if we view the evidence in this case, I would submit to you that the evidence demands and cries out for verdicts of guilty on both counts, and I ask you for those verdicts now."

CHAPTER 34

The next morning Norma and I walked into the courtroom shortly after 9:30. The trial itself was over, and all that remained was for the judge to instruct the jury on how to consider the evidence and to inform it under what circumstances it could find Norma guilty or innocent. In Norma, the tension and strain of more than two weeks of watching witnesses and listening to the evidence in her case was already giving way to an even greater tension—the anxiety of waiting for a verdict. While testimony had continued, we had always had the hope of introducing one more significant piece of evidence, of asking one more penetrating question on cross-examination, of making one last persuasive argument. We had still had some feeling of control over the trial, the evidence, even Norma's fate. Now we had none. It was entirely up to the jury.

The jurors themselves filed back into the courtroom at 9:45. Their faces were serious. They, too, had sat through more than two weeks of testimony, some of it tedious, but most of it, I thought, fascinating and enthralling. However they viewed it, the toughest part of their job lay ahead of them: they had to find a logic and clarity in the evidence, in accordance with the judge's instructions and their own consciences, and decide whether Norma was guilty or innocent. As Judge Maine read the instructions, the jurors listened intently, seeming to digest every word.

From our standpoint the most important of the instructions was the one on unconsciousness. The judge read it as he had modified it after admitting Dr. Unger's testimony,

> Where a person commits an act without being conscious thereof, such act is not criminal, even though, if committed by a person who was conscious, it would be a crime.
>
> This rule of law applies only to cases of the unconsciousness of persons of sound mind, such as somnambulists or persons suffering from the delirium of fever, epilepsy, a blow on the head or the involuntary taking of drugs or intoxicating liquor, and other cases in which there is no functioning of the conscious mind.
>
> The state of unconsciousness also contemplates persons of sound mind who suffer from some force that leaves their acts totally without volition.

It was the last paragraph that had been added to the instructions as a result of our legal argument. I wondered how the jurors would react to the term *totally without volition.* I had argued in chambers that the case law used the term *without volition,* but Judge Maine inserted the word *totally,* which gave the jury a little less flexibility in evaluating Norma's volition at the time of the crime, especially during her meetings with Hanscom. Indeed, Morrison had mentioned in his closing statement that Dr. Unger had testified that Norma's volition had been acting against the hypnotic suggestion, but that she had had some volition. The point was, however, that Unger had characterized Norma as powerless to resist the suggestion and that to the extent volition had been operating, it had been in an unconscious direction against the suggestion. I hoped some members of the jury would remember that.

The judge also gave the jury an instruction on diminished capacity. It read;

> When a defendant is charged with a crime which requires that a certain specific intent or mental state be established in order to constitute the crime or degree of crime, you must take all the evidence into consideration and determine therefrom if, at the time when the crime allegedly was committed, the defendant was suffering from some abnormal mental or physical condition, however

caused, which prevented him from forming the specific intent or mental state essential to constitute the crime or degree of crime with which he is charged.

If from all the evidence you have a reasonable doubt whether the defendant was capable of forming such specific intent or mental state, you must give the defendant the benefit of that doubt and find that she did not have such specific intent or mental state.

Within thirty-five minutes the bailiff escorted the jury to its room for deliberation, and the wait began. I didn't expect a quick verdict. Indeed, a short deliberation would suggest that the jurors had totally rejected the defense and had considered the case, as Morrison had put it, "open and shut." The evidence was too complicated for a quick judgment. It didn't surprise me when I learned through a phone call late that afternoon at my law office that the jury had been excused for the weekend without having reached a verdict and would resume its deliberations Monday morning.

Waiting for a verdict is a kind of private purgatory for a defense lawyer: it is impossible to avoid second-guessing yourself. Over the weekend I wondered about several important moments in the trial. Should I have called Unger on surrebuttal? Should I have explained the Hanscom count more clearly in summation? Had I done everything possible to remove the boyfriend issue from the jury's mind? Would the jury get stumped on the wording "totally without volition"? It was a useless exercise, of course. My job was over. I could only await the jury's decision.

Norma returned to El Centro for the weekend, working at her office on Saturday, talking to brokers, sometimes about business, but usually about the case. On Sunday night she happened to watch a special television program on women felons, which featured the only women's prison in California. She heard interviews with bitter, hardened women. She watched as the camera panned along the prison walls and the small jail rooms where the women were kept. That's when it hit her. She had lived most of the past six months and certainly all of her trial without even considering the possibility of jail. She couldn't imagine being in prison. Now she didn't have to. It was right in front of her.

"That's where I'm going," she said to herself. How would she live with those women? What would happen to her business, her customers? What would happen to Beth and David? That night Norma cried herself to sleep.

On Monday morning she and her children returned to San Diego and stayed close to my office, to be nearby when the verdict finally came in.

The jury began deliberating again at 9 A.M. on Monday; just before 11:30, we learned, the foreman sent word to the clerk that the panel wanted to listen again to the tape of Norma's interview with Sergeant Ryan. I was reached by telephone, and I didn't object to its hearing the tape and following the transcript without our presence in the courtroom. The jury also asked for a copy of the unconsciousness instruction.

Late that afternoon the telephone rang again. The court wanted us to return to the courtroom. The jury had reached a verdict on the first count, I was told, but was deadlocked on the second.

"They're deadlocked?" Norma asked, a look of anguish spreading across her face. "Doesn't that mean another trial?"

"Probably. That would be up to the district attorney to decide."

She seemed to crumple at the news. "I just don't think I could go through that again," she said.

That wasn't our only worry. In a second trial we would lose the element of surprise in the case. And we would also lose the first count, which the jury had decided. Without the benefit of the weaker Pappas count, I thought, we might have trouble describing the complete sequence of events for the jury. Indeed, I wondered what would have happened if I'd been successful in my attempt more than a month ago to have the charges separated. It might have worked against Norma.

But I found some encouragement in the news. Given a deadlock on count two, I was all but certain the jury had acquitted Norma on the first charge. If they hadn't gone with us on that one, they would have no reason to haggle over the details of Norma's meetings with Hanscom.

When we arrived at court, the judge called the attorneys into chambers and asked what we wanted to do.

"Your Honor," I said almost before I knew it, "let's give them the dynamite instruction."

Both the judge and the prosecutor seemed surprised. The "dyna-mite instruction," also known as the *Allen* charge, is something the prosecution often requests when a jury is deadlocked, in an effort to budge one juror who seems to be holding out for innocence. (It has since been declared unconstitutional when used in such cir-cumstances.) Seldom, if ever, does the defense ask for it.

"Well," the judge said after a moment. "Yes, I can give them the *Allen* charge."

"Yes, Your Honor, the defense requests it."

The district attorney did not object, and we went back to the courtroom, where the judge gave them the instruction. The jurors listened carefully.

"You should consider that the case must at some time be de-cided," he said, "that you are selected in the same manner and from the same source from which any future jury must be selected, and there is no reason to suppose the case will ever be submitted to twelve men or women more intelligent, more impartial, or more competent to decide it, or that more or clearer evidence will be produced on one side or the other. And with this view, it is your duty to decide the case, if you can conscientiously do so. . . .

"In the present case the burden of proof is on the People of the state of California to establish every part of it beyond a reasonable doubt. And if in any part of it you are left in doubt, the defendant is entitled to the benefit of the doubt and must be acquitted. But in conferring together, you ought to pay proper respect to each other's opinions and listen with a disposition to be convinced to each other's arguments."

He told them if the vast majority were for conviction, a dissent-ing juror "should consider whether a doubt in his or her own mind is a reasonable one, which makes no impression upon the minds of so many men or women equally honest, equally intelligent."

If a majority were for acquittal, "the minority ought to ask themselves whether they may not reasonably and ought not to doubt the correctness of a judgment which is not concurred in by most of those with whom they are associated, and distrust the weight or sufficiency of that evidence which fails to carry convic-tion to the minds of their fellows."

Then the judge asked the jury to continue its deliberations the next morning at nine.

As I was leaving the courthouse that afternoon, I saw two of the jurors, including the foreman, walking out a side entrance. They both seemed preoccupied, most likely with the case, and I was suddenly struck with a good feeling about that jury. Its members had lived with this case for nearly a month and were about to begin a third day of deliberations together, days intermingled with three nights and an entire weekend of mulling the evidence over alone at home. That's what jurors were supposed to do, of course, but I was impressed with their commitment. They were struggling with the evidence and with their consciences in trying to reach a verdict. Norma, I felt, could ask for no more than that.

Just before 1 P.M. the next day, Tuesday, March 25, the telephone rang in my office, where Norma and I were waiting. It was from department five. The jury had returned with a verdict.

It was less than a ten-minute drive from my office to the courthouse. Today it seemed to take hours.

"Well," I said, looking straight ahead, "we gave it our best shot."

The statement was as much for my benefit as for Norma's. And she responded as if on cue.

"Whatever happens, Milt," she said, "you did a real fine job."

Her words were distant, as if uttered by someone else. She knew at that instant that her fate had been decided. All that remained was for it to be announced.

We reached the courtroom just before 1:45. The DA was already there, as were Beth and David, who had driven down with a relative, and a small audience that had been following the case.

At 1:47 the jurors filed in and took their seats in the jury box. I scanned their faces, looking for a sign, but found none that I could rely on.

"Mr. Foreman," the judge asked, "do you have a verdict?"

"Yes, Your Honor, we do."

"Would you hand it to the bailiff, please?"

The bailiff took two sheets of paper from the foreman, turned, and handed them to the judge.

Judge Maine unfolded them slowly, as with great care. He read the verdict to himself. His expression showed not the slightest change. He handed the papers to Ralph Boyle, the clerk.

"Mr. Clerk, would you read the verdict, please."

The courtroom was silent. The jury seemed to be made of stone. No one breathed. Norma sat motionless beside me.

Ralph Boyle, a tall, graying man of fifty-five, stood facing the jury in front of the judge's bench and read in a painstakingly slow, clear voice.

"In the Superior Court of the State of California, in and for the County of San Diego, Department Five. The People of the State of California, Plaintiff, versus Norma Winters, Defendant. We the jury in the above entitled cause, find the defendant, Norma Winters, not guilty of the crime of . . ."

The rest of the words were a jumble. I glanced over at Norma. Her head bobbed slightly, and she seemed to have lost her breath. Tears began to fill her eyes.

There was a rustle in the courtroom, but it turned quickly to silence. I had been right on count one, I thought. What of count two?

"Ladies and gentlemen," I heard the clerk say, "was this and is this your verdict?" Each member of the jury nodded. Mr. Boyle slid the second sheet of paper out from under the first, and, as was the custom, read the entire caption on the jury verdict form.

"In the Superior Court of the State of California in and for the County of San Diego, Department Five. The People of The State of California, Plaintiff, versus Norma Winters, Defendant. We the jury in the above entitled cause find the defendant, Norma Winters . . ." He paused for just an instant.

". . . not guilty . . ."

Norma burst into tears. Her head fell into her hands. Her whole body shook. I heard Beth crying behind me. Then David cried too.

"Norma," I said softly, leaning toward her and touching her gently on the arm. "You can go to your children." She stood up, turned and embraced them over the courtroom railing.

I looked at the judge, then at the jury. The faces were no longer cold; they were beaming.

Judge Maine began to say something to the jurors, but I didn't hear what it was. I'm sure he thanked them, as he always did, for their care and patience in deliberations; and then he excused them.

As they rose and filed out, I stood by the gate in the center of the railing and opened it for them. I shook the hand of each as they left. Some of them simply nodded as they walked by. Others paused a moment to say a kind word. A few of them had tears in their eyes.

Maybe I did too.

EPILOGUE

As we stepped out of the courtroom that afternoon, Norma was greeted by a sheriff who promptly served her with a subpoena from the small-claims court in San Diego County. It ordered her to appear in a matter involving a ninety-dollar claim resulting from her association with a construction company. The claimant? Walter Lovell.

The claim had been improperly filed, and Norma did not pay him the ninety dollars. Nor did she pay him one cent of the more than eight thousand dollars he'd sued her for the preceding November. That suit was dropped.

Lovell was never arrested or charged with any offense in connection with the Norma Winters case, and he remains a practicing consultant near San Diego.

Beth is married and has two children. She still lives in Holtville and works with her mother in the escrow business. David lives with Norma's sister and is going to mechanics school.

Norma and Wayne Connors dated for several months after the trial, but eventually decided to make new lives apart. Norma is now happily remarried, living in a comfortable home in Holtville and working at her escrow business in El Centro.